THE GREAT I AM IS THE GOLDEN STRAND

THE GREAT I AM IS THE GOLDEN STRAND

A STORY OF GRIT, GRACE, AND NEVER GIVING UP

BUDDY MERCER

Ebook ISBN: 979-8-218-84318-2

Paperback ISBN: 979-8-218-84441-7

Book Cover Design by AuthorsHQ.com

To my beautiful wife of fifty-two years, who has walked hand in hand with me, offering unwavering love and support, and to my three children, who have made my life exciting and special.

PREFACE – MY LIFE

I am writing this to give glory to the God of the Bible, the Great I Am, for the beautiful life He has provided to me. I rely on my own experiences and observations, not religious doctrine, and I do not aim to convert others to my beliefs. That would be anti-thetical to my conviction that God has given us all free will to choose what we believe and how we live. However, I do use scripture from time to time when it defines my personal experience.

During my life, God has chosen to bless me in ways that defy logic and can only be described as miraculous. Even an atheist would struggle to dismiss what has happened to me as mere coincidence or luck. I have never been one to plan. As my son has told me numerous times, I tend to fly by the seat of my pants. I would prefer to think I have learned to let God do the planning: "Commit to the Lord and He will establish your plans" (Prov 16:3), while I just do the work.

Whichever the case, many dramatic things have happened

in my life that cause people who hear my stories to tell me that I need to put some of these events on paper to encourage others who are struggling to find hope, "for God is no respecter of persons" (Acts 10:34), and what He has done for me He can do for anyone. He will meet the needs of anyone who puts their trust in Him. No one in their right mind would waste their time reading about the things I have accomplished on my own, for soon it will become apparent that left to my own devices, I am only a man filled with weakness and prone to sin. On my own I have worked hard to have such wonderful titles as a "functional alcoholic," "oil field trash," "carnival bum," "rodeo bum," "jailbird," and finally, a "homeless vagrant" on the streets of Portland, Oregon, and Los Angeles.

My biggest regret is the hearts that I have broken and the lives I may have destroyed as I rejected the spiritual upbringing that my mother instilled in me as a child. I am beyond grateful that my sins are covered by the blood of Jesus: "For God so loved the world, that he gave his only begotten Son, that whosoever believeth in him should not perish, but have everlasting life" (Jn 3:16).

Trusting God's direction, I have since had the titles of husband, daddy, grandpa, and great-grandpa. By God's proclamation, I am the child of the King who by the grace of Jesus Christ and the convicting power of the Holy Spirit will spend eternity in a place called heaven where the beauty and splendor cannot be described with earthly language.

In my professional life since trusting in God, I have served as general manager of manufacturing facilities in San Luis Obispo, Los Angeles, California, and Portland, Oregon. I was appointed chief operating officer (COO) of the LA facility where, by the grace of God and His miracles, we took the company public. Finally, in "retirement," my wife and I started a small business, HOA Janitorial Inc., which God enlarged beyond my wildest dreams.

I was encouraged first of all by my wife, Jane, and then by friends and family, especially Dave Kimmitt, to write this story in March 2002. I was hesitant, as I didn't think it would be of interest to anyone except my family. However, if it helps to encourage even one person who is struggling to fight on or to come to a saving knowledge of the grace of Jesus Christ, it will have served its purpose. I also wrote this for myself, as I am getting up in years and want to be able to remember, and to make sure my children and grandchildren remember, how my life in Christ has brought me to where I am today.

The stories regarding my early years are written based on anecdotal evidence, but to maintain their integrity, I confirmed most of them by having long conversations with various family members, especially my cousin Beth and her husband, Buddy Van Cleave, who were familiar with that period of my life and have now passed on. I am writing this to glorify God, so it is of ultimate importance to me that it be as truthful as possible ("and the truth will set you free" Jn 8:32).

Please note that some of the names herein have been changed to protect confidentiality. And as mentioned, although the stories are true, some instances are based on my memories, which may not be exact. God is the author of this story.

1

THE EARLY YEARS IN OKLAHOMA

THE BIBLE OPENS with the words "In the beginning" (Gen 1:1). If that's a good enough starting place for God, it's as good a place as any for me to begin recounting my life's story. I was born August 7, 1943, in Marlow, Oklahoma. My mother had married a man named Glen Roy Jacobs, so I was named Glen Roy Jacobs, Junior. I understand he was quite the rounder as he was frequently found in bars and was often drunk. Shortly after my birth, he decided he didn't want to be married anymore, so he joined the military, divorced my mother, and was never heard from again.

My earliest memories begin when I was about three years old, surrounded by love from my mother, Grandma and Grandpa Prestage, aunts and uncles (especially Uncle "Fudge" (Emmitt)), and lots of cousins. They all took an interest in me and made me feel special. My grandma was very sweet and made the best cookies I've ever had. She always called me her "little buddy," so when she gave me a teddy bear, I named him Buddy.

I remember the glorious days when we would all get dressed up in our "Sunday go to meetin' clothes." On Sunday mornings I would walk with my mother and grandparents down a dirt road to a little church. I can still feel the warm sunshine and smell the cut grass. It gave me a feeling that all was right with the world. As we walked, friends and neighbors would join us. Before long, Grandpa would start singing "When the Roll is Called Up Yonder" (James Milton Black, 1893) and most everybody would join in.

After church we would go home and change out of our good clothes. While the adults fixed dinner, my cousins and I went out to play. Soon, we would be called in to a big table loaded with mashed potatoes and gravy, fried okra, black-eyed peas, and, yes, the best fried chicken. There would be goblets of cold sweet tea to wash it all down too. Once everyone was at the table, Grandpa would say grace, then he would smile and say, "Ain't God good? Everyone, dig in."

When everyone finished eating and the table was cleared, we all went out to the front of the house, where the adults talked on the porch as my cousins and I played in the front yard. After a while, Uncle Fudge would get out his guitar and start picking as the whole family sang along.

Later, Grandpa would get out the old crank ice cream maker. He filled the canister with the fixings for the flavor of the day and used an ice pick to chop the block of ice. Occasionally, he let me turn the crank, warning, "Now, don't turn it too fast because the milk won't harden, and we won't have good ice cream." My next job was to fold a burlap bag, lay it on top of the maker, then sit on it to help hold it steady. Boy, did I feel grown up and important!

As the day wound down, friends and neighbors would stop by for conversation on the front porch. As twilight settled and the sky turned inky black, I chased fireflies to put in my mason jar. Once I had caught a few to give to my grandma, she would hug me, thank me, then suggest, "Why don't we let them out, so they can be free and go home to their families?" If she thought that was a good idea, I was all for it. We would go over to her flower bed, take the lid off the jar, and watch them as they flew away to be with their families, or so my grandma told me. Then she would say "Buddy, I am so proud of you. Maybe we deserve some cookies and milk."

In the afternoons when I was put down for my nap, which I did not like because I thought I was missing play time, my grandma would come and tell me stories about Jesus and how much He loved me. Then she would sing "Jesus Loves Me," and I would drift off to sleep. Sometimes I would hold off on going to sleep, coming out of my room later to say, "I didn't think I would ever get Grandma to go to sleep."

These are just some of the memories I have retained and hold dear to my heart some seventy years later. There was lots of love for family and friends in that slow-moving, long-forgotten era.

2

MOVING TO TEXAS

SOMETIME AFTER MY FOURTH BIRTHDAY, my mother met and married Harry Mercer, and things began to change. He was not a happy, loving man like the people I was used to being around. He wasn't a bad guy, but he was very distant when I was around.

We moved to a little house across town from where I had been raised, and things were a whole lot different for me. No more walks to church on Sunday mornings, no more cousins to play with, and except on special occasions, no more sweet times with Grandma and Grandpa Prestage.

Harry's family were good and decent people, but the warm, loving feelings to which I was accustomed were missing, especially with his mother. I am not bitter toward her, but she did not like my mother. She called me "nothing but a stepchild," so I didn't like to be around her. That made Harry angry. He told me in no uncertain terms that she was his mother, and I would go with them to visit her. His father was a much older man who liked to sit on his front porch with a radio on, tuned to either the news or a baseball game. He would whittle wood with his pocketknife, never really making anything. He was very quiet, never talking much except when one of his neighbors, who was about his age, would come by for a visit.

Harry had a sister, Margie, who was married to a man named Gilford. They had two daughters, Margret Ann and Linda Sue, who were about my age. They lived in Rush Springs, Oklahoma, which is about fifteen miles from Marlow where Harry's mother lived. They were nice people who made us feel welcome when we went to their house. Unfortunately, Margie, who had severe depression, would start crying when we visited and go to her bedroom. It was scary for me because not only would she cry, she would also yell and scream. When she had one of these "fits," as they called it, the girls and I would be sent outside to play. Then in a little while we would be called back in for pie and ice cream, and she would be "normal," like nothing had happened.

I was told that later she had a complete nervous breakdown. She was hospitalized and, through treatment, recovered and lived a regular life with Gilford until he passed away in the late 1980s. The girls grew up, graduated from high school, and attended college. The last I heard, they were married and doing well.

Harry had another sister named Erma who married a man named Price Pearson. They had two sons and had moved to Los Angeles, where they were doing well. Harry also had a brother named Earnest who married a lady named Louie Mae. They had one son and lived in Shasta, California. Earnest pastored a Baptist church there. I only met them when Harry's dad passed away, and the family gathered for the funeral in Marlow in the late 1960s.

Just after my fifth birthday, my mother sat me down and told me Harry had a job in Texas, where we would soon be moving. She told me stories of cowboys and how good life was going to be. The way she explained it, I imagined Roy Rogers and his horse, Trigger, Hopalong Cassidy and Topper, and Gene Autry on his horse, Champion, riding across the prairie to my house to play with me. I realize now she was trying to sell me a bill of goods.

It reminds me of something that Ronald Reagan once said: "When your mother tells you she loves you, trust her but verify."

We loaded our belongings into a truck, looking like the Beverly Hillbillies, and made the trip to Texas. We wound up in the town of Barnhart where Harry went to work in the oilfields. It was a small community in west Texas with a combined post office/grocery store/filling station and a train depot, but there was no Roy Rogers, Hopalong Cassidy, or Gene Autry; just me and a couple of friends on our stick horses chasing the bad guys. My mother got pregnant while we were in Barnhart, and my brother Steven Harry was born.

During this time, Harry got a job with a company called Deep Rock, which became Sinclair and, many years later, ARCO. Soon, we were on the move again, and with his new job we wound up in Big Lake, Texas. The amusing aspect of that little town was that the lakebed only filled with water after a significant rainstorm.

One of the good parts of our time in Big Lake was that my mother's sister, my Aunt Lila and her husband, Roy Schilling, lived there with my cousins, Sue and Beth and an older son, Roy Jr. Uncle Roy was the pastor for the First Methodist church, so I would go to Sunday school with them. Harry and my mother weren't attending church at the time. I liked going to Sunday School because they told stories about Jesus and how much He loved us, just like my grandma said.

Unfortunately, even at such a young age, I found a way to get into trouble using my sense of humor. One Sunday the teacher was telling the story of King Nebuchadnezzar and the three Hebrew boys in the fire—Shadrach, Meshach, and Abendego. To this day I couldn't tell you what motivated me, but I said, "Oh, you mean Myshack, Yourshack and Underthebedwego." That was the moment my Sunday school teacher *lost* her sense of humor, demanding to know where I learned to say that.

When my mother came to pick me up a short time later, it was not a pretty scene. The Sunday school teacher was sure I was evil, and my mother was embarrassed because Aunt Lila was there too. At least my aunt had a good sense of humor and was smiling and winking at me. Harry, who had been waiting in the car for my mother and me, showed up to find out what was taking so long and became angry because I had embarrassed him and my mother. He made me apologize. When my cousins, Sue and Beth, arrived and heard what I had said, they started giggling. Things went even further downhill from there when Harry grabbed me and took me to the car while my mother apologized and cried. The rest of that day, there was deep discussion in our house about my future at Sunday school. I was amazed when Harry decided we needed to go to the First Baptist church instead. Perhaps

God used me that day, as He tends to work in mysterious ways.

When I turned six, I was told I would soon be starting school. This was not in my plans, so I decided that I would rather run off to Montana and be a bum than be forced to do that. On the first day of school, my mother took me to the schoolhouse, but as soon as she left, so did I. This was not acceptable to the teachers, my mother, or anyone else. I found myself being walked back to school by a police officer. In retrospect, I recognize that this event served as an early indicator of future developments. When we got back to school, I saw my mom had been crying, and I felt bad, but not for the right reasons. I knew that once Harry got home, I would get a spanking for leaving school and making my mom cry. I can assure you; I didn't pull a stunt like that again for a long time.

When I was about six, we lived in a house on one end of the block. On the other end of the block lived a lady whom everyone called Granny Maxwell. She was an old-time west Texas woman who could be as tough as nails one moment and caring and loving the next. When my mother first met Granny, she saw a large lump in her jaw. Initially, she suspected the lump was related to a jawbone issue. When she mentioned it to one of the other neighbor ladies, the woman laughed. "Vida, the next time you see Granny, that lump may be on the other side of her jaw. She's chewing tobacco."

One night at around 10:00 p.m., we heard a shotgun go off. My parents hurried down the street with me in tow to Granny Maxwell's. She was standing there with her shotgun, waiting for the Big Lake policeman and his blaring siren. When the officer exited his car, Granny assured him, "It's fine. He didn't take anything." When he asked her what she meant, she said, "There was a peeping Tom looking in the window of my neighbor's house, so I shot at him with my shotgun. I missed both times, though."

The officer was shocked. "Granny, you shouldn't just shoot at him. Be sure to aim below the knees."

Granny stared at the officer like he was crazy, then she smiled. "Sir, could you please run, so I can observe where his knees might be?" The officer was incredulous. Granny started cackling. The entire crowd that had gathered began to laugh, along with the officer, whose face reddened with embarrassment.

Granny earned her livelihood by providing laundry and ironing services for the townspeople, utilizing a large cast-iron pot over an open fire in her yard and a washboard. She was raising two grandchildren, Drucilla and Larry Joe, who were about my age. Larry Joe and I played constantly but could get angry at each other over the silliest thing, and then the fight was on. A short time later we would forget about fighting and return to playing.

Late one afternoon we were playing in front of Granny's house when things erupted into a fight. Larry Joe spotted a butcher knife lying in the yard. He picked it up and came at me, so I turned and ran home, Larry Joe right on my tail.

As I got into my yard, Harry, who was sitting on the front porch, saw what was going on and told me to take the knife away from Larry Joe and chase him home, or I was going to get a spanking. When Larry Joe heard Harry, he dropped the knife and ran for Granny's house, so I picked the knife up and started after him.

When Larry Joe got to his house, Granny, who had been watching the action, told him to kick my butt. When he came at me, for whatever reason I dropped the knife and ran back to my house. Larry Joe came after me, but he didn't pick up the knife. About halfway down the block, we were both tired, almost breathless, so we just stopped and stared at each other, both of us crying. When we looked at Granny and Harry, they were both laughing, asking us if we had enough.

One incident happened after I got older. Several of the neighborhood kids would get together in a vacant lot next to our house to play baseball. One day, tempers rose, and we threw dirt clods at each other—painful but harmless. One of the older boys, a real bully, picked up a small rock and threw it at me. It hit me on the collarbone, causing me to start bleeding. I picked up the rock and threw it back to him. The rock hit him on his ear. He screamed in pain and started crying. His father, who was nearby, saw what happened and came running, yelling at me. To my surprise, Harry intercepted him and told him that his son started it, and if he wanted to do something about it, Harry was ready to fight him. It was the first time that Harry had acted like he cared about me.

Shortly after, my mother became pregnant again and my youngest brother, Jim Randall, was born. Life was pretty good then, as we had become somewhat of a family. We resumed attending church, where I recalled the stories Grandma Prestage shared with me and those she read from her King James Bible. I could really see myself being present in those Bible stories when she read them aloud. I also thought of her beautiful voice and her rendition of "Jesus Loves Me." These recollections of my grandma and her love for Jesus helped me to fall in love with him too. Oftentimes though, it would seem like a fantasy because I could only see Jesus in my mind.

One night at church, we had a visiting evangelist preaching. He was yelling, saying Satan was after us, and if we didn't get to the altar and get saved, we were going to burn in hell. This scared me because I couldn't see or feel Jesus around to protect me. When the altar call came, I bolted out of the pew so quickly that I was the first one there. I was baptized in water a short time later.

Even though we moved around when I was young, I made friends easily, so between church and school I usually had someone to play with. The house we moved into in Big Lake had an empty lot next door. A couple of my neighborhood friends and I would get together and play some sort of baseball game we devised. As more kids came, we made some bases out of burlap bags and sand, which made it like a baseball field. We played baseball all day, only pausing for lunch and when it got dark. Soon, I started Little League, which I really liked. I played well enough to be selected for the All-Star team as a catcher when I was eleven, which made Harry very happy because he could brag about his son.

During my childhood, I developed a love for reading. I was still not a big fan of school, but I did well—maybe too well because by reading a lot, I developed a large vocabulary. In the third grade I wrote a short story for an assignment using the word "pertaining" in a sentence. When my teacher read my paper, she accused me of cheating. She said there was no way I knew what "pertaining" meant. She scolded me in front of the class and then spanked my hand with a ruler. I never used big words in her class again.

When I was about ten my younger brother, Steven, hit me with a bat. Of course, being the big brother, I took the bat from him and hit him back. Unfortunately, it was just as Harry turned the corner to witness the act. He became angrier than I had ever seen him. He slapped me across the face, knocked me to the ground, then cut me to the core with words that, to that point, I had never heard: "You are no son of mine, only a stepchild who lives here." At that moment, I felt alone and knew I didn't belong, but I just sucked it up and went back to playing. Later that day, he and my mom, who had been crying, came into my room. Harry told me he was sorry for what he had said. Even though he apologized, from then on, I knew how he really felt.

Just after I turned eleven, a boy in my class asked me why my name was different from the rest of my family, why my last name was Jacobs and theirs was Mercer. I didn't know what to say, so I just kind of shrugged it off. The next day when I got to school, that boy was waiting for me. He started pointing and calling me a bastard, and the other kids joined in. I knew I was supposed to walk away, but something in me went cold. So, I walked up and punched him in the face, knocking him to the ground. I started kicking him, which made me feel really good, so I started in on another one of the kids who had decided to make fun of me.

Naturally, my teacher saw me and told me to apologize. I refused, just glaring at the kid I had punched and kicked instead, so we were sent to the office. That day the principal administered my first school spanking with a paddle, but I did not flinch nor make a sound. I should have known it was not the end of the incident. That evening, I was sitting on the front porch by myself when the principal drove up. Without a word to me, he knocked on the door and spoke to my parents. When he left, Harry spanked me again because I had made him look bad.

A few months later, I was outside having my twelfth birthday party when my mom came and asked me to come inside. I didn't want to leave my friends and the great time I was having, but I knew better than to resist. We went inside where she and Harry sat me down and told me that Harry wanted to adopt me. It would change my last name to Mercer, like the rest of the family. My mom said I could also change my first name from Glen to any name I wanted. Instantly, I thought of when my sweet Grandma Prestage called me "her little buddy." It made me feel so good. When the adoption papers were completed, I became known as Buddy Roy Mercer.

Just before I turned thirteen, Harry had a new job offer with the same company, but we had to move to Eldorado, Texas, some seventy miles away. It sounded wonderful to me because I thought about being able to have a new start as Buddy Mercer. When we reached Eldorado, though, reality kicked in.

Eldorado was a small town on the rolling hills of the Balcones Fault Zone. It had a well-established societal order, with ranchers at the top and merchants next. Below them came the crop farmers, then the small sod farmers with pigs, goats, and sheep, and then us "oil field trash" at the bottom. I found this interesting because we had purchased a nice house in a newer part of Eldorado, my stepfather drove a snazzy new Buick, and my mother got invited to join a lady's group at the First Baptist church that we were attending. This social structure began to make me aware of the inconsistencies present in society.

When school started in September, I enrolled in the Eldorado High School Eagle band. I was a sophomore, and once again, I found myself an outsider. The other kids had lived in Eldorado most of their lives and had their little cliques, which I was not invited to join. After being in the band for a bit, I must have impressed the band director because he put me in as first chair.

I had started playing the trumpet when I was in the third grade in Big Lake and found that I had a natural talent for music. I had taken lessons, and since I enjoyed playing the instrument, I practiced religiously every day. I became quite proficient with all types of music, including rock and roll, classical, jazz, and church music. I was good enough to be invited to play with the high school band as a freshman at my previous high school in Big Lake.

My promotion to first trumpet did not sit well with the rest of the trumpet section, especially a guy named Eddie Taylor, who was a senior and had been first chair for three years. One day he started mouthing off about me and my "oil field trash" parents, so I caught him outside the band hall and popped him a couple of times. When the band director got wind of my actions, he took me into his office to give me a lecture, but I was in no mood to listen. I walked out and went home, not saying a word to my mother about the incident.

The next day when I went to school, I was called into the principal's office where the band director and the principal explained that fighting was not acceptable at school, no matter what caused the trouble. The band director then told me he had a great solution: the band needed someone who could play the baritone. He thought I had the ability to make the transition from the trumpet with his tutelage. I knew what he was really doing, but I didn't care, so I agreed. The change of instruments resulted in my selection for the all-star band as a baritone player later that year.

My love for reading continued, and with my strongly developed vocabulary, I was able to enlarge my writing skills too, writing poetry and short stories. This talent soon made me somewhat popular, but it also created a problem for me. In a west Texas town, guys who wrote poetry were looked upon as, shall we say, "having a little sugar in their tank." This didn't really bother me, but in this small town with a bunch of narrow-minded people, rumors abounded, which troubled Harry.

I guess I confounded the rumors because I was popular with the girls. They were used to boys who became football players and acted tough and manly, but my poetry was basically about the love of God and His goodness, which flowed through real men. This didn't fit the rumors. I also found it amusing that some of the guys asked me to write poetry for their girlfriends and book reports for their English literature class. I agreed to do it for a few dollars.

The biggest surprise came when I joined the football team as a fullback. I also tried riding calves at the junior rodeo. Now all I had to do to be fully accepted was to start chewing Beechnut chewing tobacco, smoking Lucky Strike cigarettes, and drinking Lone Star beer, which was cheap, tasted awful, and caused bad headaches. All these extracurricular activities didn't allow me much time to study, especially unimaginative subjects like mathematics. Since I detested it and the math teacher, my math grades went downhill, especially when I was learning about algebra.

In those days we received report cards with alphabetical grades. My grades were usually A's or A pluses in English Literature with a nice comment on my report card from the teacher. I earned C's or D's in the rest of my classes with teacher notes about how I needed to work harder. My math grade was usually a D or an F with a nasty comment on my report card. I wasn't really concerned, though, because when six-week exams or semester tests came along, I found a way to do well enough on the tests to bring my grades up to a respectable level.

We were required to take our report cards home and get them signed by our parents. I had a girlfriend who would sign them on my behalf, after which I would return the documents to school. I also discovered a way to ensure my parents saw my "good" grades by getting a hold of some blank report cards. I had another girl fill them out for me with good grades like they were from the teachers. I would take these home for my mother to sign. We thought it was great fun until one day my friend came by my house after school when I wasn't home. He told my mom not to worry, that he had failed Algebra too, but we would work really hard to make the grade up. Needless to say, when I got home, the feces hit the rotating oscillator, and my life at home and school changed immediately.

I felt a new lack of confidence from my mother. It was my first almost criminal act in her mind because I had deceived everyone—my mother, the teachers, and the school. The teachers hadn't noticed that the report cards had been slightly mutilated to help cover up the girl's handwriting. It was a complete deviation from the truth, and I got caught. I told them that I wrote the report cards out myself.

"We know you aren't telling us the truth," they said.

"Then why are you asking me the question?" I countered. "It's evil to snitch."

That didn't happen again, not because of the consequences at school but because of my mom. I was suspended for two days. Thankfully, the girls who were helping me were never found out. This made me a good guy with the girls and my friends.

To join football and band, I needed passing grades, so I began doing my homework. It turned out to be kind of fun because the girls who helped me doctor my report cards came to my house to study, and we became good friends.

During this time, I also found relief in going to church. It was my place of refuge from the world outside. I could get alone, read my Bible, and feel the love of Jesus. When I was elected president of the Royal Ambassadors church youth group, I felt like I finally belonged somewhere. I thought no one could take it away from me. Unfortunately, I forgot about my temper. When a kid called my mother an oilfield bitch, I clocked him, and that did it—no more Royal Ambassadors president for me.

The rest of my sophomore year at school went okay with playing football during the fall, practicing with the band, and running a paper route, delivering the San Angelo Standard Times early in the morning, until Harry and I had a serious falling out. I bought an old Indian Scout motorcycle with my own money. I didn't really know how to ride, and I had a serious accident. A guy was riding on the back, and his leg got busted up, so he had to wear a cast.

When Harry got home and heard about it, he took a sledge-hammer to my motorcycle and busted out all the spokes in the wheels. Then he came in and started yelling at me, saying that as long as I lived under his roof and ate his food, I would abide by his rules. If I didn't like it, I could get out. I told him there were no rules about how I spent my money, so I would get out.

I had a friend who had a motor scooter that he wasn't riding because his dad had purchased a car for him. I explained the situation with Harry and asked to borrow his scooter to main-tain my paper route. He agreed, so I hopped on the scooter and went down to the local hotel and café. I told Mrs. Henderson, who owned and operated it, what had happened and said I would wash dishes and keep the hotel clean in exchange for room and board. She looked at me like I was crazy but laughed and agreed to have me do the work. Just like that, as a sopho-more in high school, I was living on my own.

The next morning, I was up and peeling potatoes in the kitchen at 5:30 a.m., as we had agreed. Then I did the other tasks that she wanted done and went to school. After school, I attended football practice and then went to the hotel to change clothes before beginning my evening shift, washing dishes. When I entered the café, to my surprise, my mother, Harry, Mrs. Henderson, and the local sheriff, Orville Edmiston, were all waiting for me. As soon as I walked in, the waitress who was working that evening closed the door behind me and then hurried out into the hotel lobby.

My mother and Mrs. Henderson were standing with tears rolling down their faces. Sheriff Orville came over to me and said we needed to talk because I was not old enough to be living by myself, and besides, Harry and my mother wanted me to come home. Mrs. Henderson told me that it broke her heart when I showed up and asked for work in exchange for room and board. She said she would not be able to use me anymore because she knew how broken-hearted my parents were over the situation. His entire body shaking, Harry apologized for damaging my motorcycle and admitted he was frightened by my accident. Then he shared that he had lost a brother in a motorcycle accident some time ago.

Harry's emotional apology caught me off guard, and I felt compelled to accept it when he offered his hand. When I told him that I was riding a motor scooter for my paper route, he said he already knew it, and he appreciated me telling him about it, but the decision for me to return home was final. I spoke to Mrs. Henderson, who agreed I could keep working for her before school, provided things were going well at home. That worked out well for me because I would go to the café at 5:00 or 5:30 a.m. to help get the kitchen ready for the day—peeling potatoes, preparing the coffee, and doing other menial tasks.

One extremely cold winter morning, I was busy peeling potatoes when I heard a tap on the back door. I opened it to find a small, older black man standing there. shivering, so I invited him to come in.

"I saw your light on, and it shore is cold," he said. "I would really likes to get a cup of your hot coffee, which I can pay for 'cause I gots money."

I told him to sit down, and I would get him a cup of coffee, and he wouldn't have to pay anything. When I brought him the cup of coffee, he took it graciously, then asked, "Could I get a saucer?" That surprised me, but I got him a saucer anyway. Much to my amazement, after he put the cream and sugar in the coffee and stirred it, he poured his coffee into the saucer and began to sip it from there.

As he drank his coffee, I peeled potatoes. Suddenly, Mrs. Henderson came storming into the room with a broom. She began hitting the little old man, calling him the N-word, and yelling at him to get out. The poor little old guy dropped his saucer and ran out. As he was making his escape, she scowled at me and said, "N-word lover. If you ever let another N-word in here, I'll kick you outta here." As she stormed out, I thought, *This is one of the ladies who sits in the Amen corner of the Eldorado First Baptist Church where the preacher assures us that we are all created in the image of God. Mrs. Henderson and the other people always shout a loud "Amen."* It was the first time I saw racism face to face, but it wasn't the last.

Just before I started my junior year of high school, I decided to get along with everyone at school, including teachers, and complete my homework. I even decided that I would play football. I wasn't very good at it, but I filled a spot, and if that made Harry and some other people happy, that was good. Sadly, it meant I had to sacrifice the marching band because I couldn't march in the band and play football at the same time. Nevertheless, I continued to practice, as my primary passion lay within the field of music.

Everything was going along well until one day in the middle of October when my speech teacher, Mr. Bowen, came into the class, all excited. "I have come up with a challenge for everyone in here," he said to the twenty or so students in the class. "You're going to write a soliloquy about whatever you want to write about. You pick the title, you pick the topic, and you write the soliloquy. Unlike a monologue, which is directed at the audience, the soliloquy is directed at yourself. It must be at least ten minutes but no longer than twelve minutes. You've got two weeks to get it done. When we finish, you will present your soliloquy to the class and the English Literature teacher. We will select the best one, and it will be entered in the district competition. They're going to decide from there on whichever one's the best."

The assignment didn't really thrill me, but it sounded like something I could do. In my early teens, I read a lot of Shakespeare, who was known for his soliloquies. The most notable were Hamlet's "To be or not to be," MacBeth's "Tomorrow, and tomorrow, and tomorrow," and my favorite, Mark Anthony's "Friends, Romans, Countrymen, lend me your ears."

Later at home, I began thinking more about the assignment. Suddenly, I remembered reading Ayn Rand's *Atlas Shrugged* in eighth grade. Shortly after I did a book report on it, I got called to the office. My mother was there, and I asked, "What's going on?" They wanted to know where I got that book because it was banned in the Eldorado Public Library. "I got it in San Angelo," I said. "We were up there, and I saw it, and it piqued my interest, so I bought it. What's wrong with it?" They explained that it was written by an atheist, and it was about the love of money. "Okay," I said. "What's wrong with that? I'm not an atheist, and it's okay to work for money. Why do you work if money's bad?" That didn't sit well. So, they suspended me for one day and told my mom to take me home and straighten me out.

I had kind of forgotten about reading *Atlas Shrugged* until my junior year. During that time, there were other censored books like *To Kill a Mockingbird* and *Catcher in the Rye.* I was able to get my hands on them and read them, and I didn't see anything evil in them, but it got me thinking. An atheist doesn't believe in God, which I could not fathom. The best I could see, science had never disproved it. There were no facts given to prove that God doesn't exist. However, in the Bible, it says, "In the beginning God," and nobody had disproved that. So, I believed in the Almighty God who created the heavens and the Earth. In *Atlas Shrugged,* the main character is John Galt. He created a motor that would turn the world. The other main characters include Hank Reardon, who is the head of the steel mills, and Dagny Talbert, who is the head of the railroads. They are depicted as independent thinkers who earn other people's respect through honesty rather than manipulation, and I thought, *Buddy, you have not been doing that, but maybe it's time.* This encouraged me to write the soliloquy.

That book became sort of an anthem for people my age. I was inspired not to fall into collectivism like we were encouraged to do in Eldorado. Everything we did was supposed to be for the good of the community, the school, or our parents. But then they told us that they wanted us to be thinkers. It was confusing because as I watched the people of Eldorado, they didn't seem to be following that rule. I put it all together and encouraged myself to become an independent thinker. Because of our young age, though, we couldn't be trusted. We still had one year left to go in high school, and then we were out and off to college or to work. Being independent thinkers could have given us recognition for traits such as honesty, diligence, and self-reliance.

As I read and studied, I developed my own philosophy. I could not go along with collectivism, but I did not agree with objectivism, as I believed that reason is supported by faith, which I considered essential to the process. For me, everything I did had a certain amount of faith in it, even if I was doing something as simple as turning on a light switch. I had faith that there was going to be light if I flipped the switch on. I had faith that it was going to be dark if I flipped the switch off. I trusted restaurants would have food to order. So, to do away with faith was not reasonable.

This is when I came up with the idea that I was born alone, I would live alone, and I would die alone. I am not trying to be maudlin, but it is true; I was born alone, a screaming, bawling little brat. As I grew up, people came into my life, but they also left me, and I left them. That was just part of life.

As I got older, it became apparent that I thought differently from other people, and now there I was, a junior in speech class. I have an opportunity to express my innermost thoughts, not directed at the class, Mr. Bowen, the English teacher, or anybody else. I shared my honest thoughts as an independent thinker. This went against the grain of a lot of people in Eldorado because they wanted me to be what they wanted me to be.

I was tethered to Eldorado and to my parents by several factors, the most prevalent of which was financial. I had to respect the rules and laws of my home and my town, but I didn't have to respect their opinions, even though I was only a junior in high school. I had my own thoughts. It was time that I started working them out and making my way because I had that year left and then my senior year, then I'd be off to the work world or college.

My soliloquy was honest, but it would create a problem for some of the people in Eldorado, because hypocrisy ran rampant there. I pointed that out. There were people in Eldorado who supposedly walked and talked well, but their walk wasn't as good as their talk. The Bible tells us that the truth will set us free. If that was good enough for the Bible and Ayn Rand, who wrote the same thing in *Atlas Shrugged*, then it was good enough for me. Between the two, I could come up with a philosophy of my own and how I wanted to walk through the world as I grew older.

When it was finally my turn to present our soliloquies to the class, the English teacher, and Mr. Bowen, it got awfully quiet. The tension was thick because I had garnered quite a reputation for not only my writing talent but also my caustic attitude. As soon as I was done reading it, everyone sat in stunned silence for a full minute. Then the kids erupted in applause. That didn't sit well with Mr. Bowen.

He came over and snatched the paper away from me. "Mr. Mercer, did you write this, or did you plagiarize it from somebody?" he asked. "You know, that's illegal."

I stood up to face him. *You know,* I thought, *what I just read, my soliloquy, is about people who are honest and truthful. And now here you are, a phony hypocrite, because I've seen you in precarious positions with different people.* "Mr. Bowen, I wrote it. It's mine, and reflects my thoughts. You told us that whoever wrote the best one was going to present it in the school contest, and I believe that'll be me."

The next thing I knew, I was going to the principal's office. They explained that my soliloquy was far above my ability to think and reason. "Well, that's what I wrote," I said. At that point, it dawned on me that I was not going to be allowed to present my soliloquy, that Mr. Bowen had other ideas.

"Buddy, I'm going to give your soliloquy to one of the girls who's a senior and mentally more impressive, and I'm going to have her take it to the district contest.

"You know what?" I replied. "You can do what you want to, but you'll never take those words away from me. They're my words from my heart, my soul, and my mind, and you're a phony hypocrite. So, go ahead and take it, and see what happens."

He did take it to the senior girl, but she came to me and said, "Buddy, I am sorry."

"Judy, I want you to take it and do the best you can," I replied. "You will be performing my work because I wrote it, but it's going to be you who sells it."

Sure enough, she took it to the district competition and won. When she competed at the regional level, she placed second among more than thirty contestants from the entire state. After she returned from regionals, she wrote a piece for the *Eldorado Success* newspaper. "I was pleased to have taken Buddy Mercer's soliloquy to the district and regional contests," she wrote. "His writing moved me forward with my life." Upon reading that, I reflected on the implications. *I don't care what anybody else thinks. I know who I am, and I know what I am, and that's what's going to get me to go from here.* There were pros and cons to my situation, but at the end of the day, I was complete within myself. However, after that confrontation with Mr. Bowen, I adopted a different view of what my junior year was going to look like.

I continued to practice the baritone and trumpet daily. That didn't work out so well, though, because both require that I apply my mouth to the mouthpiece in different ways; apply a different embouchure, that is. So, I dropped the trumpet and continued with the baritone. I also continued to play football, and I did well enough to make the team.

Football in the South, especially in Texas, is more than a game. It's a religion. Such was Eldorado. Our little town only had about 1,700 people, but when the farmers and ranchers and spectators from the other town came in on Friday night, we'd have 2,500 to 3,000 people in the stands. There were some perks to being a high school football player. If we played on a Friday night and won, we got to go play pool at the pool hall on Saturday morning. We also got free milkshakes at the drugstore.

One Saturday morning after a successful football game, we were shooting pool, having a good time, when we heard the town marshal bragging about how he had some fine watermelons in his backyard. He was being very protective of them because one of the thrills around Eldorado was stealing watermelons. When we heard him bragging about his watermelons, that put an idea in our mind that we might want to take one of them. But then we heard him say, "if they try to steal watermelons out of my yard, they'll have a surprise coming." That just fanned the flame of challenge in our hearts.

A couple of nights later, after midnight, we snuck to his house, which was on the edge of the town. When we got to his backyard, it was about one hundred yards from the fence to his house, and in the middle of that was the watermelon patch. Just as we got to the watermelons, we hit a tripwire, but we grabbed a watermelon and ran. Suddenly, the porch light came on.

We dropped the watermelon and took off. Just as we jumped over the fence, we heard a gunshot, and it was not a shotgun. We were used to being shot at with buckshot or bird shot from a shotgun, but this was a whole other deal. He was firing it .30-06 (pronounced "thirty ought six"). That was one time I outran the other two guys. Normally, they were faster than me. I also knew that bullets couldn't turn corners, so I ran to the nearest building and ducked behind it.

The next Saturday, we were in the pool hall, and the marshal was talking about his watermelons, saying he thought he knew who did it. "I didn't shoot at them with the shotgun. I shot a .30-06," he said.

"Well, what if you'd have killed them?" someone asked.

"I didn't shoot to kill," the marshal replied.

"You know with your aim, anything bad could have happened," someone else said, chuckling. Everybody got a big laugh out of it.

Toward the end of October, we had our homecoming football game against our archrivals from a town called Sonora, located about twenty miles away. A couple of buddies and I decided we would go to Sonora and burn a big E on their football field for Eldorado. In the middle of the night, we snuck down there and poured about twenty gallons of gasoline in the shape of a big E on their football field. Then we lit it on fire and took off.

The next day, there was a big to-do about what had happened in Sonora, but nobody knew who did it. They had their suspicions, of course, but they weren't able to prove anything.

Our schedule also included games against Ozona and Big

Lake. We got wind that players from all three teams were going to retaliate by burning a big S, O, B on our field for Sonora, Ozona and Big Lake. So, some friends and I went out to our football field and waited. Right on cue, a few cars showed up. As they carried the gasoline cans onto the football field, we turned on all the floodlights, and the war was on. They ran like hell, but we caught up with some of them. Some punches were thrown, but we let them get away, then everyone went home.

The next day at school, we were identified as those responsible for the "big E incident." As punishment, we had to go to Sonora and apologize. But it was worth it because some of their guys looked a little raggedy due to our earlier confrontation.

The following spring, there was no football. I didn't play basketball, and I refused to run track because I wasn't fast enough, so we started playing baseball on Sunday afternoons, but it wasn't any fun. Some weird guys would come to the field, and they just wanted to goof around. I really liked baseball, and I was pretty good at it, but I wanted to play with more serious guys. Then someone told me, "If you want to play baseball, go to the town where the black folks live," a place that was kind of like a suburb to Eldorado.

"Buddy, what the hell are you doing down here?" one of the black guys I knew asked when I showed up.

"I came to play baseball," I replied.

"Oh, white boy," he said, "you come on over to enjoy a baseball game is what you did, so have fun with us."

And it was fun. But later that day when I got home, my mother confronted me. "Buddy, you can't be going there. We're oil field trash already, and now you're taking us another level lower, so you can't go back there." I agreed to abide by her wishes. It wasn't prejudice or racism on our part. It was the fact that we had been termed oil field trash, and anything I did reflected on my parents. So, I just focused on my academics until the end of the school year. I received my grades through my own efforts.

I got a job in the summer and performed well. Seeing as I was making money, I bought a car. It was an older vehicle, but it got me around town.

That summer a girl showed up from a town in North Texas. She was the granddaughter of a rancher whom I knew, and we happened to go to the same church. She was visiting her grandparents for the summer. For some reason, she took a liking to me, which was okay because she was pretty. We would meet at the drugstore and have milkshakes, and we'd go out to the roadside park and have some fun.

One Sunday her grandpa, the rancher, came up to me and said, "Buddy, I understand you're dating my granddaughter."

"Although the idea did not originate with me, that is acceptable," I replied.

"Boy, you better treat her like gold, or I'll be after you," he warned. I got the point.

She began to get serious about us and what we could do together after our senior year. I was only trying to make it through the rest of the summer. I hadn't even thought about my senior year. Then, just before she left for home, we had a big party. The girl announced that she was in love with me and that I was going to be her boyfriend, even though she had to go back to North Texas. We would have to see if our long distance "relationship" went anywhere.

After she left, I started running with some rowdy kids, and

somehow I became the leader of the pack. We didn't do anything really bad, at least not as I saw it, but in that small town, I was looked down on by the "better than thou" folks. I guess it was the "do as I say, not as I do" attitude that didn't sit well with me, so I rebelled. I had been noticing things at school that I knew were wrong. The male history teacher was making it with the school secretary. The principal was making it with the PE teacher. And I caught the speech teacher drinking from his whiskey flask just before class. I quickly realized that the word "hypocrite" was meant for Eldorado adults. Worse yet, I caught a deacon with a woman from the church in the backseat of a car in the school parking lot. I often thought the song "Peyton Place" was written about Eldorado.

Eldorado was in a dry county, meaning liquor could not be sold anywhere. The nearest place for Eldorado residents to buy liquor was twelve miles away in Sutton County at a liquor store named Brushy Top, which got its name from a big, tall tree that stood above it. Naturally, I had to see what was going on.

One Saturday evening I parked my car in an oak thicket some distance away and walked up with my trusty Polaroid camera, then hid from view. Sure enough, I got pictures of deacons and elite businessmen who sat on the front row of the church coming out of Brushy Top. It was at that point that I began to question God's existence. If these people lived like they did, why should I waste my time going to church?

Even though I was having an agnostic crisis, I still wanted to have a good time outside with my friends. One day my friend Ikey decided we needed to make what he called apricot brandy. He said he knew how to do it. So, we went and got a gallon jar, then we got some apricots and strained them and got the juice out. We added sugar and all the other stuff that goes into the drink, then we wrapped it up in a burlap bag and went in search of a warm, humid place for fermentation. My parents' house had a closet for the hot water heater that had just enough room for that gallon jar, so that's where we hid it.

Later, my parents hosted a domino party with friends. They had four couples over for the evening. They would barbecue and then after supper they would play dominos. My friends and I decided we weren't going to leave just yet because we wanted to eat the barbeque. Everyone was chatting when, suddenly, there was an explosion. Ikey looked at me and said, "Oh, crap!"

"What was that?" one of the parents asked. "It sounded like an explosion."

"I think we have a bit of a problem here," one of the dads added. "I smell alcohol."

They checked the hot water heater closet and found apricot brandy all over the floor and all over that hot water heater. The adults appeared to find it amusing, so they proceeded to play dominoes. Ikey and I just sat out on the front porch, waiting for all hell to break loose. Sure enough, after everyone went home, there was no sleeping that night for me. I had to stay up and clean apricot brandy from all over the floor and the walls.

As summer wound down, I vowed that I was not going to play football during my senior year because I had been notified that I might be getting a music scholarship to North Texas State in Denton, Texas. That was exciting to me because it was a well-known party school. More than that, it had a great music program. That was going to be my goal for my senior year—to get that scholarship.

I skipped football practices when they commenced in August, but I did not contact the coach regarding my absence. One night when I got home, my mom said, "You got some company coming." It was the principal and the football coach.

Oh, I know what they want, I thought. I told my mom and Harry that I had decided that I wasn't going to play football, that I was going to try to get a scholarship to North Texas State. It meant more to me because I wasn't good enough to get a football scholarship. Amazingly, for once in my life, Harry and my mother agreed with me. When the football coach and the principal came, they started talking about how my grades probably wouldn't allow me to graduate.

"Hey, you know, I don't care what you do," I said. "I'm not going to play football, so make your plans. I'm not that good. You can replace me with anybody. Besides that, I have some information about teachers doing things they probably should not be doing. Maybe we should talk about that."

That lit a fire. They weren't happy with my attitude, but they took off, and that was the last I heard about it. Instead of playing in the football games, I was part of the marching band, and I had a great time doing that.

It was a pretty good senior year. The girl from North Texas continued to call and write, and I talked to her on the phone. When she told me that she loved me. I thought, *Okay, let's see what's going to happen here.*

At Christmas, her family and mine gathered together. It was kind of an awkward situation because her daddy was a big-time jeweler in a North Texas town, and they were well to do. There we were, little, old oil field trash. It wasn't uncomfortable for us because we knew who we were and what we were doing, but it was very uncomfortable for them. Our parents got along well with each other, though, which helped.

When they got ready to leave, her daddy said, "I want to talk to you for a minute." He and I went outside, and he said, "You know, I don't know what my daughter sees in you, but she has her mind made up that you guys are gonna continue on after school's out and that things are gonna probably lead up to getting married."

"Well, I don't know about that," I replied.

"Consider it," he countered. "Because if you marry my daughter, you will never have to find work. You can work for me in the jewelry store. You will be making a lot of money, and you can have a house that I have up there, and everything will be set for you. So, just take that into consideration." I was stunned because that just was not going to get it with me, but we went ahead with the rest of the year.

By springtime, all I wanted to do was make it to the end of the school year. I had figured out that I probably wasn't going to get a scholarship to North Texas State, so I had no desire to go to school because nothing there held my interest. I did what I needed to do, and I placed twenty-seventh out of twenty-eighth in my class, graduating by the skin of my teeth.

3

FROM HIGH SCHOOL TO JAIL

ONE NIGHT RIGHT AFTER GRADUATION, a friend of mine came by and said, "Get some money and some clothes together. We're going for a ride."

"Okay, cool," I replied. "Where are we going?"

"I got a surprise," he said.

So, I got some money and clothes together, and we took off.

By the time we got to Texarkana, we had had a couple of drinks, so I asked him again where we were going. "We gonna go to Murfreesboro, Tennessee, the home of Middle Tennessee State College," he replied. "And, Buddy, they got beautiful women there. It's just like a banquet. Maybe more like a smorgasbord 'cause you can pick what you want. We're gonna have a ball."

That sounded like a good idea to me, but we didn't quite make it to Murfreesboro. Instead, we made it to a place called Printer's Alley in Nashville. We had some drinks with the

Tennessee boys, and things quickly got rowdy on both sides. Suddenly, my friend and I are standing on the table, singing "The Eyes of Texas Are Upon You." We got thrown out, not down the stairs but up the stairs. They put a pretty good whipping on us.

When we got to the motel and got cleaned up, we looked at each other and said, "We ain't gonna go to Murfreesboro." So, we turned around and headed home.

I went to work for a guy named Marvin Looney who was building a service station in Eldorado. He was quite a character. Marvin taught me how to lay bricks. He liked my work, and I worked hard. I had a lot of fun with the money I was making too.

During that time I made a couple of decisions that created problems for people. The first one happened when I called my girlfriend in North Texas and told her that I didn't want to see her anymore. She blew up, bawling and squalling, and told me that her daddy had already planned on us getting married. Invitations had been sent out, and they planned to discuss it with me later. She told me that we could get married in August, on my birthday.

"Well," I replied, "I'm sorry, but I'm not gonna be there. If you got a problem with that, I'm sorry. I've got other plans. I'm gonna have a job. I don't want your daddy's money, and that eliminates you."

The thing I knew, her daddy called and told me he was going to do terrible things to me and that I'd regret this decision. He was going to put a restraining order on me. I didn't know what that meant, but I also thought he was going to put a hit job out on me the way he was talking. "If you ever come to North Texas, around his town, you'd better be careful," he warned. I had no plans to go there, so that didn't bother me. Her rancher grandpa ran into me in the pool hall and told me he was unhappy with the decision too, which made me nervous. Later that year, I was in Austin, Texas, with a friend, checking out the girls who went to the University of Texas, and I nearly ran smack into that girl and one of her friends on the sidewalk. I did the only thing a guy could do: I ran like hell.

The other decision I made was about my original plans to go to North Texas State. I hadn't heard anything about that music scholarship, and I was enjoying my job and its perks. So, I told my parents that I wasn't going to go to college. I was going to continue to work at my bricklaying job until the service station was finished. Then I'd be moving on because Marvin had another job lined up in Big Spring, Texas. After all, I had graduated from high school, I was on my own, and I was paying my own way, so I thought it was time for me to go. As always, the storm came, and my mother started crying.

I didn't realize it, but they got a call from my uncle Roy, the Methodist minister. A couple of days later, my mom and Harry were so excited to tell me that I had a music scholarship to McMurray College in Abilene, Texas, thanks to my uncle. That made me wonder if I did get a scholarship to North Texas State, but somehow the only one that I heard about was from McMurray. I decided that to eliminate the problem of my mother being upset, I'd go to college. Little did I realize that decision was a serious mistake.

In early August, my friends and I went to San Angelo

College to take the SAT for college admission. My parents were out of town. The night before, a couple of my friends came over, as we were all going to ride to San Angelo, which was about forty-five miles away, then we were going to party there together afterwards. My buddies brought over three or four bottles of Silver Satin charcoal-filtered wine. It had to be the cheapest of the cheap wines, but when a group of guys are getting ready to go to college, they're bound to have a little fun. They're going to have their libations.

We began by drinking wine and setting off some bottle rockets. The night watchman happened to come by while we were out in the middle of the street, setting them off, and asked what we were doing. The guy was like a Barney Fife character, so we had a little fun with him, then sent him on his way. Then along came Bill Tillison, the route manager from the San Angelo *Standard Times* newspaper that I delivered in Eldorado. "What are you guys doing out here?" he asked. "How'd you guys like a little shot of Jack Daniels?" That sounded good, so we had some Jack Daniels, and we had some more of that wine. Then we realized, hey, we're a little bit drunk, so we better get some sleep because it's going to be a hard day tomorrow.

When we woke up the next morning, we realized we were in no condition to take the SAT. However, you do what you gotta do. So, we jumped in the car and drove to San Angelo. Now, the problem with cheap wine is when you drink water, it hits you again. And we were thirsty. So, as we drove to San Angelo, we drank some water, and sure enough, not only did it play with our minds, it also played with our stomachs. We were not feeling good, but we got into that room to take the test. The windows were open, but it was still warm in there. They handed out the test, which consisted of multiple-choice questions, and we had to mark our answers in little circles. Trying to hit those little circles was not working.

Suddenly, Ikey ran to the door. I heard him vomiting as he went down the hall. Initially, I was amused, only to realize I had to chase after him with the same issue.

Eventually, Ikey and I made it outside, but our other friend, Jimmy, didn't come out until later. We were lying on the grass when one of the professors came out. He took a look at us and said, "Are you boys okay? Oh, my God, you're drunk." That ended our testing for the day.

When we made it back home, our parents were not very proud of us. We got an invitation to go and take the SAT again. We passed, so we could go to college.

In the last part of August of that year, my parents had to take me to McMurray because we had been informed that I wouldn't be allowed to have my car there. It wasn't running very well anyhow. When we got to McMurray, I saw right away that I was out of place because I was probably the only guy there wearing a Levi's belt, cowboy boots, snap-button shirt, and a Stetson hat. Most of the other guys were wearing slacks, button-down shirts, and slippers. *Well, this is a fine how do you do,* I thought.

We checked in, then met the band and director Doctor Raymon Bynum, who was enthusiastic about playing Sousa marches. I think he thought he was John Phillips Sousa reincarnated. When I walked into the band hall, Professor Bynum took one look at me and asked, "Who are you?"

"I'm Buddy Mercer," I replied.

"You're the baritone."

"That's what I'm up here to be," I said. "I believe I have a scholarship."

"Well, I must explain to you that when you come to college, you become a man," he said. "You don't come up here in cowboy clothes because we don't have cowboys here. You will wear slacks and a button-down shirt. Let me think here. You said your name is Buddy?"

"That's correct, sir," I replied.

"Well . . . . Buddy's not a real name. What's your middle name?"

"Roy."

"Okay, from here on, you will be known as Roy Mercer."

I laughed. "No, I don't think so. I'm Buddy. I've always been Buddy."

"Then you will not play in my band," he replied. "Because I don't allow scholarships to young men who are named Buddy."

"Then I'm not here," I countered and walked out.

As I started trying to figure out how to get home, it hit me: I didn't have any place to go. While I was walking out of the band hall, one of the seniors, a trumpet player and the leader of the band's brass section, approached me. "You will be learning a new way of life. Be Roy in the band and be Buddy everywhere else." He mentored me to become a member of the band in the eyes of Professor Bynum. I got the hint right away. Dr. Bynum truly accepted me when he heard me playing, especially when we played the Colonel Bogey March from "The Bridge on the River Kwai." I played the baritone part well.

It was quite a year because the band did a lot of traveling. I will credit Dr. Bynum with one thing: he knew how to put on halftime shows. They were quite exciting, and it was fun to march in them. We'd also go out of town and play in Methodist churches, billeted in people's homes.

That part was all well and good, but I also discovered colleges have sororities and fraternities and all that kind of stuff, which I had no intention of joining. That was for the "real" college boys, and I wasn't one of them. I looked at things a bit differently, and I still thought about rodeoing and having a good time.

I found out that the college football players, or "animals," as they were called, had a club of their own called the "Dirty Shirts." I got a special invitation to join. It was a lot of fun, but the hazing was brutal. We had to carry a paddle with us, and they'd give us a swat every once in a while. We also had to repeat slogans about freshmen.

"A freshman is so low, he could crawl beneath the belly of a snake with a top hat on and never tickle the snake's belly."

"A freshman could dangle his feet over the edge of a sheet of paper and never touch the ground."

Freshmen were viewed as slime, the lowest form of life. They gave us a paddle. They gave us a whack. There were some other things that weren't fun, but we also had some great times.

Some of these great times probably shouldn't have been going on at a Methodist campus, but they had beer-drinking parties, and we partied a lot. One night we had a great idea. I had heard about these things called panty raids. Three or four of the football players thought that'd be great sport, so we decided to let the girls know we were going to do a panty raid. That put a kibosh on it right away because that wasn't going to happen at a Methodist college.

Then a serious thing happened—the Cuban Missile Crisis. President John F Kennedy was speaking on television, and it looked like we might be going to war. All the guys decided we needed to say farewell to the girls in a fine way. The funny thing was, a campus assembly was called in the main hall. The girls were told, "These boys are not going to be going to war, so they don't need to be making love before they go to war. They're going to be staying here and going to college. So, ladies, keep your legs together." It was an unusual way to be told such a thing in a co-ed Methodist College.

One of the defining features of my life is the constant presence of unusual events. One day I was out with a couple of the guys, walking the streets of Abilene, when we happened to go into a pawn shop. While looking around, I spotted a valve trombone. I'd never seen one before. I talked to the guy who was running the shop, and he said, "I dang near give that thing away because nobody wants it, but if you can give me fifty dollars for it, you got it." My colleagues and I pooled our money to reach fifty dollars, and I bought that valve trombone, case included.

As soon as we got back to campus, I went to the band hall and started playing it. It used a baritone mouthpiece, which I played well. I discovered that, using the valves, I could make it sound like a slide trombone, and it had a great staccato sound. Professor Bynum liked me even more, as he now had a valve trombone in his band.

But as usual, things fell apart when we had some issues with some other colleges in the area—Abilene Christian College (ACC), Howard Payne, and Hardin Simmons. Some of us from McMurray got together with some fellas from Howard Payne and Hardin Simmons to toilet paper ACC, and it turned into a big deal. They decided they wanted to get a bit rowdy, and the fight was on. The Abilene police were called, and we were hauled in. I don't know why we got hauled in, and the boys from ACC who started the trouble didn't, but it got around that we were troublemakers.

Dr. Bynum found out about the incident and called me into his office. "I can't have that in my band," he said. "Either you straighten up or we're going to have to revoke your scholarship."

I knew my parents would be broken-hearted and that Uncle Roy had been instrumental in getting me a scholarship, so I didn't want to add to it, but at the same time, I had the opportunity to play in a dance band. This was off limits for a McMurray student, but I figured I could handle it as long as it stayed secret. The sad thing was that the guy who led the band loved to play Tony Bennett's, "I Left My Heart in San Francisco," which was okay, but it got a bit old. He liked my abilities and really liked having my valve trombone in his band, so I was accepted. Then things started going sideways because when we played in those places, the ladies would come around and offer drinks. I didn't dare go on campus with the booze on my breath because I didn't want to get kicked out of school, so I quit the dance band.

By the end of the first semester, I felt that being at McMurray was a waste of my time and a waste of a good dorm room, but I didn't have a choice. I had to push through until the end of the year. There were times when things got quite interesting. A lot of the animals, the athletes, stayed in the same dorm as me on the lower floors. So, there was always something going on, and I was involved in it. We had a lot of fun, but the only interest that I had academically was in band and in music. When Professor Bynum figured out that I was going to stay, he put me in some places in the songs because I picked up music quickly, and I was doing well in music class. Outside of music, though, my interests lay with having a good time.

Frenchie Poe, my roommate, was older than me. He was a premed student. He had this idea that we could get by with one hour of sleep at night (midnight until 1:00 a.m.), then rest fifteen minutes every two hours. I went along with it, but all it did was screw up my sleep pattern, so I missed some of my classes. He turned out not to be a good guy. The next thing I know, the FBI came and got him. He had deserted from the Army, I guess, so they took him away.

In the dorm we had a guy named Hickory McGowan, who was quite the character. He would often sit on the commode, sound asleep. When he wasn't sleeping, he was messing around in the science lab. He was a smart guy, but he liked running tests in the lab. One day we heard a huge explosion. Hickory had mixed something that shouldn't have been mixed and blew up part of the science lab. He went to the hospital, and then he went home—for good.

In the room next door to mine at the dorm was a football player named Morrow Hunsaker. He was six foot five, weighed 240 pounds, and was meaner than a junkyard dog. He was really good at football and went on to play for the New York Giants. We were both freshmen, and Morrow was rowdy and liked to have a lot of fun.

His roommate was a serious medical student. He had gone out and caught seven rattlesnakes, wanting to milk their venom. That night he brought the snakes back to his dorm room in a burlap bag, which was tied up with twine. When Morrow came into their room a bit later, he had been drinking and was a bit tipsy. When he saw the bag, he decided to find out what was in it. He opened it and saw the rattlesnakes. Instead of closing it, he jumped up on his desk and started yelling. There he was, standing on the desk in his boxers, screaming like a little girl.

Someone else heard him screaming and went to find out what was going on. When he opened the door, he saw rattlesnakes all over the floor. Instead of closing the door behind him, he took off, and the rattlesnakes went out into the hall, going every which way. The dorm supervisor called the police, but they wanted nothing to do with rattlesnakes. So, they called a guy who caught snakes for a living. He caught five of the snakes, but he couldn't find the other two, leaving everyone too scared to sleep in the dorm.

Shortly after that, in a move that was completely out of character, Professor Bynum put together a stage band to play for a televised polio telethon that was to be held in the school auditorium. He included me in it with my valve trombone. McMurray College would get some good promotion out of our stage band playing on live TV. The entertainment for the telethon included the cast of the *Beverly Hillbillies*, including Max Bayer, Donna Douglas, Irene Ryan, and Buddy Ebsen. They had just come on the scene in Hollywood, and they were showing off. It was a fun time, except things got a bit out of hand. Bette Davis was also there, and she was a diva. She stormed up to Professor Bynum and told him that if he didn't get a professional band, she was leaving.

"Well, there's the door over there," he replied. "Go ahead and leave."

She threw a fit. The dean of men came over and proceeded to calm her down. He promised that they would do something for her but that our stage band was doing well. We were getting calls from the television audience, saying they liked the music that we played, so they were going to stay with us. She stormed out.

We still had the *Beverly Hillbillies* to entertain us. We decided to take up a little offering. For some reason, we decided we were going to talk to Donna Douglas about buying her pants and then selling them for the polio telethon. Right there, just off stage, she dropped her pants. Fortunately, she had some bloomers on or something, and we put her pants up for sale. Somebody bought them, and then we made up a deal that we were going to give her five dollars a kiss. It turned out to be a bad idea because Max Baer was not happy. He was a big old boy, and he got a hold of one of our guys and kind of threw him across the stage. It was a mess.

Shortly thereafter, we were invited to play at the Sweetwater Rattlesnake Roundup. It was a big deal in West Texas; Sweetwater had been holding the event for many years. They brought in celebrities, and they invited our stage band to participate. The entertainment included two comedians, Red Buttons and Moms Mabley. Moms was an African American lady who had come out as a lesbian, and she used a lot of profanity. None of this was normally accepted in West Texas, but people loved their acts.

After we finished our set, some of the rattlesnake rustlers came up to us and said they needed a rattlesnake catcher. One of them looked straight at me and said, "I think you would make a good catcher." When I asked him what I would have to do, he said, "Hold the burlap bag open while I catch the snake with my gig and put it inside." It sounded pretty simple, so I gave it a shot.

What they didn't tell me was that they had a rattlesnake den up on the side of the hill, loaded with rattlers. When we got out in front of the den, a couple of guys who were up on the hill above the den poured gas into the den. Then they dropped a flaming rag into the gas, causing an explosion that set things on fire and sent the terrified rattlesnakes slithering out of the cave.

"Stand still, and they'll leave you alone," the guy said. "They want out of there." Then he grabbed a rattlesnake right behind the head and dropped it into my bag, tail first. A man saw a rattlesnake around his boot and took off running and yelling. The rattlesnake thrashed as the man screamed. They finally caught the guy and pulled the snake off his boot, then chopped the snake's head off. After the rattlers were caught, they were taken to guys who milked the venom out, then they killed them and made rattlesnake steak barbecue. I hadn't tried that delicacy before, but they said it tasted like chicken. Everything tasted like chicken in Texas, so I decided to try it. It was so good I didn't even know I was eating rattlesnake.

At the end of the year, after the spring semester was over and my days at McMurray were done, I packed up my bags and left with no regrets. I had a job at home doing road construction waiting for me. I knew the foreman, and he was going to teach me. I would be driving a bulldozer and handling related tasks. I was looking forward to that.

When I got home, I went directly to work, and I learned a lot. It was difficult because I was playing with dynamite and dynamite holes in the side of the hills. The foreman told me that handling dynamite could lead to headaches but indicated it was an expected aspect of the process. "You'll get over it," he said.

Then I got a phone call about a scholarship for the Cisco Junior College band. I talked to the guy from the school. He knew me from my days in Eldorado, and he said he could get me a full scholarship because the school was starting a marching band. There would be a stage band too, and he said the director was a fantastic guy whom they were fortunate to have. He thought I'd be a good match. I told him I didn't think so because I wanted to stay in Eldorado. However, my friend from high school called and said he had also received a scholarship and hoped I would go, so we could be roommates. I told him I would consider it, but I thought we should drive up and check out the campus first.

Cisco Junior College (CJC) was a small school that had been built on top of a hill overlooking the little town of Cisco, Texas, where Conrad Hilton started the Hilton Hotel chain. He built his first hotel there in 1919. The only other thing of note about the town was the "Santa Claus Bank Robbery" that took place on December 23, 1927.

To reach the campus, we had to drive up the hill on a small, narrow, winding road. CJC had only about fifteen buildings, some of which were near the edge of the hill. Upon arriving on campus, the first sight that caught my attention was about thirty pretty girls in shorts and skimpy tops performing on the campus parade ground. It was the girls drill team, known as the Cisco Jr. College Wrangler Belles. After this impressive welcome, we met the band director, who looked like he was not far removed from college himself. We soon found that he was a highly respected musician and instructor. He gave us a tour of the campus and then excused himself, as he had some school business to take care of. We were left to explore the small school on our own. We went to see some of the classrooms in one of the newer buildings, which sat on the edge of the hill with a great view of downtown Cisco, which was not impressive at all.

We asked a guy who was a professor where we could find the guy who had called us, offering us the scholarships. He was very congenial, welcoming us to CJC and was quite informative. He told us that the guy who had called us was very excited that we were coming and was looking forward to meeting us. He directed us to the building and said the office was down the hall on the right. Upon entering the building, we did not find an office to our right. Instead, we noticed a staircase directly ahead. We proceeded upstairs, assuming the office would be located on the right at the top of the stairs. Suddenly, all hell broke loose.

It turned out we were in the Wrangler Bells dorm where they were showering and getting ready for lunch. They started screaming and throwing things. We were in the wrong place and not welcome, so we beat a hasty retreat. Later, we went to the cafeteria for lunch and met the band director, who was dying with laughter, as he had heard about our escapade in the dorm. Then to add insult to injury, he introduced us to a very pretty lady who was not only his wife but also the director of the Wrangler Belles. She was also laughing, but she made it very clear that her girls were off limits.

We got our food and went to a table, but before we sat down, he introduced us to the girls, who received us with giggles. They told us they hoped we would join them at CJC. I took one look at my friend and knew I was ready to give college another try. This choice turned out to be disastrous because it was, once again, just one party after another. In retrospect, it amazes me how I could turn something good into something evil, which had a devastating effect on the rest of my life.

Once again, I made friends easily, and shortly after school started, half a dozen of my new friends and I decided we should have a panty raid on the girl's dorm, the two-story building where the Wrangler Belles were housed. We figured it would be great fun so one evening we put our plan into action. Unfortunately, just as we started the raid, a thunderstorm with lightning, thunder, wind, and hail struck the area, but we were not to be deterred. Undaunted, we began raising the ladders. The girls cheered us on. Suddenly, all hell broke loose because someone had snitched on us, and the Cisco police, campus police, and fire department lit us up. We all started running, forgetting the area was covered with cactus, thorns, and rocks. It was an ugly scene as guys were falling off the roof and off the side of the hill. We forgot that some of the buildings were set on the edge of a hill, which had an over sixty-foot drop. Thankfully, no one was badly injured, but many had bumps, bruises, sprained ankles, and so on. The injuries made it clear about who had participated. The dean of men put me, the ringleader, on probation. "Your reputation has preceded you, and we will not tolerate this kind of nonsense," he said. Fortunately, the band director stepped in and saved us, but he made it clear he expected us to get our act together, or the college would revoke our scholarships.

After that dust up, we kind of settled down. The band

performed well, and all the members were skilled musicians. They also had a sense of humor. We had a lot of fun, and we marched in parades all over West Texas. Earl Hesse, the band director, would occasionally request our absence from school on short notice to participate in activities aimed at developing the band. These efforts received positive feedback. The dean of men praised our band. He was very proud of us, especially when we got an invitation to play at the Tri-State Stage Band competition at Stephen F. Austin University in Nacogdoches, Texas. It was going to be an overnight trip. We really looked forward to it.

That was in November, and although we were eagerly anticipating it, other activities kept things engaging. We had a rodeo club, a yachtsman club, and all sorts of other clubs. The animal athletes were just about as bad as they were at McMurray, but the CJC football team was quite good. The games were rowdy, and like in Abilene, we had about four other colleges nearby. There was significant competition in that context. We had a lot of fun, and it didn't create any problems.

The morning of November 22, 1963, we played in the Tri-State Stage Band competition and won first place, which was a great thrill, only for us to be devastated that afternoon by the assassination of President John F. Kennedy.

A few days later, our homecoming game was to be played against Ranger Junior College. Some toilet papering and other activities took place. The cheerleaders and the Wrangler Belles decided we needed to have a big bonfire. We gathered cardboard and wood and stacked it up. The pile grew and grew until it was nearly two stories tall. We were out there one evening, completing the pile, when someone suggested putting an outdoor outhouse on top. Everyone agreed that'd be a great idea. The daddy of one of the guys owned a towing company. We took out a tow truck and spotted an outhouse fairly close to the college. We didn't check anything; we just backed up and put a cable around it, then turned on the winch. There was just one problem: it had a porcelain commode inside the outhouse, attached to a base, which nobody had ever seen. And by the time we realized it, it was too late. The outhouse had come off the foundation, taking the porcelain toilet with it.

When we got it back to where the bonfire was, the only way to get it up on top of the pile of wood was to hoist it by hand. The football players and everybody else pitched in. Unfortunately, the porcelain commode was still inside, and it broke loose, shattering into pieces as it came tumbling down. A piece of porcelain struck one guy in the shoulder, and another piece nearly cut off my pinkie.

The next morning, our soon-to-be bonfire had an outdoor toilet on it, complete with a porcelain commode, or what was left of it, when the police showed up. The poor old lady who owned the outdoor toilet wanted it replaced, so we all chipped in and gave her the money to install a brand-new outhouse toilet. Later, the band director came up to me and said, "I do not want to hear that you were involved. Please tell me you were not involved. No, no! Do not lie to me."

The end of the year came, and I was at loose ends, so in June I went to Abilene. I had some friends I could stay with until I could figure out what I should do. But those guys were as goofy as I was, and it turned out to be a huge mistake. When I got to their place, we decided we needed to go to a club to have some fun. It turned out to be anything but fun. Shortly after we arrived, some guys decided they wanted us to leave. A fight broke out, and the sheriffs were called to the scene. When one of the guys grabbed me, I swung instinctively and connected with a sheriff's jaw, breaking it. Needless to say, that was a no-no. Since this was before the phrase "police brutality" was in vogue, they whipped me pretty good, then took me to the county jail.

A few days later, I found myself in front of a judge with enough charges that I expected to do some time in the prison at Huntsville. I was scared beyond belief because Huntsville was known to be a horrible place. The judge asked me what I had to say for myself, but before I could answer I heard a lady's voice saying, "Your Honor, we would like to speak before this goes any further." I turned to see who was speaking, and to my amazement, it was the deputy sheriff and his wife. Everything in me froze, and the whole world stopped. I thought they were going to ask for the strongest punishment possible. But then I heard the lady say, "Your Honor, we are Christians, and we have checked Buddy's past. He has never been in serious trouble, and we believe he is a victim of circumstance. We ask that you have leniency and that the charges against him be dropped."

It was deathly quiet, and my heart stopped as my whole life hung in the balance. I closed my eyes as I waited for the judge's decision. He cleared his throat and said, "Take the defendant back across the street to the jail while I take this under consideration."

I waited in that cell for what seemed like eternity. I was all alone, my heart pounding. I wanted to scream, but nothing came out. Then the cell door finally opened, and a deputy brought me back to the courtroom, which was empty.

The judge entered, but instead of going to his bench, he came to where I was standing and stared at me for a long time. "I see nothing in you that is redeemable," he said, "but Deputy and Mrs. Trammel tell me that they see a young man whom God loves, and they believe if I send you to Huntsville, you will be destroyed. They tell me that if I release you to their custody, they will be responsible for you. It is my desire, and I have every right by law to send you to Huntsville for two to ten years for striking an officer of the law." He paused, then shook his head. "But I cannot go against their wishes, so I am going to sentence you to ninety days in the county jail. When you have served your time, a deputy will drive you five miles past the city limit sign and let you out, never to return to Abilene again. I will not release you into their custody. I just want a piece of trash out of my city."

Ninety days later, on a cold winter day, a deputy followed the judge's orders but added his own farewell by hitting me twice on my shins with his night stick. Then he got back in his car and left me standing there.

Luckily, a fellow in a pickup stopped and picked me up. He was going to Odessa, which was a little over a two-hour drive. We drove in silence for a while, then he asked how I had wound up on the highway on a cold, drizzly day with no baggage. I was silent for a few moments, thinking that if I told him the truth, he would probably kick me out. But somehow I knew I had to tell him the truth. I began by telling him about the fight in the club and how I had unwittingly broken the deputy's jaw. I also told him how the deputy and his wife came to talk to me, saying they were Christians. They said they forgave me and would pray for me. I told him how the judge wanted to send me to

Huntsville prison, but the deputy's wife asked the judge for leniency. I also explained how the judge had his deputy drive me out to where he picked me up and how the deputy hit on my shins before he drove off.

When I stopped talking, the guy told me his name was Cliff Waggner. Then he said that he and his wife were Christians too, and they believed God works in mysterious ways. He told me that, normally, he would not pick up a guy standing on the side of the road, but something in his spirit caused him to stop for me. Then he told me if I wanted, he would like me to stay with him and his wife until I could get on my feet.

When I met his wife, Mildred, she told me she was so happy her husband had been obedient to the Spirit and that I should just enjoy my time with them. Then she told me to wash up, as supper was ready. When we sat down to eat, we bowed our heads, and Cliff prayed a blessing over the food and thanked God that I was with them. After supper, they took me to a department store and bought me some clothes, underwear, socks, and toiletries. When I tried to assure them that I would repay them, they just smiled.

The next day, Cliff called one of his friends who had a construction company. The guy came over, and after we had talked for a while, he asked if I had any experience in construction. I told him that I had worked construction on a road job and could run a D6 Caterpillar. He laughed and told Cliff that God had just answered one of his prayers. He had just had to fire his Cat operator, so he would like to give me an opportunity to see if he could use me.

I got the job, and I was making more money than I had ever made. I worked for the guy for the next six months and lived in

Cliff and Mildred's garage apartment, paying rent and repaying them for the money they had spent in the beginning. At the end of the six months, I thanked them all for everything. I wanted to go to Kermit, Texas, because I had a job offer in the oil field. They told me that they would pray for me, and if they could ever be of help, they would be there for me.

4

FREE FALLING INTO HELL ON EARTH

WORKING in the oilfield on a drilling rig is hard, dangerous work performed by hard, dangerous men who played as hard as they worked. Most of them were in their late twenties and older. Once again, I did not fit in. I was much younger and had no experience. They always gave me the dirtiest, most dangerous jobs, making me prove I had the guts to be one of them. Finally, I won their approval and was invited to go drinking with the crew after work. I had been working with them for about three months and was doing well. The money was good, but I was getting restless and tired of the same thing day after day.

I did not have a mailbox and would pick up my mail at the post office window. One day when I went to pick up my mail, the lady asked me to wait outside until she could get things taken care of. The next thing I know, the Kermit police were handcuffing me and walking me back into the post office. When I protested, they told me to calm down, as they had to straighten some things out. After a few minutes, the police officer told me that another Buddy Roy Mercer had lived in Kermit for a long time, and he accused me of trying to steal his mail. I laughed and told them that if they would let me get my wallet out of my car, I could prove who I was. About that time, the other Buddy Roy Mercer showed up. They determined that two people named Buddy Roy Mercer lived in Kermit. The other Buddy was about twenty years older than me. He told me that he would get his own mailbox, which would alleviate the problem. So, the cops took the handcuffs off and sent me on my way.

One night I met a pretty girl and asked her to go out with me. She readily accepted, so we headed for a bar to go dancing. Unfortunately, she didn't tell me she had a boyfriend whose daddy was the chief of police in Kermit. When he spotted us, the fight was on. He had a couple of friends with him, so I grabbed a pool stick to even things out, but that didn't help too much. Soon, they had me in the alley, and they worked me over. They left me, thinking I was done, but I had a surprise for them. I went to my car and grabbed a link-chain weapon, then I went back to the bar and whipped them. Just as I got to the last one, the police showed up. They put me in handcuffs and finished the beating on me. I spent the night in jail, then the next morning they loaded me and my clothes into my car and escorted me out of town, warning me not to come back.

I moved on to another little town, got a job with an oilfield crew, and was doing well, staying out of trouble. The local fair was going on with food booths, carnival rides, and a rodeo, so I went looking for a girl I knew, wanting to spend some money and have some fun. After we connected, I played a carnival game to win her a stuffed animal, joking with the carny who ran the concession. After winning her the animal, I thought, *These guys make money, travel all over, and party a lot.* It sounded like my kind of job.

I returned to the concession and asked the carny how things worked. He introduced himself as Kevin Mazure from West By God, Virginia, and he owned four of the concessions. He told me to hop into the concession booth, so I could give it a try. It didn't take me long to start making money, so he had one of his employees take over, and we walked down to the cook shack to talk. He asked me if I would like to join the carnival, work for him, and have a chance to buy one of his concessions. Without hesitation, I shook his hand and became a "carny bum," as we were called.

When it came time to go to the next town, the girl I was with, asked if she could go with me. How could I say no? So, we packed up some of her stuff, and away we went, going to Carlsbad, New Mexico, where we partied all week. Then we headed for Moab, Utah, and started all over again. By then I was tired of the girl who had gone with me, so I gave her a hundred dollars and a bus ticket back to Kermit, thinking I would be able to party with the local girls. I didn't expect her to get angry. She explained, in no uncertain terms, that she was only sixteen and underage, so she wasn't leaving. Now I was in a royal mess, so I agreed she could stay with me. The situation lasted for a couple more months, but she couldn't put up with my constant partying and finally agreed to go back home. That left me free to party with the local girls (making sure they were of age, of course).

While traveling with the carnival, I also entered myself into the bull riding event at the rodeo. The entry fee was only twenty dollars, and the winning rider collected five hundred dollars. I would like to say I won, but I got bucked off just outside the chute gate. I wasn't deterred, though; I knew there would be another opportunity at the next fair.

Every week it was another town and another party, which suited me just fine. But I kept thinking about my mother, who I hadn't spoken to for nearly a year. I knew I should call her, but I was sure by then that everyone in Eldorado would know about my shenanigans at college and my time in jail, and I couldn't bring myself to talk to her after letting her down and, in my mind, ruining her life.

We pulled into Belen, New Mexico, a little town on Highway 66 just outside of Albuquerque, for a three-day fair. On a free day, I decided to go to the bar and see if I could win money shooting pool. I was doing well when I heard a voice say, "Buddy Mercer, you're dead." I looked around, expecting to see someone with a weapon of some kind. Instead, I saw a friend of my mom and Harry from Eldorado, some five hundred miles away. He turned as white as a sheet upon seeing me.

"Johnny Barnes, what is going on?" I asked. "Let's go to a booth and talk."

By then he was shaking like a leaf, and the story he told me chilled me to the bone. "The rumor is that you were on an offshore oil rig that went down in the Gulf of Mexico, and they never found your body. Your mother grieved for nearly six months but has turned the corner and is busy helping at the high school because your brother is in the band." Everything inside me was in turmoil. I started to explain what had been going on in my life, but he stopped me short and said he had no desire to know my business. He also said he would never tell anyone about seeing me. He added that he would never have stopped at a bar, but it must have been the Holy Spirit that led him to stop and get a Coke. "You don't look like you understand what I just said," he added. Then he stood up and stared at me, shook his head, and walked away.

When he was gone, I just sat in the booth, thinking. *Well, I won't call my mother if she has already basically buried me.* It was such a weird feeling. *What did he mean about the Holy Spirit leading him to stop and get a Coke?*

When I left the bar, I was totally confused, so I headed back to the carnival grounds. I felt completely empty because, all of a sudden, I was dead. It also meant that my mom had been grieving, as had my favorite grandma and grandpa and my favorite uncle. I knew I had been doing wrong and that I had let everybody down, including me. Because of all the trouble I had been in, I knew I couldn't go back and face them. That left me with one choice—to continue on with the carnival and see where it led me.

When I got back to the carnival grounds, the owner's son, Frank, approached me. "Hey, Buddy, we're going to be opening the show in Shiprock tomorrow, but we'd like to take a couple of rides down. I'd like you to go with me. You drive one truck, and I'll drive the other. When we get there, we can get a car and go over to Farmington. We don't want to be on that reservation tonight." (The fairgrounds we were going to were on an Indian reservation.) That sounded good to me, so I grabbed some clothes, hitched up the tractor to the ride that I would be hauling, and then we headed for Shiprock.

It was a whole different world. When we pulled into the fairgrounds, the chief and his cohort came out to meet us. They spoke broken English because on the reservation they only spoke in their native tongue. They didn't give us a very friendly greeting, but Frank just winked at me. "Hang on a minute. I got something for them." He went to the trailer he had pulled and came out with four large stuffed teddy bears or different sorts and sizes. They were thrilled, and they welcomed us to the northern Navajo Tribal Fair, telling us to enjoy ourselves.

"I got a better idea," Frank said once we parked the trucks. "Let's unhook one of the tractors, and we'll run over to Farmington."

By the time we got there—Farmington was twenty miles away—it was past the dinner hour. Neither of us were hungry, so we decided we might as well go to the Copper Penny Bar, where we knew people from the previous time we were there. We had some drinks, shot some pool, and had a good time with the guys in the bar. It was getting late, so we headed for the motel.

The next morning, we got up and headed back out to the fairgrounds in Shiprock where the Navajo police welcomed us with open arms. We started setting up the rides, which took the better part of the day.

When we headed back to Farmington that evening, we happened to bump into a guy I knew. He was a bit rowdy, but he was a lot of fun. After having some laughs about some of the things we had done when we were there before he asked, "Hey, how'd you like to go get some Twister wine?" Twister wine was a favorite of the Indians on the reservation. It was cheap and quick.

"What do you think you're going to do with Twister wine?" I asked.

He laughed. "We're going to go sell us some wine to some Navajo Indians and make us some money." I told him that we were not going to do that because that was a federal rap. "It's a federal rap only if you get caught," he retorted. That made a lot of sense to me because we were not going to be there for long. Frank was all in for the idea, so we went to the liquor store, loaded his car with several cases of wine, and headed back to Shiprock and the fairgrounds, leaving the tractor at the motel.

When we got to the fairgrounds, we were waved in by the Navajo police, who remembered us, then we drove to the back of the fairgrounds where we had parked the other truck. Sure enough, the Indians came out to see what was going on, and they wanted to know if we had any wine. We sold a lot of wine very quickly. They were having a good time, but word got out that there was wine on the reservation and that some guy had it in his car. We jumped into the car and headed back to Farmington, feeling good. We had picked up some extra money, and it appeared that we were in the clear.

The next morning when we returned to the fairgrounds, the rest of the carnival was pulling in, with the show scheduled to open that night at 6:00. The owner of the carnival came up and asked Frank if we had had any problems with the Indians. Frank assured him that we hadn't. At that moment, one of the Indians who had already been drinking came up to Frank and me, asking if we had some more wine. I looked at Frank, who was frozen as his father, carnival's owner, glared at us, waiting for an answer. I laughed and told the Indian man that we only had enough for us and that he should leave before we had a problem.

"Where are your brains?" Frank's father asked. "You guys

have been selling wine to the Indians on the reservation when you know that it's against the law. You could go to jail on a federal offense, and the carnival could have gotten kicked off the reservation, costing me everything. When these Indians start drinking, they go crazy, pass out on the highway, and get run over." After he finished yelling at us, we assured him that it wouldn't happen again, then we took off to help set up rides and concessions.

At 6:00, we opened the show with loud music. Carnival rides started turning, and Indian men came to the midway dressed in their finest western boots, Levis, and gaudy western-cut shirts with lots of silver and turquoise adornments. The women wore their finest ribbon skirts with dressy tops, moccasins, and all their silver and turquoise decorations. Everyone appeared to be in a festive mood. It was looking like a wild time with some of the young men dressed in their native costumes and doing their ancestral dances. We didn't know whether they were doing war dances, peace dances, or if they had already been drinking and were just having fun.

Later in the evening, they had teepees set up at each end of an arena. In the middle, the medicine man had his teepee with powwow drummers surrounding it. The lights around the arena were dimmed, and the drummers began to beat the drums and chant. We went to watch the ceremonies. Men with migraine headaches were in the teepees on each end. When the medicine man came out of his teepee and started dancing and chanting, they brought the guys with the migraine headaches out of their teepees, and they sat cross-legged on the ground. Then four guys in native costumes entered the arena and started chanting and banging on something like tambourines.

Suddenly, two of the guys bolted to a teepee at one end of the arena, and the other two ran to the other teepee. They ran up to the guys with the headaches and started beating their instruments and yelling. It was humorous to us, and we started laughing, though we felt sorry for the guys with the headaches. It looked ridiculous.

Almost instantly, two Navajo policemen pulled us away from the arena and threatened to put us in handcuffs. "We don't laugh in your cathedral," they told us in broken English, "and you don't laugh in ours." Fortunately, one of the guys who helped us set up rides recognized us and came over and spoke to the police. He explained that the ceremony was to remove the evil spirits that caused the headaches from the men. That was not a good way to start things, but we were forgiven and went back to the rides where we belonged.

From then on, the rest of the week went pretty well. We were making money, and no more was said about the wine or our problem at the arena. Close to the end of the fair, I told Frank I needed to get off the reservation because all I had seen was dark-haired and dark-skinned women. I wanted to see some blondes for a change. I was getting restless. I said I wanted to head to Taos, New Mexico, since that was the next place the carnival was going. After some conversation, he agreed. "But don't get in any trouble up there because we're going to need you to run a couple of the rides," he said.

I laughed. "I'm just going to sack out in the truck tonight." I knew it was going to be late when we finished tearing down the rides.

"I'm going to sack out in another truck because I don't want to go to Farmington tonight either," Frank replied. That seemed to be the best course of action for both of us.

At about 1:00 a.m., some of the Indian men came and started messing around the trucks, which woke us up. We got out of the truck to deal with the situation, but it was obvious that they were loaded on something, and when we tried to talk to them, they became hostile. They wanted to run us off the reservation, but we couldn't let that happen, so the fight was on. I hit one as hard as I could, square in the side of his jaw. He tumbled backwards but then came right back at me. Frank yelled that he had hit one, but he didn't stay down either. It was obvious they were on something stronger than wine, which meant trouble. When the one I had hit came back for more, I kicked him in the privates, and when he doubled over, I caught him under the chin with my knee and sent him sprawling. To my surprise, he came at me with a long knife called a pig sticker, and he was angry. I knocked him down again, and he started to get up, so I hauled off and kicked, aiming to hit him in the face, but I caught him in the Adam's apple with the point of my boot, and he spit blood. Frank finally got his guy down, and the other one took off running. When Frank saw my guy spitting blood but still getting up, he grabbed my arm. "Buddy, we got to get hell out of here!" So, we headed for Farmington in one of the trucks.

The next morning, we got up early and went back out to the reservation, stopping at the Natanni Nez Lodge restaurant for breakfast. We were sitting at the counter when a New Mexico state trooper walked in, a friendly sort of guy that we kind of knew from before. He sat a couple of seats down from us. He ordered a cup of coffee and then smiled at us. "Boys, I heard they had a little problem out here last night. Apparently, things got really rowdy around the carnival trucks." We assured him that we didn't know anything about that because we spent the night in Farmington. "I'm sure happy to hear that because one of the Indian boys had a problem with his throat being kicked in. He's in the hospital in Farmington. I guess he's going to be okay, but he's going to be there for a while because he must have busted his Adam's apple or something.

"I don't have jurisdiction on the reservation, so I want to help because those Indians were loaded on peyote and felt indestructible, so if you know who did the damage, I hope you tell them to get off the reservation. Right now, they are thinking it was Navajo on Navajo, but they are going to start talking to the carneys, and it's going to get ugly." He finished his coffee, then told us to have a nice day and left.

We waited for a minute and then we headed to the fairground. Frank had to tell his dad that there was a little problem, and we had protected the trucks, but in the process one of the Indians who was loaded on peyote had been badly injured, and now the Navajo police would be blaming us. His father listened to our story, then handed Frank the keys to one of his cars and told us to get out of there. He said he didn't want to hear from us or see us until he got to Taos.

The interesting thing about Taos in the 1960s was that it was home to a hippie commune, with signs like "Make Love, Not War," "Smoke Grass," and "Free Love." Frank said we had better be careful because we're going to get in trouble there. We checked in at the motel and then went to a restaurant to get something to eat.

We were sitting in the booth talking when a blonde-haired

beauty and her friend walked in. She looked around, then walked up and asked if they could sit with us. She told us her name was Starr Stapp, and her friend was Daisy Flower. "You boys look like you're new in town. Maybe you're a little lonely. We sure would like to spend some time with you." I could hardly turn that down, so we headed for their little hippie commune.

It was a sight to behold, free love and drugs everywhere, but we told Starr we didn't want to be involved in that. She was insistent that we stay there and surprised us both when she said they didn't really want to have sex; they just wanted to have a good time. We spent the night sitting around a firepit under a black sky filled with stars that twinkled like diamonds, drinking beer, talking, and singing while Daisy strummed her guitar.

When we woke up, we decided to travel forty-five minutes up to Red River, which is a beautiful town with mountains all around. We spent the day there partying, tubing on the river, and riding rented bikes with Starr and her girlfriend. It was a great time.

When we got back to Taos, some of their friends had fixed us up a place, as we would be staying there for two weeks, which was a nice gesture, but I felt very uncomfortable because it looked like we were expected to spend that time with Starr and Daisy and the rest of their hippie friends who were all about making love and doing drugs. It looked to me like we were heading for nothing but trouble, so I told Frank that I would meet the carnival in El Paso. The season was over after Taos, and all the rides and concessions would be taken to El Paso for the winter where we would rehabilitate them, make sure they were safe to operate, paint them and otherwise prepare them for the following spring.

Working on the rides was boring, though. There was nothing to do except work on rides all day, and the only thing we got paid was room and board plus twenty-five dollars per day, which was a lot of money for the owner to shell out. At night everybody sat around and played poker or got drunk. Some people wanted to go across the border to Juarez where things could get wild, drinking Dos Equis beer, which cost only twenty-five cents a bottle, and having sex with a prostitute for two dollars, but disease was running rampant, so I didn't want to go there.

Then one day out of the clear blue, the girl who went on the road with me when the carnival left Carlsbad but had lied to me about her age called me. After we had talked for a while she said, "Buddy, I've been thinking about you. I keep missing you, and I want you to come to Portland, so we can enjoy some time together." She also told me that she was actually eighteen. There was nothing else to do, so I told Frank that I was going to Portland.

"Have a good trip," he said. "It's going to be rainy and cold, but enjoy it. When you get bored, come back, as you'll always be welcome at our carnival."

When I got to Portland, it was rainy and cold just like Frank had said, but Rhonda, the girl, was waiting there for me. She was living with her mom, and her brother was there too. After having something to eat and visiting for a while, her mom said, "Why don't you just stay here? I have an extra bedroom for you upstairs." I told her that I appreciated the gesture, but Rhonda and I had some things we needed to clear up before I made any plans, to which Rhonda agreed. I told them that I was going to get a motel room and go to sleep, as I was exhausted, but I would return the following day, and Rhonda and I could discuss what was going to happen.

Early the next day, I returned to Rhonda's. She met me at the door and asked if we could go to a restaurant and have breakfast, so we could talk in privacy, which suited me fine.

On the way to the restaurant, we made small talk, but after we were seated and the waitress had taken our order, she became very serious, talking about how her life had changed since the last time we had been together. She worked as a nurse's assistant in the hospital during the day and did babysitting in the evening, saving up money so she could become a licensed vocational nurse. As she spoke about how her life had changed, it was apparent she was not the same girl who had left her life in Carlsbad to go on the road with me. I was impressed with how much she had changed and how sincere she was with what she wanted out of life.

I told her about my life and how it was rumored that I was dead. I said I was having a hard time trying to find my way and figure out what I wanted to do.

"Buddy, I don't want to scare you away, but I have to be totally honest and transparent," she said. "When I called you and asked you to come to Portland, I was sure that I wanted to spend my life with you. I know you're probably not ready for that, but I hope we can work things out."

I told her that to be fair, I didn't know what I wanted, but if we could take things slowly maybe it would work out. She said she was willing to work with me, hoping we could have a life together.

We agreed that living in the same house was not a good idea, so she told me that one of the nurses at the hospital had a small apartment above her garage that I could use for no cost for a month, which was great.

We drove to the nurse's place, and the lady greeted me warmly. She gave me the key to the apartment and told me to make myself comfortable, saying if I needed anything, I should let her know.

It was a small but comfortable place with a bathroom, a refrigerator, a small stove, a coffee pot, and all the utensils. Rhonda was beaming. "Now if you can take me home, you can start your new life," she said.

When I got back to the apartment, a strange feeling came over me as I was all alone with nothing to do but watch television. My first thought was to go to a bar and shoot pool, thinking maybe I could make a little money, but that thought didn't really excite me, so went to a liquor store to get a bottle of Jack Daniels whiskey, thinking it would help me to get used to the situation, but for some reason I didn't want to do that either.

Then I was overcome with thoughts of the life I had been living, which took me back to the trouble that I had gotten into when I got into the fight in Abilene and nearly went to prison for breaking the deputy's jaw. I was also reminded of the girls I had been involved with and then left them without saying goodbye, how I had hooked up with Rhonda, and after I got bored with her, I just wanted her to leave. The worst of all was having my parents' friend pop into my life in a weird way in Belen, New Mexico, of all places to let me know of the hurt and pain I had caused my mother and my grandparents. Then there was what had happened to the Indian whom I had kicked in the throat.

As these memories flooded my mind, it dawned on me that I had basically become a man with no soul, not caring about anyone or anything, destroying anyone who made the mistake of getting close to me, but here I was in Portland, thinking about starting a new life. It hit me so hard I began shaking, screaming, and crying because, in reality, I was empty and void of any of the values that my mother and grandparents had instilled in me.

I must have cried myself to sleep because the next thing I knew the sun was shining into the apartment where I lay, demanding that I wake up, pull myself together, and face the guy I had become.

I got up and took a hot shower, hoping I was washing away some of my ugly past and that maybe I could become the man I ought to be.

After my shower I got dressed, made a pot of coffee, and turned on the TV. That was a big mistake because there was a preacher on one channel talking about the kind of life I had been living and how God could give me forgiveness, love, peace, and joy. I turned the TV off and then turned on the radio to a country-and-western station, which played songs that I could identify with.

That day while Rhonda was at work, I looked at the ads in the paper and found one for a job at a sawmill. It was a small mill that made lumber up to twelve feet in length and two inches in width. The job didn't pay as much as the large sawmills, but it was close to where I lived, it was out of the rain, and I had to start somewhere, so I took the job. The problem was, it was a little dangerous because if one of those logs got loose off the belt, the buzz saw would grab it and shoot it out the end where I was receiving the product for stacking. If one of those logs smacked into someone, they'd wind up in the hospital. The boss, called a millwright, liked my work, so things went well, and it was nice to be out of the rain and the cold.

I worked there until spring, then I went to work for a large lumber mill in Portland that paid a lot more money. It was a union shop, which meant I would be on probation for ninety days before I could join. Once I began paying my dues, I earned union wages, so I was doing really well.

My job was working in the yard, stacking lumber. When it was stacked to the proper specifications, I would band it together, then a guy would come on a forklift and take it to where it would be loaded on a flatbed truck for delivery. One day I got my load stacked, and I didn't have anything else to do, so I jumped into a forklift to move the stack, which would allow me to work on the next one. Suddenly, some goofball came running out, turned the forklift off, then pulled me out of the cab. I landed on my hands and knees on concrete, and it hurt, but I looked up and his privates were right there, so I nailed him, and when he bowed, I got him under the chin and laid him out. I was standing there trying to figure out what had just happened when the shop steward came at me, screaming that he was going to do something bad to me, and I thought I was going to have another fight.

Then a guy in a suit came out of the office building, yelling for the union guy to get back into the shop where he belonged. Then he told me to come with him.

We went into the office building where there were several

guys in suits. As soon as we walked in, they laughed and told me that I had just earned a job without having to do an interview because the guy I had fought with was what they called a union enforcer, whatever that was.

The guy who had come out to get me took me into his office and closed the door behind us. He was the president and owner of the company. "Buddy I don't know where you came from, but I want to put you on the payroll. First, I need to get your information, so we can get you out of here before the union guys find out any more than they already know. Here's a check for the work you did today. A guy is waiting to take you down the back stairs, so you can get your car out of the parking lot before the union guys get to it and to you. I will be in touch with you later." The check he gave me was for five hundred dollars, which was way more than I was supposed to be paid, but I didn't bother to ask questions, I just wanted to go home.

Later that day, two of the men in suits from the office showed up and wanted to talk to me about coming to work for the company as management. I told them that I had planned on leaving Portland and wouldn't be available. They smiled and said if I ever wanted to go to work at the company there would be a place for me in management. After they left, I had a good laugh, imagining the management position I would have with the union boys.

A couple of weeks later, Rhonda and I had a serious conversation about our lives and the future. "Buddy, we just need to get married and start making our way in life," she said. "We've been seeing each other for a couple of months, and everything is going well. I'm working to become an LVN and will be making good money, and I'm sure I want to spend the rest of my life with you." I was tired of coming home to an empty apartment and had saved up some money, so after further conversation with her, I agreed. She told me that she knew of a preacher whom we could talk to about marrying us, and we could have a small ceremony at her mother's house.

The next day we went and talked to the preacher, but he said he didn't want to marry us because he didn't know anything about us. He said his spirit was uncomfortable with it.

"Well, do you think for one hundred dollars we can find somebody else to marry us?" I asked.

He laughed. "If you're so bound and determined, I'll marry you at Rhonda's mother's house but not in my church and ask God's blessing on you."

A week later we got married, and I moved out of the apartment and into Rhonda's mother's house where we had a room with a bathroom and a shower. It seemed to be working well, as we all got along, eating meals together and spending time in conversation.

We started talking about finding a place of our own, which everyone agreed would be good. One of the maintenance men at the hospital told Rhonda that he had a small but nice trailer on his property. "It's on my land, so you don't have to pay any rent," he said, "but I'll warn you it's butane powered, so it's going to be expensive to heat. And you got to make sure those tanks are filled all the time."

It didn't sound like a problem for me, so we took him up on the offer. Although it didn't have the finest furniture, the place was furnished, and all of a sudden, we were married and had a place to live. He and his wife had us over for dinner to get better acquainted. They said they would be happy to help if we ever needed anything. He was a mechanic, a maintenance guy, and he was always tinkering with the mobile home, making things better for us. He also helped me with my car.

Shortly afterwards, I told Rhonda that I had decided I was going to go to work in the woods, setting chokers on a logging crew. It was a bit dangerous, and I didn't know what I was doing, but they paid good money. She was getting her nurse's cap. We were going to be doing well.

I went to work, setting chokers in the woods, and it was going well. Then one day we got up there, and there was a deep snowfall. When everybody got out of the crew vehicle, I said, "I ain't going out there, working in snow that's nearly over my head."

"Then you'll walk back into town," the owner said.

I didn't walk into town. I walked down the mountain to where they had the logging trucks on what they called a landing. That was where they took all the logs and then loaded them onto the trucks. Truckers would haul them down the hill. If you haven't had a ride in a logging truck going down a hill, I wouldn't advise it, When I asked one of the guys for a ride. He laughed and said, "You can ride if you can. I'm going to drive it, so jump in." I saw what he meant because there was no seat on my side. All he had was a five-gallon bucket. He invited me to sit on that, then we started down the mountain.

He didn't seem to think there were any brakes on that truck. All we did was slip and slide while he shifted the gears up and down. I looked over the edge at what appeared to be a 5000-foot drop. Meanwhile, he was singing and having a good time. That was my last experience up on Mount Hood.

I went to work in construction instead. We were doing well,

as Rhonda had her LVN cap by then, and we were making money. We had an opportunity to rent a duplex. We could live in one side and sublet the other side. Later that year we bought a cherry wood bedroom set that cost us $2,000. I made a deal with the man who owned the little trailer we had lived in and started buying and selling used cars, which he would fix. When I sold the car for a profit, I would give him a commission.

From construction I went to work for a large tree farm that grew fruit trees. I learned the business quickly. The owner was an older man but full of energy with some great ideas, which he shared with me. I made a deal with the owner, who gave me a small plot of land to work. I would go out and pick seeds, then we'd plant them, and they would grow the seedlings. He would get his pick of the seedlings that first year, then I could sell the rest. After that, it'd be my business.

A little later he put me in charge of managing his nursery. I learned how to graft trees, turning flowering trees into fruit trees. I also worked in the greenhouse. It was really good, and the money was flowing.

One night I didn't come home until nearly 9:00 as it was freezing cold, and I had to stay and cover the seedlings, so they wouldn't freeze When I got home in, Rhonda met me at the drop room, where I took off all my muddy clothes, and demanded to know where the hell I'd been. She was having a party, and I should have been there.

The party broke up at about 10:00. One of her friends, Kathy, stayed over. Rhonda went to bed, but Kathy and I sat up and had some beers until early morning. Rhonda was sound asleep when I went into our bedroom, so I got undressed and went to sleep.

When I woke up, Rhonda was gone, and I assumed she had gone to the hospital for work. When I went to the hospital to see her, though, I was told that Rhonda had called in sick. I went over to my mother-in-law's. She explained that Rhonda was angry, thinking Kathy and I had done something in the living room while she was asleep in our bedroom. She had gone to Bend, Oregon, on the other side of the mountain. Her mother said if I wanted Rhonda, I'd better go get her. But something inside of me said that was the end of us.

I went back home, packed up my stuff, sold the cherry wood bedroom furniture, and sold my seedling business to the nursery owner for $2,000, which was half price. I also sold a couple of cars. At the end of the day, I loaded Rhonda's clothes in my beautiful 1957 red-and-white Buick convertible and drove over to my mother-in-law's house. I told her that I had sold everything, then I laid $2,800 on the table.

"What's this?" she asked. I explained what had happened and that I had sold everything we had together.

"This is one half of what's left of our marriage," I said.

Her brother, who had been standing there listening, decided he was going to do something about it, and he came running at me. Unfortunately for him, he led with his nose. My fist connected with it, and he went down.

I left my Buick to Rhonda and went to the Greyhound bus station and caught a bus for Las Vegas. I had heard that I could go to work for a casino, making a lot of money. I got a job as a security guard at one of the casinos. I was really more of a bouncer, called on to remove drunks from the property. If someone was caught trying to cheat the casino, I was to walk him out front and, in full view of the public, teach him a lesson.

I was also responsible for taking care of the working girls whose job was to get the money doing whatever the customers wanted. Things weren't nearly as rosy as I had pictured them. The problem was, the casino industry was heavily influenced by organized crime. I decided that was not the job for me, so I quit, which did not sit well with the guy who hired me.

One night I was in another casino, playing blackjack. I was on a hot streak when a pretty girl came and sat on the stool next to me, asking me to buy her a drink. I knew she was a set-up girl, and I was in trouble. I grabbed my chips to leave the table when two security guards grabbed my arms. I thought I was going to get some of the treatment that I had given to others. To my surprise, they merely told me I was not wanted in the casino and escorted me out. When we got out in front of the casino, they made a big deal of telling me to have a wonderful night and that if I was ever back in Las Vegas to be sure to visit their casino.

I was staying in a hotel just down the street. As I walked toward it, I kept my head on a swivel, still expecting something to happen. Only when I got to my hotel did I realize my wallet, which had been in my hip pocket, was gone along with the fifteen one-hundred-dollar bills that were in it. That left me with less than two hundred dollars, which I had in my front pocket. I started to go back to get my wallet and my money, but I knew it wasn't going to happen.

The next morning when I went to check out, the desk clerk told me that someone had dropped off my wallet. I knew my money would be gone, but at least my driver's license and a few other things were still there—including a note that told me to get out of town and never come back.

I was in a mess, but I had heard that California was the land of milk and honey, and I could go to work in the oil fields there, which paid a lot. I put all of my clothes in one suitcase, then threw the other one with the remainder of my clothes in a dumpster. I headed for Greyhound down the street and bought a one-way ticket to Los Angeles, determined to put Las Vegas behind me.

When I got off the bus in downtown Los Angeles, I still had about $150 dollars in my pocket, and the sun was shining. I got a room in a cheap hotel, so I could get a good night's sleep, then in the morning I would find out where I needed to go to get a job. I set my suitcase down while I was renting the room, but when I turned to pick it up, it was gone. When I told the clerk what had just happened, he told me I was in downtown LA where stealing was how people made it. Now I was in a mess. I had no clothes, my money was getting low, and I had no one to turn to.

I discovered that the oil field work I was looking for was in Long Beach, quite a distance from where I was, but I found work as a dishwasher in one of the downtown restaurants. It didn't pay much, but I made enough to eat and have a room in a cheap hotel. Then tragedy struck! I woke up sick with a fever and a cold. I went to work, but the owner took one look at me and said he couldn't let me work and that he would have to replace me. He gave me what money I had coming and told me to leave.

It didn't take long, and my money was gone. I started sleeping under the freeway. I pulled a piece of cardboard up to where I was sleeping to serve as a wind break. If someone decided to come up to where I was, I would be able to hear them, and I had rocks to send them away. I went to the mission where they fed the homeless and got some clothes because the clothes I was wearing stunk. That's when it finally dawned on me that I was in serious trouble.

I managed to survive by going to the mission to get something to eat, but I hated it because before the meal, which normally consisted of a small bowl of beans, cornbread, and coffee, the holy rollers would come in and sing some songs. They wanted us street people to join them in praising God for His wonderful blessings. That exercise was haunting, for it brought back to me the days of my childhood and the love I experienced. Plus, I felt like they were just doing their duty and didn't really care about us. I heard them talking about how they had ministered to us poor, wretched souls, giving us hope in the Lord and letting us know what God had done in their lives. Then they would leave to go to their homes and families, and I would feel more alone and emptier than ever.

I was losing weight, and I knew I couldn't go on like that much longer. I had seen the cops find a body on the streets and throw it in the back of a wagon. It looked like my end might be coming, for I was getting weak from hunger. I stayed up in my little wind break and slept a lot. The worst part was thinking about my mama and grandparents. Oh, how I missed them.

One cold, misty afternoon I felt the need to go to the mission and get something to eat, but fought it, as I didn't have the energy to go down the freeway embankment to the mission, sit through the holy rollers for a bowl of beans and cornbread, then crawl back up the embankment to my shelter. But I couldn't shake the desire to go to the mission.

I crawled down the embankment, slipping and falling

because my feet were covered with cardboard and wrapped in plastic, as my shoes were mostly gone, but I made it to the streets and headed for the mission. When I rounded the corner, I saw a line of guys standing outside the mission and was told the kitchen was not working but it would be fixed, and meals would be served in about an hour. My emotions erupted, making me laugh, cry, and scream at the same time. That happened frequently to guys on the street, so no one paid any particular attention, as they had their own problems to deal with.

"To hell with it," I said, cursing the desire that had driven me to leave my shelter and come down to the street. I headed back, dreading having to crawl back up to my shelter, when I spotted a wallet under the bushes by the sidewalk. I picked it up, expecting to find it empty, but to my joyful surprise, there was a crisp ten-dollar bill inside. As I headed to the little store on the corner, I thought about the sardines, Vienna sausages, and crackers I could buy. Then a diabolical plan came to me. Instead of food, I bought a fifth of cheap whiskey, a package of Salem cigarettes, and two tins of sardines. I hid my treasure under my coat, so nobody would try to take it from me, then headed for my shelter under the freeway with a spring in my step, for now I had a way to escape my horrible existence.

5

A NEW BEGINNING

WHEN I FINALLY REACHED MY shelter, I checked to make sure no one had followed me, then secured the cardboard as best as I could. I opened the tins of sardines and wolfed them down. Then I opened the bottle of whiskey, unwrapped the cigarettes, and put my plan to work. I thought if I downed the bottle, I would pass out, and I would never wake up, as alcohol poisoning would claim my life. I had seen other guys use it as their escape. Since I had no identification on me, when they found my body, they wouldn't be able to identify me and call my mother or anyone else.

I tilted the bottle back, took a big swig, lit a cigarette, and waited for a warm glow to hit my stomach, thinking it would all be over soon. My stomach began to feel the effects of the first swig, so I tilted the bottle and gulped down several large swallows before lighting another cigarette. When I looked at the bottle, it was nearly three quarters gone, and I was beginning to feel the effects of the booze cutting off the oxygen to my brain. I lit another cigarette and poured the rest of the booze down my throat. At that point I hoped the end would be near, but the next thing I knew, I was wide awake, clearer headed than ever, in a clean, warm peaceful place where I saw three trails before me.

I looked down the first trail, which was filled with garish lights. I heard screams mocking me, telling me I would be joining them soon in hell. Even then I felt no fear. I looked down the second trail, and although I had never been near Folsom Prison, I saw it in detail and felt myself being drawn to it. But once again, I felt no fear. I looked down the third trail, and in the dim light I saw three people on their knees, weeping, crying out to God, and praying for me. They were my mama and Grandma and Grandpa Prestage. Then I was terrified and cried out, "God have mercy!"

I don't have any idea how long I was out, but when I awoke, I could tell it was early morning, as the trucks on the freeway above were moving fast. I looked around, saw the empty bottle and package of Salems with three or four cigarettes gone and the two empty sardine tins. I was still alive. Nothing had changed. My plan had failed.

I didn't know if what I had seen when I was out was a dream, a vision, or my mind had been blown by all the alcohol I had consumed. Why wasn't I dead? Suddenly, nothing mattered, as I was alive and knew without a doubt that I was leaving the streets that day. I didn't take time to analyze where the feeling came from, as I wanted to get to the mission to have some oatmeal, toast, and coffee. This time I had no problem going down the freeway embankment. Also, to my amazement, I saw the sun shining in the morning sky.

I walked into the mission, got my oatmeal, toast, and coffee, then found a table where I would be by myself. For once I didn't gulp my food but ate slowly, enjoying every morsel. When I finished, I took my tray up to the window, then turned to walk out when I heard a voice say, "Hey, cowboy, you need to get cleaned up for your trip." Someone led me to a back room where I found a bag of clean clothes, including new underwear, socks, and a pair of work boots. Most importantly, there was also an assortment of snacks, including candy bars. There was another bag with shaving stuff, toothpaste, a new toothbrush, a comb, and a pair of scissors. On a shelf were clean towels and wash cloths.

My first thought after seeing the stuff was "Where did it come from?" But I decided that, as the old saying goes, not to look a gift horse in the mouth. I peeled off my old clothes and threw them into a corner. I used the scissors to cut my hair short but sort of even. Then I shaved and got into the shower. It was the first hot shower I had taken in a long time, and I enjoyed every minute of it. I dried off and put on the new underwear. The clothes were used, but they were nice and clean. Then I sat down, put on the new socks, and slipped my feet into the work boots. When I stood up, I wanted to cry from happiness, as I looked and felt like a brand-new man.

When I went to dispose of my old clothes, they were nowhere to be found, so I picked up the bag with the rest of the gear and headed down the hall to thank the caring man who had helped me out. A guy who worked at the mission stopped me and asked what I was doing back there. I started to tell him about the guy who had helped me, but he stopped me and said something left me confused. "First of all, you are not allowed back here, as this area is only for people who work here. Second, I know everyone here, and no one who looks like the man you describe works here, so get out and stay out."

I followed his advice and left, feeling no need to argue. I had what I needed and was heading someplace to get off the streets, never to return. I didn't stop to consider who the guy was who had helped me.

I walked some seventy blocks to the corner of Avalon and Florence where I spotted a state employment office. Inside, people were sitting at tables, filling out forms. I was looking around to see where I could find a form when I heard a lady say, "Hey, cowboy, you want a job?" I turned and saw an older African American lady behind the counter smiling and waving for me to come over. We exchanged pleasantries, then she handed me a sheet of paper and said, "These people need a janitor, so get over there and go to work."

I grabbed my bags and walked to the corner of Central and Slauson to a large building with the name Bonded Engine painted on the wall. I hid my bags, walked in a big roll-up door, and saw an older guy staring at me. I walked up to him, handed him my paper from the employment office and said, "I'm your new janitor."

He took a couple of steps backward, got a strange look on his face, stared at me, then yelled at a guy standing behind the counter. "Get this boy a mop and a bucket, and put him to work." The guy took me back into the plant, showed me some trash receptacles that needed to be emptied, got me a broom, a mop, and bucket, then left me alone to figure things out on my own.

About an hour later the guy returned with a troubled look

on his face and told me that the owner, Mr. Lou, wanted to see me in his office. As he led me through the building, which was huge, I thought they had found out about my past and that I would be fired or maybe even arrested.

When I entered the office, I felt a sudden urge to run because there were four men in suits who looked like detectives. Behind a large desk sat the man I had spoken to when I entered the plant. It was eerily quiet and tense with everyone just staring at me. Suddenly, my street attitude took over, and my apprehension turned to anger. "Why you staring at me?" I asked. "What's going on? You're scaring the hell out of me."

The guy behind the desk held up his hand to stop me. "Sit down and shut up. You're scaring the hell out of us." As I sat down, he continued. "I fired the old janitor not an hour before you walked in. We didn't place an order with the employment office, and when we called to find out what was going on, the supervisor told us that no lady with the name that is on the work order works there. Now, who the hell are you?"

"I have no idea what you're talking about, as you have the signed order," I replied as I stood up. "I don't know what's going on, but I can just leave." Then one of the other guys spoke up.

"Hey, sit back down, and let's figure this out."

I did so, then the guy who had taken me to get the mop and bucket started laughing, as did the guys in the suits, which infuriated me because I thought they were mocking me.

The guy who had brought me up to the office finally regained his composure. "The guy behind the desk is my father, the owner. These guys work for us at Bonded Engines as salesmen. You're not the problem. It's just we've never seen anything like this, and we don't understand what's going on."

"I have no idea what's going on either, as I've told you the truth," I replied. "I really want the job, but if you think I'm lying and don't want me, I'll just leave."

Mr. Lou stood up. "Enough of this. You all get out of my office and go to work. Marvin, if you want to be responsible for this guy, have him fill out the employment papers, get him some uniforms, and put him to work." Marvin looked at me, then smiled and shook his head, saying if I wanted the job, I should follow him.

I filled out the paperwork, got my uniforms, then went back to work. Later, I saw Mr. Lou watching me. Then he shook his head and walked away, still in disbelief.

Just before 5:00, Manuel, the parts manager came and asked me how it was going. Then he proceeded to tell me that I was the talk of Bonded. He said Mr. Lou was rough but had a big heart. If I showed up on time, did my work well, and didn't cause problems I could grow with the company.

After work, I waited down the street where I thought no one would notice me and then collected my bags. I walked down a side street, looking for a place where I could sleep until I got paid. Bonded Engine was in an industrial area where I found an empty building that suited my needs perfectly. After I found everything I needed to make a bed, I opened my bag, found the goodies, and relived the day.

I was off skid row with a job and uniforms to wear, a place to stay until I could get a room, and enough food to sustain me. It seemed like I was living in a dream.

The next morning I went to the plant, waiting outside for someone to open the doors, so I could go to work. When the break buzzer sounded at 9:00 a.m., everyone went to the coffee wagon, but I had no money, so I just found a place to sit. I waited until the buzzer sounded, then went back to work, oblivious to everyone around me.

Just before the lunch buzzer sounded, Manuel said he would like to buy me a burrito and a cup of coffee, which sounded like music to my ears. However, to be polite I thanked him and said, "No thanks." But he insisted, saying he would like to talk to me. So, we went to the coffee truck where he ordered two burritos and two cups of coffee. Then he asked me to follow him to his office. I sensed he was trying to find out more about me, but I wasn't about to open up just yet. Then he dropped a bomb, saying I needed to fill out a timecard and that the company held back a week's pay, meaning I wouldn't get a check until the following Friday. It shook me, but I didn't flinch, saying I would be just fine. Then he smiled and said it was time for him to get back to work. I had eaten only half of the burrito, so at least I had lunch for the next day. I had been in much worse shape before, so I went back to work.

The next day was Friday, and they would hand out paychecks when the 5:00 buzzer sounded, meaning it was quitting time. At about 4:30, Manual told me that Mr. Lou wanted to see me in his office, but not to worry. When I knocked on the office door, Mr. Lou yelled at me to come in, then motioned for me to sit down. Once again he stared at me, but this time he looked perplexed. "I have watched you work," he said. "My son says you're doing a good job, but I can't figure you out." I listened intently as he spoke with a New York accent, not about to interrupt. "I want you to let me know what's really going on because I know you have no money and are sleeping in an empty building down the street. Talk to me."

I found his demeanor encouraging, feeling I could confide in him. So, I let him know I was just off of skid row. I explained that I had walked from downtown to the employment office, about the lady that gave me the paper, and that I had walked from the employment office to Bonded. He knew the rest. Without another word, he pulled out a roll of money, peeled off five twenty-dollar bills, then handed them to me and said there was a small hotel a couple of blocks away where I could get a room. Then he stood up, smiled and told me to get the hell out of his office. I started to thank him, but he told me to get out of his office and not to tell anyone what we had just talked about.

I got my bags and headed for the hotel. When I got there, the guy behind the counter said, "You must be the Texan that Mr. Lou called me about. Here's the key to your room. It's paid for a week." That was nearly too much. For the first time in months I would be in a clean room with a lock on the door and sleeping between clean sheets. I couldn't hold it back any longer. Tears ran down my cheeks until I fell asleep.

I was doing well at Bonded Engines and getting along great with Mr. Lou and Manuel and even some of the employees who appreciated the fact that I was cleaning the place and was being more than helpful. The janitor before me hadn't operated that way. The floors were always oily, which made it dangerous for the guys to work, always slipping and sliding. I developed a schedule that allowed me to take care of the entire plant in less than a day, which made the guys who assembled the engines very happy, as they could be more productive with less labor, which also made Mr. Lou happy. I started looking at things that I could do to make things better for the employees. I got a kick out of it because Mr. Lou's son came up and said he was very happy that his father didn't remember ordering a janitor. Of course he was joking, but it was all fun anyhow.

One morning I was mopping the loading dock because it got oily out there. The trucks that the drivers loaded the engines onto were three-quarter-ton bobtail trucks backed up to the loading dock where there were hoists. They would wheel the engines out of the plant on hand trucks, check them over, then load them onto the trucks. When they wheeled them across the dock, there was oil in the engines from when they had been tested on a testing machine. They were wrapped in plastic, but the oil still dribbled down. I kept the loading dock mopped, so the truck drivers wouldn't slip and fall.

"Hey, boy!" someone called. When I looked up, I saw a truck driver staring at me. They called him Tiny, even though he was anything but. He was about six foot four and weighed around 250 pounds. He didn't look very solid, but he was big.

"What's up?" I replied.

"I want my place mopped," he said. "You got to get over and get this done now."

"I'll be over there in a minute," said, but he came over and grabbed hold of me. "Boy, I said, *now.*" That didn't sit too well with me. I had my mop in the bucket, which was full of hot water and detergent, which was semi acidic. I told him he had better turn me loose. I guess he didn't quite understand me, so I dipped my mop in the bucket and slopped it on his foot, He started screaming and yelling at me, then he took a swing.

I ducked, then jumped up and kicked him in his privates. When he bent over, I got him under the chin with a good elbow, and he went reeling backwards. He lost his balance and fell up against the cinder-block wall, hitting his head. It seemed to disorient him, as he slid down and lay motionless. Everybody who had been watching moved away, watching from a distance. Then the general manager came out. "I knew it," he said. "I knew you were no good, and I'm gonna fire you right now because fighting is never allowed." I told him I was fine with that, as I wouldn't allow anybody to talk to me like that.

Just then Mr. Lou's son came out and told the general manager that he would take care of the situation. He led me back to Mr. Lou's office, smiling the whole way. "Don't worry about anything," he said. "It's all under control."

"I hear that you knocked Tiny out," Mr. Lou said once we were in his office.

"Well, he tripped and fell and hit the wall," replied, "and that's probably what happened."

"I'm thankful for what you did because we've been wanting to get rid of him for a long time, but he's threatening to sue us for a problem with his back, which is as phony as hell. Now we're gonna get him for lying down on the job and starting a fight. Go change your clothes, and put on some clean uniform because you're gonna have to take over for him as a truck driver."

Mr. Lou's son laughed. "You just got a promotion and a raise, but don't be fighting anymore."

Once I was all ready, they introduced me to the dispatcher. "I'm so happy you're going to be driving for me," he said. "I won't have to put up with Tiny's bullying." He gave me a quick course on how to do the paperwork and a Thomas Guidebook, then introduced me to another truck driver. He took me out to the loading dock where some of the other guys came over and assured me that they would help with everything I needed to know. One of them shook my hand.

"You just became a hero out here now that we don't have to put up with the bully anymore."

I loaded the truck with three engines for three nearby stops. When I returned to the plant a couple of hours later, the dispatcher checked my paperwork, then gave me one more engine to deliver. After that was done, the dispatcher laughed and said that was all he had for me, so I asked if I could go help the guy who had taken my place as janitor.

When Mr. Lou came out and heard what had happened, he called me into his office. He was just dying from laughter. "Not only did I get me a new truck driver, I got one who wants to work." Right there on the spot, he gave me a fifty-cent-per-hour raise, which in those days was quite a bit. "I guarantee that you'll be getting overtime and making even more money," he said, "if you want it."

6

MORE UNBELIEVABLE CHANGES

UNFORTUNATELY, old habits die hard, and soon I found myself going to the bars and shooting pool after work. There are always girls around to keep me company, but I was cautious to hold my temper, so I wasn't involved in so many fights.

One night I was in my favorite hangout having a good time. A band was playing country music, and there was lots of my favorite booze and plenty of girls who wanted to dance and have a good time later. Then in walked a pretty lady dressed in the fashion of the day, a classy top with flowers, hot pants, and go-go boots. Instantly, I saw she was not the typical bar girl, and she had my undivided attention. I stopped dancing with the girl I was on the floor with, walked to the bar, took a shot, then told the bartender to watch me. I strode up to the girl and said, "My name is Buddy, and you probably came in to dance with me."

"No thank you," she replied, then walked to a booth with the girl she had come in with, leaving me standing there like an idiot.

I was about to return to the bar when I saw the bartender and the girl I had been dancing with having a big laugh at my expense. So, I sucked it up and went back to the booth where the girl and her friend were sitting and asked if I could buy her a drink. She just shook her head and continued talking to her friend. She didn't know who I was, but even worse, she didn't care to know me.

I went back to the bar, facing derision from everybody who had just watched me be turned down flat, but before I made it to the bar, something told me to go back and talk to the girl. "I'm sorry if I offended you," I said. "Can I sit down and talk? Because I really am a nice guy."

"If you really just want to talk, okay," she replied.

After we talked for a while she said, "I really shouldn't be here because I'm in the middle of a divorce, and I have two little girls at home who mean more to me than anything in the world. I'm not here looking for what you want, but you do seem like a nice guy. So, I'll give you my number. and if you choose to call me, knowing about my girls, we can talk."

I accepted her number, then gave it one more shot. "How about we get out of here? We can go to the beach, have a long, peaceful conversation, and really get to know each other."

"No way," she replied. "You have my number if you want to talk. Now excuse me." With that she slid out of the booth and disappeared out the door.

The next day I couldn't get her off my mind because she was different from the girls I was used to being around. I couldn't put my finger on what it was, but I really liked it.

A couple of days later I called, expecting she would just

hang up, but to my pleasant surprise she sounded happy to hear from me. We talked for quite a while. I didn't lie to her about who I was, but I didn't go into my sorry past. It seemed to get her attention when I told her I had graduated twenty-seventh in my senior class. I omitted the fact that only twenty-eight students graduated. I was reminded of being legally right but morally wrong, but oh well. Then she asked if I would like to come to her place for dinner. "Just give me your address and what time you want me there," I replied.

The next day I was looking forward to having dinner with her and her girls at 6:00. But then at about 4:00, a strange feeling came over me. I couldn't figure out why I was so apprehensive. Then it hit me: this was real life, not at all the kind of life I was used to living.

I was at her door promptly at 6:00. When I rang the doorbell, my stomach had a severe case of butterflies. The door mysteriously opened, but no one who opened it. Then I saw the girl, Jane, standing in the middle of the room with a huge smile on her face. I looked down and saw a little blonde-haired girl staring up at me. I was speechless. "Buddy this is my three-year-old daughter, Dena. She wanted to open the door for you," Jane said.

I quickly regained my composure, then stuck out my hand and smiled. "Hi, Dena," I said. To my surprise, she took my hand and pulled me to the kitchen-dining area to introduce me to her little sister, Stacey, who was in her highchair, eating some Cheerios. She wasn't at all interested in me.

After dinner, we took the girls to a shopping center where there were some rides set up for little kids. We put them on a little merry-go-round, then watched them while the ride turned. Stacey was holding on for dear life, even though they were strapped in, but every time they passed, Dena smiled and waved, yelling "Watch me!", which I did.

When I dropped them off at home afterward and said good-night, I asked Jane if she had had a good time. She assured me that they had had fun, so I asked if I could see them again. She smiled and said yes, which was all I needed to hear.

We began to spend a lot of time together. On the weekends we would go to the beach or to a park or drive into the mountains for a picnic. It seemed like no matter what we did, we had a good time. Whenever it was time to say goodbye, I hated it. I loved being with all of them.

One Saturday we went to the park for a picnic. The girls wanted to play on the playground equipment, so we put our picnic stuff on the grass in a spot where we could keep an eye on them. As Jane and I talked, I felt something come over me, making me feel completely vulnerable. "Jane, I think we ought to get married," I heard myself saying. "I don't really know what love is, but in my mind, I love you and the girls. You need a man to help you raise the girls, and I need income tax deductions. If you marry me, I promise you I will never cheat on you, and you will never be bored." I felt like a complete fool, for although I truly wanted to marry her, I had not planned to say those things. They were completely honest and true, but they sounded so stupid.

"Well, that's not the proposal I wanted or expected," she said, "but I totally understand."

"Please, I didn't mean for it to come out that way, but it's all I have," I said.

She smiled. "I do want to marry you, so, yes."

I was speechless for a moment, my mind racing to understand what had just happened. I was confused by the fact I had not planned to propose to her that day or in that manner. It was as if those words had come from my innermost being and been voiced by someone else.

When I finally regained control of my emotions somewhat, we talked for a long time, oblivious to what was going on around us. I wanted to know how and when she wanted to tell the girls, for in my mind, they were the most important thing we had to discuss.

"We're hungry." The two little girls had just put everything into perspective. Jane and I started laughing because food was the most important thing at that moment. Everything else could be taken care of later.

After we ate lunch, Jane and the girls fell asleep on the blanket, leaving me alone to gather my thoughts. While watching them sleep, I felt a sense of peace that I had not felt for a long time, if ever, and my thoughts returned to my childhood. I vowed that those girls would never have the word "stepchild" directed toward them, that I would love and protect them the best I could and that they would see their mother respected and loved to the best of my ability.

Unfortunately for Jane, when we told her ex-husband's parents about our plans, they came unglued. They said Jane was making a horrible mistake and putting herself and the girls in danger by marrying a rodeo bum and a guy who was not far from being homeless. But Jane maintained her composure. "I've been left on my own to make this decision, and you have no right to tell me, from now on, how to live my life," she replied.

Her parents, while probably not overjoyed at her decision, accepted me with open arms. Her brothers were happy for us, but they let me know I had better treat her and the girls right.

7

A NEW AND WONDERFUL WORLD

JANE and I were married November 14, 1973, at the courthouse in downtown Los Angeles. Afterwards, we went to pick the girls up at daycare. We had talked to them beforehand, and they said it was okay for us to get married. When we picked them up and told them the news, Dena reached out her arms for me to pick her up. "Does this mean we're all married?" she asked. All I could do was hold her tight.

"We're married forever!" I replied.

We moved into a small apartment and started life as a family, Jane and I working and the girls going to a babysitter. After work, Jane would pick up the girls, and by the time I got home, it was play time. After dinner we would watch television until it was time for the girls to have their bath and get their nighties on. Then I got to brush their hair.

One night out of the blue, Jane informed me that I would have to give the girls a bath and help get their nighties on, as she had to go to the store. I was mortified, for I had never dreamed I would have to do that. I tried to explain to Jane that I didn't want to, but she smiled and said, "You'll do just fine," then she walked out the door.

The old saying "Necessity is the mother of invention" may not have been perfectly applicable to that situation, but fear made me come up with a solution for Dena, who was now a "grown up" four-year-old. "Dena," I said, "I bet you can give Stacey a bath and help get her nightgown on." She smiled and nodded in agreement, so I went in to run the bathwater while she got everything ready. I kept an eye on them, but she did a great job, and when she was finished, she paraded Stacey out for me to see. I clapped and praised her effort, then asked if she could give herself a bath while I brushed Stacey's hair. She smiled, then went to get her things while I ran her bathwater. When she had finished bathing and put her nightgown on, she came over, handed me her hairbrush, then sat at my feet while I brushed her hair. Then, to my surprise and joy, both girls crawled into my lap and watched television with me.

When Jane got home a few minutes later and asked me how it went, I told her I handled it well, but I also told her what a great helper Dena had been and how my crisis had been averted.

One Saturday morning I was out in the parking lot when Jane's ex-husband and his girlfriend pulled up. When he got out of the vehicle to take the child support check to Jane, I asked if I could talk to him for a minute. I told him of my desire to raise the girls as my own. If he would agree not to try to see them, he would not have to pay child support, which would make it easier for him and his girlfriend. I also suggested he should talk it over with his girlfriend, which he did. He came back with the concern that we would turn him in for not paying child support. I explained in no uncertain terms that if he kept his part of the deal, he would never hear from us again. To my surprise, he agreed, then got in his vehicle and left.

I was elated, thinking I had gotten what I thought was best for us. But then I wondered what in the world made me do that without speaking to Jane first. To my surprise and relief, when I told her what I had done, she gave me a kiss and a hug and said, "Thank you, for I never wanted to see him again."

It was imperative that we get another car, as I was riding the bus to and from work or getting a ride from my friends. One of the business owner's sons had a nearly new Chevy Vega that he needed to get rid of, and he was selling it for $1,000. It was a good price, but I had very little cash and virtually no credit.

One morning I turned on the television and saw an ad for car loans at Bank of America. I knew it was a long shot, but since the bank was open until 6:00 that evening, I talked to Jane about applying for the loan. As the saying goes, "Nothing ventured, nothing gained."

Later that afternoon, she met me outside the bank. When we walked in, a pretty, young lady came over and introduced herself as Leilani. She took us to her desk and asked how she could help us. I told her we needed to buy a car but that I had no credit, Jane had just gone through a divorce, that we owned nothing, and we were renting. Then I asked if she thought she could help us. She smiled and told us to fill out the information sheet, and she would see what she could do. As I watched Jane fill out the paper, I figured there was no way they would loan us a dime, much less a $1,000 for a car.

Jane finished filling out the paper and handed it to Leilani.

She smiled, asked a couple of questions, then asked us to excuse her while she went to see what she could do.

She walked over to a man dressed in a business suit and handed him the paper. They talked for a moment, then they came over to her desk, where we were waiting. The man introduced himself, shook our hands, then asked if we had the car there. When I told him no, he chuckled. "Normally, I wouldn't approve this loan without seeing the car first, but Leilani says she has a good feeling about you folks, and after meeting you, I agree. So, we're going to give you a loan, so you can get the car. However, I would appreciate it if you would bring the car by so I can see it."

Jane and I looked at each other in astonishment. I stood up, shook his hand, and assured him I would bring the car by the following day after work. I asked if he wanted the title to hold, but he just smiled, shook Jane's hand, then went back to his desk. Jane and I just looked at each other, too astonished to speak.

Leilani disappeared for a moment, then returned and slid the application across her desk, asking us to sign it in a couple of places. Then she gave us a check, asking me to sign it on the back, which I did without even looking to see how much it was made out for. When that was done, she opened an envelope, counted out ten one-hundred-dollar bills, and handed them to me. Then she stood up, walked around to where we were, and gave us both a big hug. "I believe this is the best loan we have ever made," she said. "The manager and I agree you are blessed, so thank you for giving us the opportunity to serve you."

The next day, I drove the car to the bank, so the manager

could see it, and I could thank Lelani again. When I arrived, Leilani was nowhere to be seen, but the manager was behind his desk. As soon as he saw me, he smiled, then came over with his hand extended. We went outside so he could see the car, I asked him again if he wanted the title. He just shook his head. "Leilani told me to tell you how much she appreciated you and your wife, as she couldn't be here to tell you herself. She was here yesterday because the regular loan agent was sick. Normally, she works at a branch in Torrance as the assistant branch manager, and I couldn't argue with her insistence that we make the loan. You were just lucky enough to come in on the right day." As I have since learned, "God will make a way where there seems to be no way" (Is 43:19).

Our first Christmas together as a family was wonderful. Mr. Lou gave us $200 as a wedding gift. I was overcome with happiness as I watched the girls play with the things "Santa" had brought them.

One morning during this time, I woke up early, so I took my coffee out onto the patio to enjoy the sunshine. As I sat there, my mind returned to my childhood and my mother. For the first time in a long while, my heart ached with a longing to see her, but I stuffed my feelings down, for it was not time to go home.

Things went well for me at work, with the company's name changed from Bonded Engines to Bonded Motors. I was promoted from truck driver to parts man. I received a nice raise and was given more responsibility, which made things easier at home.

The following summer, Jane had a week's vacation, so I asked if I could take off at the same time. Mr. Lou not only said it was okay; he also gave me $200 out of his own pocket and told me to make sure Jane and the girls had a good time. I asked Jane if she would like to go to Oregon. At first, she was apprehensive, but then she got excited and started packing. It was a good trip, as the girls slept a lot, giving Jane and I time to talk. They loved staying in motels, so they could play in the pool. We went to Sandy, Oregon, just outside of Portland on the slopes of Mt. Hood. It was beautiful. The Sandy River meandered through gorges as the snow melted from Mt. Hood, producing lush green foliage along its banks. Tall pine trees pierced the blue sky, standing guard over the whole scene.

We were talking about the majestic natural beauty all around us and the lazy pace around the outskirts of Portland when Jane surprised me by saying, "Buddy, I'm going to pray that when we get old, God will make a way for us to retire and move up here to live." Why did it surprise me? Two reasons. First, Jane was a California girl, and her family and friends lived there. Second, it was the first time she had mentioned prayer since I met her.

Shortly after we returned from Oregon, Jane met me at the door when I came home from work with a large smile and said, "I'm pregnant. Now we're going to have a child of our own." I was stunned by the unexpected news, and I did not receive it well. I said I was happy just having the girls and did not want another child, but Jane told me everything would be just fine. What could I say? I just had to suck it up, be a man, and move on. When she told the girls, they jumped around and laughed, asking all sorts of questions. I sat there feeling like a jerk, for it had been selfish on my part to have been so negative.

In preparation for our new arrival, we moved out of the small apartment and into a rental house. Fortunately, her pregnancy was without major problems. The girls were ecstatic, feeling their mother's stomach and feeling the baby move. By then I had asked Jane to forgive me for being so selfish, my excitement was also growing. On November 6, 1975, we were blessed with a bouncing blue-eyed baby boy whom we named Brent Ira Mercer.

The following summer, Jane became insistent that we try to buy a house. She wanted to have a home that she could call her own. I was happy renting with no mortgage and less responsibility. Nevertheless, to placate her I agreed to look for a house that we could buy. Even so, I tried to make her understand we couldn't afford to buy a house, as we didn't have enough money, but she insisted we at least look.

One day Mr. Lou called me into his office to discuss my future with the company. By then I had worked hard to learn the business, and I was a key player he could count on. He said if I continued to learn, he would be able to use me as a salesman, and I could make more money. Then he said, "Buddy, it's about time you bought a house for Janie because women like a home of their own, and you can make money as the house increases in value."

I sat there for a minute, pondering his words. "Have you been talking to Janie?" I asked. "Because she's been bugging the heck out of me to buy a house."

"Hell no I haven't been talking to Jane," he replied. "I just know more about your wife than you do. Besides, so you won't be so likely to cut and run, I'll loan you fifteen hundred dollars for a down payment. Now go buy that woman and those kids a house they can call their home."

The next weekend we found a nice house in a good neighborhood that we could purchase with $1,500 down and payments we could afford. I was now a homeowner with a mortgage. Jane finally had a place to call her own, and the girls had their own bedrooms.

One Saturday I was sitting on the porch of our new home when I was overcome with feelings I had not felt for a long time. I thought of the days before I turned my back on God, and Jesus was my best friend. The days when I was a little boy walking to church with my grandparents, mama, and the neighbors. In my mind, I could hear my grandpa singing "When the Roll Is Called up Yonder I'll be There." Once again, my emotions overtook me. I went into the house and found Jane in the bedroom, folding clothes. "Jane, I think we ought to start going to church," I said. She looked at me as if I were nuts.

"Buddy, I don't think I'm ready, for I'm filled with guilt about my past," she replied. I understood what she meant, for I was racked with guilt about my past too. However, I knew the kids would love Sunday School as much as I did, so after a little more conversation, we decided we would check things out. I looked in the Yellow Pages and found the First Baptist Church of Southgate. The next morning, off to church we went.

We attended off and on for the next three years, but it was hit and miss, as we were going to the beach and the mountains. Then we got hooked on going to Pismo Beach, which we all enjoyed.

One Saturday Jane took the kids to visit her parents in Gardena while I stayed at home to do some yardwork. After I finished, I sat on the porch, enjoying the sunshine and the smell of fresh-cut grass, thinking how lucky I had been over the years. My mind took me back to the courtroom in Abilene where the deputy and his wife asked the judge release me into their custody; to skid row in downtown LA where I had planned to end it all but instead had a dream or vision of my mama and grandparents praying for me; to the guy at the mission whom nobody knew who helped me get off the streets; how I had walked about six miles or so with no idea where I was going and wound up at an employment office at where a lady who I found out later didn't exist sent me to Bonded Engines for a job that wasn't really available. More recently, I had been able to get a car loan with no credit and buy a house that we could call our own. With luck like that, I thought maybe it was time to go home and see my mom, so she could see that I was alive, and she could be proud of me.

When Jane and the kids got home, I talked to her about my plan. She thought it was a great idea also, so we started planning a trip to Texas. Then one day when I got home from work, she was crying, and she told me her sister Jeannie, who lived in Texas, had called her and said my mother had died. Jeannie had heard an announcement on the radio, wanting any kinfolks of Vida Mercer to get in touch with the sheriff in Eldorado, for there had been a death in the family. When I heard the news, I thought my luck had just run out, and there was no need to return to Texas

By early January 1977, I had made great strides in learning the business, and was promoted to parts manager at Bonded Motors, receiving a nice raise. But the promotion also came with new responsibilities including purchasing parts and maintaining inventory, which meant dealing with the vendors who supplied us with what we needed to build the engines in the plant. The guy who had been doing the purchasing was unhappy with my promotion because he had anticipated becoming parts manager, and he was used to doing his job with no budget or inventory control and no supervision.

The Saturday after I took over, I went into the plant, which was closed on weekends, to take inventory. With me was Robby, one of the guys whose job was to stock shelves and keep the parts department clean. It quickly became apparent that my helper was capable of much more than stocking shelves. He was intuitive, intelligent, had common sense, and most of all, he was ambitious.

It didn't take long for me to realize the lack of supervision and inventory control was costing the company a lot of money. The shelves were overstocked with expensive parts, many of which were not necessary. When I mentioned this to Robby, he shrugged and said he wasn't supposed to tell me what was going on. He asked me if the purchasing agent knew we were taking inventory on a Saturday when the plant was closed. When I told him no one knew what we were doing, he laughed and said, "Buddy, I won't have to tell you anything because you'll see for yourself."

By lunchtime I was appalled at what I was finding. We were in a closed-off area where parts could be hidden and removed without anyone noticing. When I asked Robby if this was what he wasn't supposed to tell me, he just grinned and nodded.

We ate at a small restaurant that made the best burritos. It was there that Robby relaxed and started asking questions that indicated he wanted to know if he had a future at Bonded. I told him my story and how Mr. Lou helped me get off the streets and let me advance with the company, assuring him that if he worked hard and was honest and faithful to the company, he would have the same opportunity I had been given. He looked me straight in the eye and said, "Buddy, when you move into sales, I'll take your place."

When we got back to the plant after lunch, Robby asked me to follow him to an upstairs mezzanine, which was full of old machinery and office supplies. To my surprise and shock, there were also pallets of engine parts covered and hidden with colored plastic. It was all too clear that we had a theft problem that had to be corrected immediately, but we had to do it covertly. We took an inventory of everything in the mezzanine. It was time consuming and dusty, but it had to be done.

After we finished our project, we still had to take care of the parts department where all the engine parts were supposed to be in order by number. However, the purchasing agent had his own idea of how the parts should be inventoried.

By then it was around 6:00 p.m., so I thanked Robby for all his help and told him that he could go home, but to my surprise, he said he would stay if he could call his wife and let her know he'd be home late. That reminded me to call Jane to let her know I'd be home late too.

We worked all night, stopping for some more burritos and sodas, finally finishing at 5:30 a.m. on Sunday morning, at which point I sent Robby home. I stayed until about noon, putting a complete inventory on paper. I put one copy on the purchasing agent's desk and another one on the accountant's desk, then kept a copy for myself.

On Monday morning, I was in the plant at about 4:30 a.m., working on a budget for the parts department to give to the accountant and the purchasing agent. When I finished just before 8:00, I went up to the mezzanine, so I could see what was going to happen.

Shortly after 8:00, the purchasing agent raced into the parts department, frantic with worry, and went straight to the closed-off area where all the extra parts were stored. Then he went through all the shelves, which were in numerical order, after which he went to Robby. But Robby just shrugged and walked away.

I went to the accountant's office to explain why I had changed the parts department. "Good morning," I said, but that was as far as I got before he cut me off, wanting to know what the hell was going on and why I had given him a copy of a budget when he was the one who did the budgeting. I told him I would get back to him momentarily, then headed to the parts department to see if everything was okay.

When Robby saw me, he smiled and waved, then went out into the plant to take some parts to one of the rebuilders like everything was fine. I continued to the purchasing agent's office. He was flustered, wanting to know what was going on and why I was meddling in his parts department. I told him that since I was now responsible for the parts department, I wanted a numbered inventory, so it would be easy for me or anyone else to find the parts we needed. "And as far as it being *your* parts department," I added, "it's not yours. It belongs to the company, and I'm here to make sure it operates profitably."

I was on the way to my office when I was paged to go to Mr. Lou's office, which I was expecting, so I went straight there and entered without knocking, a smile on my lips. I greeted him with a cheery good morning, but he was confused and angry, especially at my demeanor. "Buddy, what the hell do you think you're doing?" he asked. "This place is in an uproar. The accountant is angry that you're meddling in his department, giving him a new inventory and budget, even though you don't know what you're doing."

I sat down across from him, still smiling. "You're in for a very unpleasant surprise, which you have helped to create due to lack of supervision. You have allowed the purchasing agent to purchase whatever he wants. You asked me to become the parts manager, so I decided to do an inventory, and what I found is horrible for your company. So, do you want me to show you what I found, or should we let the parts department continue to lose money?"

He indicated I would continue with my story. As I did, his demeanor went from angry to defeated as he slumped in his chair. After I told him everything that I had discovered, I waited for his response, and when it came, I was totally surprised. "Buddy, did you have someone with you, so you can verify your findings?" he asked. "Also, what do we do about this?" I told him that I was going to terminate the purchasing agent. I would assume that role for the week while I searched for someone to replace him. Mr. Lou agreed, but when I went to the purchasing agent's office to fire him, to my surprise, he was already gone, and his desk was empty.

To avoid any delays, I went straight to the parts department and asked Robby if he would like to become the purchasing agent if I taught him the job. He was stunned but said he would do whatever I needed.

That night after the plant closed, I spent several hours showing him the ropes of parts purchasing. For the rest of the week, I did the purchasing during the day, and after the plant closed, I trained him. The following Saturday, his training was complete.

On Monday morning, I sat with Robby to make sure he was confident he could do the job, then I told him that I would be there if he needed me. When Mr. Lou came in, he was astonished to see Robby doing the purchasing, but when I explained what we had done, he agreed to give him an opportunity

Mr. Lou and the accountant met with me the same day that the purchasing agent left, and it was decided that we would let things continue as normal for a while and see what transpired. We discovered that the purchasing agent had been selling parts to backyard mechanics in his neighborhood who were taking them to Mexico. We agreed that we would not make a big deal of the situation, so we could avoid any further disruption at the plant.

Over the next couple of years, I continued to serve as parts manager, and Robby did a fantastic job as purchasing agent. He did so well, in fact, that I told him when I went into outside sales, he could take over my job.

Soon after, Mr. Lou asked me to come to his office to discuss the possibility of moving into outside sales. He inquired if I had considered how the transition would proceed, noting the importance of avoiding issues due to my absence from the plant, since my responsibilities as parts manager included acting as a liaison with the plant manager, John Rush. We worked well together with great communication, which made for a harmonious relationship, and Mr. Lou did not want things to fall apart.

I told him that I had expected that I would be going into sales, as we needed to grow, and that I had been training Robby to take my place for the past year. He and the plant manager worked well together, which I expected to continue, as both guys understood their roles. I added that we had been grooming a parts man to replace Robby as the purchasing agent. Robby was very comfortable with the guy's performance, and he would be right there to help him if needed. Mr. Lou laughed. "You've been planning all of this for quite a while but didn't tell me." I told him that he appeared to be extremely busy with his father and the rest of the business plus some outside interests they were involved with, but we had had general conversations about the company and what was going on.

"Thanks for your efforts to help the company grow," he said. "I'm sorry for not being more involved, but I promise we'll have more meaningful conversations moving forward. Now, can we continue with your plans to put all of this together? We need to get you out into sales."

We came up with a plan that would allow me to begin working in sales within two weeks. I requested that I be allowed to speak to the plant manager and everyone else involved to ensure the transition went as smoothly as possible. He agreed to my request, asking only that I keep him in the loop.

I met with everyone involved, and soon we had an agreement in writing. When I went to Mr. Lou's office and told him what had transpired, he laughed and said, "If this keeps going, soon you'll be replacing me!" I smiled and told him I liked what I was going to be doing and that if I did well, I would be in the plant just once a week to meet with everyone involved in the transition to ensure everything was going smoothly, then I would meet with Mr. Lou to go over my sales report. He was impressed with my plans to keep him involved with everything, but I was actually doing it out of self-preservation because he was terrible at dealing with people.

The next day I started my new position as an outside salesman. I was really looking forward to it, as I had been dealing with customers over the phone, helping to take care of problems, and now I would have the opportunity to meet them in person. I had developed a reputation as being knowledgeable and honest, so I figured it would be a pleasant change from the daily pressures that I had been dealing with in the plant. I would also have the opportunity to generate new customers and create extra sales, which the company needed to grow.

Things went even better than I expected, and within a couple of weeks I picked up several new customers. I also met most of our regular customers. When I went into the plant, there was a more positive attitude among the employees because they saw that with increased business, their jobs were more secure. Mr. Lou was delighted with the progress I was making in sales and with the input I gave him regarding what was happening in the plant with the plant manager, parts manager, and the new purchasing agent.

I was also delighted because he would not be meddling with the guys in the plant and causing me more problems. He was a nice guy, but he had a real problem dealing with people, which I found was typical of business owners.

In the spring of 1979, I took my family to Pismo Beach for a three-day weekend and had a terrific time at the beach, touring San Luis Obispo's Mission, walking through the eucalyptus grove near Pismo, where thousands of monarch butterflies were fluttering about in the eucalyptus groves. When it was time to leave, nobody, including me, wanted to go.

"I'm going to pray God will make a way for us to move here," Jane said. I thought that was okay, but I told her and the kids not to get their hopes up, as there weren't many employment opportunities there. Instead, I promised we would make lots of trips to the area.

Things went really well for me at Bonded in early 1980, and I was making more money than I had ever hoped. Jane was also working and finding success. We were able to take three-day weekends quite often, including trips to Pismo Beach. One morning I was contacted by a vendor that I knew well. He wanted to meet me for lunch, but he said not to tell anyone.

"Buddy, if the owners of Bonded ever hear what I'm doing I will be in serious trouble," he said, "but I've been contacted by a small company in San Luis Obispo who want to talk to you about running their business as general manager."

I could hardly breathe, much less think straight. I owed Mr. Lou everything. He had given me my first job the day I got off the streets, helped me start my new life, loaned us the money to buy our first house, and allowed me to work my way up to where I was. Then I thought about how my family wanted to move to the Pismo Beach area. I told the guy I would have to think about it, but in the meantime, I would keep it a secret. He gave me the phone number to the company that had head-hunted me, Performance Machine, then left me alone with thoughts.

I drove to a park where I could be alone, so I could try to get my mind under control before talking to Jane. As I sat in my car, I worked out the options. From that process, it became clear that I should talk to the people at Performance Machine. At the very least, my family could enjoy the weekend at the beach.

That evening, I told Jane about what had transpired. "The kids will be excited to go away for the weekend," I added.

Fred and John, the brothers who owned Performance Machine, were happy to see me. They took me on a tour of their small plant, which was very impressive, with all the latest machinery. Then Fred invited me into his office where we spent the next three hours talking about their needs and how they were sure I would be able to help turn their company around. At the conclusion of the meeting, they made me an offer, which included the same salary that I was making at Bonded plus moving expenses.

"We don't want to rush you, as we're sure you need to talk to your wife about this," Fred said. "If possible, we'd like an answer within two weeks. Now, if you're comfortable with it, I'd like to pray, asking God to give us wisdom regarding this situation."

Afterward, I told Jane everything that we had discussed, including how Fred had prayed over the situation. "We have a lot to discuss," was her reply.

One morning a couple of days later while we had our coffee and discussed the options, it became clear that I should take the job. I called Fred with my decision, laid out what I thought would be a doable time frame, and asked if that was acceptable to him, and he agreed. We put our house up for sale and, to my surprise, received an offer within a week that met our asking price, but they needed a thirty-day escrow. That more than exceeded our wishes.

Then it was time to face the task I dreaded: telling Mr. Lou about my decision. When I told him, he was upset, but he understood our wanting to move to that area and wished us well. I told him we were very grateful for all he had done and if they ever needed me, I would come back, thinking it would never happen.

Now I had to get busy in my time off, finding a place for us to live, booking a moving van, and doing all the other things that went into moving. When I called a rental agency, my heart dropped as the lady told me there were no rentals available in the immediate area. Then Mr. Lou's son called, wanting me to work in the plant to help ease my transition out of the company. Jane had given a week's notice, but her company asked if she could make it two weeks. Suddenly, everything that had been going so smoothly fell apart. Then, to my amazement, the rental agency called to say an apartment had become available, but it was furnished, so we would have to store our furniture. As luck would have it, a storage unit was available at a reduced price. Plus, Jane's company found an applicant who needed very little training, so she could leave in one week instead of two. Our luck had changed for the better, and we were able to move as planned.

After we got moved in, the kids were ecstatic, pronouncing everything to be perfect. Jane told me she had found a church we could attend too. I still wasn't sure how God fit into our life, but I knew things were better when we went to church.

8

PERFORMANCE MACHINE,
SAN LUIS OBISPO

ON THE DAY of my original visit to Performance Machine, the owners took me on a tour of their plant, which was small compared to the plant I was used to. It had the latest technology, and it was extremely clean, the work benches and counters shining with costly stainless-steel coverings. The lighting was perfect, and to my amazement the room where the engines were assembled was enclosed with Plexiglas to avoid any particles from the rest of the plant contaminating the engines and reverse enclosed fans above the assembly area. After the engine was assembled, it was moved to another enclosed room, which had a computerized testing machine to ensure the engine was free of any problems. After the engine was approved, it was double bagged with heavy duty-poly plastic bags, then transported to another enclosed room to await a sale to a customer.

During my tour, I was impressed with the diligence of the men at the workstations. They appeared to be very intelligent, knowledgeable, and professional. As I stopped to talk to them, they were friendly and open to any questions that I had. Each man I spoke to appeared to be happy to be employed by Performance Machine.

I also sat with the accountant, Leslie, a bright young lady who was friendly and answered any question I asked. When I looked at the payroll, it was obvious that the overhead was way out of line for an engine rebuilder, but when I brought it to her attention, she just shrugged and told me I needed to address that with the owners.

I understood that the employees were very talented and wanted to be paid well for their abilities, but the cost to produce their engines was way out of line, and it was quickly apparent that I needed to have another chat with the owners, but I wanted to have further conversation with Leslie. When I asked her about Fred and John's background she replied, "You really need to have a conversation with both owners separately."

I THANKED her for her time and then followed her advice. When I sat down with John and talked to him about Fred, he dropped his head. "I love my brother," he said, "but his background is he owned a pipe shop. If you noticed, he don't get his fingers dirty, he is way above us, and he has this Christian attitude that he's the know all and be all. It's been that away since we were little kids, but now that we're in business and our dad wants to do this together, it's creating a problem." I thanked him for his time, then I went to interview Fred, who was quite aloof. "Oh, my brother is a mechanic," he said. "He works twenty hours a day on his stuff and everybody else's stuff. He's brilliant, but he's not a people person, which is creating a problem." I thanked him for his time, then walked out to my car. I realized I had a problem.

When I got home, I told Jane about my day with the brothers and their sibling rivalry. She responded by telling me about two sibling rivals from the Bible, Cain and Able, with Cain killing Able which made me think, "If I'm lucky, one will do the other one in. I had resolved these kinds of problems at my previous position at Bonded Motors so I figured I could handle this as Fred and John wanted the company to succeed.

On my first day at Performance Machine, Fred and John called all the employees together to introduce me as the new general manager. Right away I knew that there were a lot of problems, for it was apparent that the employees did not respect the owners. After I was introduced, I gave a little talk about what I had seen in the plant and had heard about the high standard to which Performance Machine adhered. I also told them a little bit about what I would be doing there to help turn the company around, mainly in sales. Unknown to the employees, Fred and John were borrowing money from their father in Bakersfield who had done well and wanted to see his sons succeed, but he was about to cut them off if they didn't turn the company around.

After I finished addressing the employees I invited Fred and John into my office. It was located in the plant and was enclosed in glass, so I could keep an eye on what was happening on the floor. Before I could get a word out, they started arguing with each other in plain sight of the employees, so I excused myself and went to talk to Leslie, the accountant. She asked if I had had enough of Fred and John's act yet. I asked her if such arguments happened often. "Yep," she replied. I was reminded of

Mark 3:25, which says "A house divided against itself cannot stand."

I went back toward my office and asked the brothers if we could step outside for a minute. As we walked out, I saw the employees were having great fun at our expense. Once outside, I told the owners that if they wanted me to stay and help turn the company around, such temper tantrums could not happen again. If they couldn't agree to that, they needed to let me know and I would leave right then. They looked at me as if I were from outer space because they weren't used to being talked to like that. But they agreed that if they needed to argue, they would not do it in front of the men.

I went to my office and began to make notes, noticing most of the men were curious as to what I was doing. Pretty soon one of the men came to my office, asking if we could talk, so I invited him in, told him to take a seat, then waited for him to say something. However, he just stared at me, so I thanked him for the visit, then went out into the shop to talk to another guy who kept looking at me. The guy who was in my office yelled for me to come back, but I just waved and then asked the other guy who had been staring if he had a problem I could help him with. He apologized and said he didn't realize he had been staring at me. I returned to my office where the other guy was standing outside. Instead of acknowledging him, I went into my office and closed the door behind me. I sat at my desk, leaving the guy staring at me. It was apparent that these guys who had appeared so professional on the day of my walk through with Fred and John were not happy that I was there, and they were going to see what I was made of.

I made it through the first day of my new position at Performance Machine, even with all these guys pulling any shenanigans that they could come up with to irritate me. Each time they did, I found a way to make them look small and played the game with them. When we made it to quitting time, I wanted to wish them all well when they went out. It was then I discovered they didn't have a time clock, so there was no way to record how long they worked, and they could put anything on the timecard they wanted. Over on a bench I also saw a suggestion box. I decided that if Fred and John had been running the company out of a suggestion box, that was going to have to come to a screeching halt, but I didn't say a word that night.

On the way to my car, to my surprise, I found the men outside working on cars, doing whatever they wanted to do. *Okay,* I thought. *I'll work on that later.* I didn't say a word, just got in my car and went home.

The next morning, the starting time was at 7:00. I got there at about 6:30 and was at my desk, watching out the window when the workers came in, goofing around, but they didn't do any work. About 8:00, they went to their workstations and started piddling around. When they saw me in the office, I didn't say a word. I just smiled and waved.

At about 10:00, one of them knocked on my door, and I invited him inside. He wanted to know why I was there so early. I told them I had a bit of work to do and that I'd let them know what was going on a little bit later.

At lunchtime, I went out and asked if anybody had any plans for the evening. When they said they didn't, I said, "Good. We're going to order some pizza and beer, and we're going to have a mandatory company pizza party. They all giggled at that. "We'll have you out of here at about seven o'clock," I added.

At 5:00, the pizza showed up. I wasn't drinking that night, so I had a soda instead. Unbeknownst to them, I had a wastepaper basket full of water and a cardboard box that said "Suggestion Box" on it. As they ate their pizza and yucked things up, I lit the suggestion box on fire and watched it burn. That quieted them down. Then I dumped what was left of the box in the wastepaper basket.

"You know, fellas," I said, "I'm trying to save this company. You guys wanted to play and see what I was made of. Well, here's the deal, Fred and John have given you a job that you cannot get anyplace else on this coast. They're paying you money that matches your abilities, but we have to either start making money, or they're going to be out of business. And if they go out of business, you won't have a job that pays what you make here. I can go back to LA and take my old job back, and I'd be more than happy to do that, but I want to see you guys succeed. Fred and John are the owners, and they'll do well no matter what. So, it's going to be up to you, but from now on in the morning when you come in, you will punch in, and we're going to start at seven o'clock sharp. You will work until five o'clock, then you will punch out. Then we're going to lock the door, and you can do whatever you want to do after that. Now, if any of you have any questions or concerns, maybe we should step outside and settle this thing."

"What do you mean?" one of them asked.

"You guys were pretty rough today, and I didn't appreciate it. Now, it's time that we turn this company around, so you can continue to have a job after I'm gone. The day that I first walked through here with Fred and John, I was amazed at your shop. You have the finest equipment throughout the United States.

I've been to over a half-dozen of the best engine rebuilders in the United States, and nobody that has the equipment that you have. The stainless-steel coverings on your workstation, the air sections over your workstations, the tools and the computers. It's all the latest technology. Fred and John have spent a ton of money on this. I went into your assembly room, and you have air induction to keep dust particles from entering the engines. You also have a fine computerized test stand that gives all the information to make sure that every engine is free of defects. Once the engines come off the test stand, they're put into a room where there is no contamination after they're double bagged in polyester. That's impressive.

"Moreover, when I did the walk through, I stopped and talked to you men, and each one of you came across as intelligent, knowledgeable, and affable, and you seemed to enjoy your work. Today, you seemed upset, but we'll move forward. I'm working on a plan for the future. I'm not a religious guy, but I do know that the Bible says in First Corinthians 14:33 that God is not a God of confusion but a God of order. There is no vision here and no rules that you adhere to, but we're going to make a change here. We're going to establish order. I'm going to put together a vision for you, but then you are going to take time to talk to me about what you see. This is your plant, and I work for you. I will continue to work for you until we get this thing going, and then we are going to go out, and I'm going to find new customers, so this plant will be around for a long time. You'll have jobs that will allow you to create a good life for your families, not because of me but because you're going to take charge of things. Fred and John brought me here to make sure that happens because they don't want to go broke.

"So, if you have nothing else to say at this point, I think it's time we go home. I'm going to put this plan together tonight, and we're going to start talking about it tomorrow. If you don't want to be involved, let me know in the morning, and I'll be more than happy not to include you. But if you do that, you have no right to tell us when things are right and wrong. Goodnight, and we will see you in the morning."

When I got home that night, the kids were in bed, but Jane was waiting for me.

"It looks like you've had an interesting day," she said when I walked in. I told her what happened, and she suggested we pray for guidance and wisdom in finding the best solution—and she did pray.

I didn't understand how it was all going to work, but I knew I had to come up with something to give the men, so I sat down, prepared to work all night, if necessary. It struck me that Proverbs 29:18 applied to this situation: "Where there is no vision, the people perish." Despite having great equipment and talented staff, success required a clear plan. Once everyone understood the rules and helped shape them, we could work effectively together.

The next morning, I woke up feeling fresh and ready to go. I got to the plant at about 6:30 a.m., and I was amazed to see some of the guys in their cars, waiting outside. When they came in at 7:00, they didn't go to their workstations; they came over to my office instead. I was curious to know what was going to happen, but I got exactly what I expected. They wanted to talk, so I agreed to listen for however long it took. After about an hour of discussion, we had a clear plan and a set of guidelines for employees.

Following the meeting, I called Fred, John, and Leslie into my office, so their employees could see their involvement, especially since much of it concerned money. I explained what we were doing and how the employees and I had come up with a plan. Fred was adamant that that wasn't going to happen, but John said, "Get off your high horse. This is what you brought Buddy up here to fix. Now he's doing it, and our employees need to be involved." He was spot on.

I asked Leslie for her insights on our finances and was pleased when she pointed out that we were overspending on premium racing engine products, which cost four times more than the standard parts typically used by engine rebuilders. Fred started to object, but I asked him to hold his thoughts until the accountant finished her report. As Leslie continued, it was clear that it was going to be a contentious but profitable meeting, as her next concern regarded salaries. When I asked how the payroll got so high, Fred objected once again, but I was adamant that we all needed to understand what had happened and how to fix it. Leslie became upset and wanted to leave, but I encouraged her to stay and give her input because the truth will set us free (Jn 8:31).

After I got her settled, I told Fred and John that, apparently, they were part of the problem. They had to come clean, so we could find a way to fix whatever the problem was, but they clammed up. Suddenly, a thought hit me like a bolt of lightning. Before I had a chance to think, I heard the words coming out of my mouth. "This beautiful shop with all of its expensive equipment, stainless steel, and top-of-the-line tooling isn't paid for, and it's not on the books, correct?"

The tension in the room was so thick I could have cut it

with a butter knife, Fred and John were frozen, their faces white as if the blood had stopped flowing through their veins. Leslie's hand shook as she reached into her briefcase and pulled out some papers, but I stopped her and looked at Fred and John. "Either one of you guys have something to say?"

"We got the money from our father when we opened Performance Machine on a promissory note that is coming due at the end of the year with a personal guarantee," Fred replied, "which means our father can close us down, according to his lawyer."

John was quiet at first, then he said it was his fault; they never should have included the business in the loan. I told them I didn't care what had happened in the past, but they were responsible for their employees' livelihood, so whatever the situation was, they had to fix it.

By then Leslie had regained her composure. "Since you've come on board, I have spoken to our attorney. With the plan you're proposing, the involvement of the employees as a fiduciary committee, and weekly reports to their father's CPA, Fred and John will need to put their homes up as a personal guarantee. If that happens, Performance Machine will be free and clear of the loan payments. You can arrange this by talking to their father. All of this is in these papers." She handed them to me.

I thought Fred and John were going to pass out, but I didn't care. I skimmed the papers, then handed them to Fred. "You and John created the problem, so here's your opportunity to face reality. Leslie has done the hard work, so now all you have to do is sign on the dotted line, showing you have faith in the company to succeed." Fred grabbed the papers and signed them, then slid them to John and sat with a menacing glare as he adorned them with his signature. I thanked Leslie for her strong leadership in the matter, but she shook her head.

"My job, which I love dearly, was on the line, and when I heard you were coming, I began to pray for God's wisdom and courage as to what I could do to help things work. He guided me through every step, so I give Him all the glory." Her words hit me hard. I realized God had been involved with every aspect of Performance Machine and its potential turnaround. According to her, He had orchestrated everything, even answering my concerns before I could voice them

I told Fred and John to go home for the day and reflect on what had just happened. Then I asked Leslie to stay in my office while I called their father.

After the brothers left, I commended Leslie again and asked if she would be okay with what had just happened with the brothers going forward. She laughed and told me she had known their father since she was a little girl, and he treated her like his own daughter, so the brothers had better pray everything went well.

I called their father, expecting to get a receptionist, but I was surprised when he answered. "Thank you for your part in this drama," he said after I introduced myself. "Leslie will be well taken care of. If you have another problem with one of my boys, kick his ass and fire him. Have a nice day."

After he hung up, I stared at the phone in stunned silence. Leslie laughed again and said, "Buddy you have a friend for life"

I went back to the employees and asked for their input. To my surprise, most of them went along with everything. But one employee decided to be a jerk. He said he hadn't been invited to the meeting, and he started giving me a hard time. I reminded him that all the employees were invited to participate in the meeting. Furthermore, I told them beforehand that if they didn't show up and speak their mind, they didn't have a right to say anything afterward.

"If that's the deal, I quit," he replied.

I asked him to wait in my office for a few minutes. Then I went to Leslie and told her to give me the guy's final check. "You better talk to Fred and John first," she replied, "because this guy had been there for quite a while, and he's one of their favorites."

"No, I'm not talking to anyone," I replied. "I'm running this company now. This man said he was going to quit because I didn't let him have his way. So, write me a final check."

She wrote the check, then I returned to my office. "Here's your final paycheck," I said.

"What do you mean?" he replied.

"You said you were going to quit, so thank you very much for your time. Now, get out of here, or I'll call the cops because you're trespassing."

After he left, the other employees came up and thanked me. "We needed to get rid of him," one of them said. "He was a problem."

From then on, our quality and our production improved, lowering the cost of the engines we produced. As for the employees, I told them they would have to weather a 10 percent decrease in their paycheck for the next sixty days. "But at the end of sixty days, if we do it properly, you'll get the ten percent that you gave the company, and we'll move on. In the meantime, do your part. Make this thing run right, and I'm gonna start working on sales."

From that day forward, things started running as smoothly as possible. The men were excited because things were going well, and they could see there was a plan in place. We would stop production regularly and have a visit, during which we exchanged ideas that we would implement on the fly, making it more exciting. Sixty days later, we were almost profitable, so we decided to refund the money that the guys had "lent" the company.

Now that the plant was running smoothly, I went out into the field to call on customers and boost sales. It was a beautiful thing. Everybody loved our equipment and our products, but they couldn't put up with Fred. He was arrogant, egotistical, and argumentative. When I explained that he was one of the owners, one of the customers said, "Well you got a problem," to which I readily agreed. But I had an idea.

I went in and talked to Fred, and sure enough, he denied all of it. So, I went to Radio Shack and bought a recorder, then I returned to our customers. "We already told you what we thought," one of them said. "Why are you back here?"

"I just want to make sure I have your words correctly. Then I'll go see what I can do about it."

Afterward, I went into Fred's office and told him what I'd heard. Once again, he denied it. So, I put the recorder on his desk and turned it on. After he heard three or four customers saying he was a problem, he picked the recorder up and threw it against the cinder-block wall and stormed out. Before he left, I told him that wasn't too smart. He had just cost the company sixty bucks. (I used company money to buy the recorder.)

Before I went back out into the field to call on customers, I had another meeting with Fred, John, and Leslie to make sure everybody was on the same page. The plan we had created would require some cooperation from all of us. "Fred, you're going to have to work closely with me, as you're one of the owners," I said. "However, I think you'd be much better off going to your pipe shop. I think you'll enjoy that. I'll expect you to come in for a weekly meeting with us, so you still have input, but we've got a man here whom I can train as customer service rep. He will be able to take care of the customers' needs, as he's very knowledgeable about what goes in the plant.

"John, you're going to have to calm down and learn to work with the men. We know you're way smarter than they are. You've got talent, but you're hard to work with. If we're going to succeed, it'll require both of you to work together. Cain and Abel didn't get along, and the result was tragic. I know you want to make this place succeed, and I'm telling you how we can do that.

"I'm going to be going out into the field to drum up new business. We started this during the first of June, and now it's the middle of August. We need to pick up sales because winter is coming. Everyone's livelihood is at stake, so I expect full cooperation from all of you, and I'll give you mine."

Over the next little while, I traveled up and down the coast, calling on customers. It was a joy ride. I'd take Jane with me, and we would go to lunch. The ocean and the hills around San Luis Obispo were beautiful. It was almost like a vacation. We could pick the kids up after school and go enjoy the parks. It was a beautiful life.

As things got going, it looked like we were going to be there for a bit, so Jane said, "I found the church for us to attend, and I think we should give God all the glory." I agreed, even though I didn't know what that meant. The kids wanted to go to Sunday school, and they loved to talk about Jesus. It was a wonderful time.

By the end of September, we were picking up business from customers who had stopped buying from us because they no longer wanted to deal with Fred. I was also able to pick up a line of rebuilt import engines from Japan that I could sell with no production cost, which enhanced our financial situation. I told Leslie that she was going to have too much money. "And you're going to have to count it more quickly because Fred and John are going to want a raise." Everybody laughed. The employees were happy, and everything was humming along, just like it should be.

By November, business slowed down somewhat, so I told Fred and John that I was going to take a week off. We wanted to go to LA to spend Thanksgiving with Jane's parents. The owners agreed and wished us a happy Thanksgiving.

Just before Christmas I received a call from one of Mr. Lou's friends, telling me that Bonded Motors was in trouble, and they needed me to come back and help. My heart sank because my family was enjoying living in Arroyo Grande, but I had promised Mr. Lou that if he ever needed my help I would be there for him.

When I broke the news to Jane, she was disappointed, but she understood why it was necessary. That evening after dinner, I told the kids what was going to happen. As expected, they were devastated, especially our oldest daughter, Dena, for she had made many friends at school.

The next morning, I left for Los Angeles to find out what had gone wrong and how my return could benefit Bonded. I told Mr. Lou that if I was going to uproot my family and come back, I needed to have some control, so I could help fix the problems, and he was quick to agree.

The morning after I returned home, I went to Performance Machine to give my two-week notice. Fred told me that he had already felt in his spirit that this would be happening. He said they would be happy to pay me for the two weeks and allow me to prepare to return to LA. On my way home, I wondered what Fred meant when he said he had felt it in his spirit. Was it like a premonition or maybe a hunch?

Jane and I agreed that I would go to Los Angeles by myself, leaving her and the kids in Arroyo Grande, so the children could finish the school year and avoid any unnecessary trauma. It was difficult leaving my family, but I would visit on weekends as often as possible, and they would come down on holiday weekends and stay with Jane's parents in Gardena. That made the kids happy, for they loved their grandparents.

My life was quite busy as I worked to help get Bonded Motors back to the level it was operating at before I left. It didn't take long to ferret out the problems. The first issue was that Mr. Lou had decided he should be involved in running the plant, which was usurping John's authority with the employees. I had to go between the two of them to get things back on track, so the employees would know that John was the plant manager, and he was in charge. It was amazing how two grown men were creating problems with production, causing engines to be delivered late and forcing customers to go to another supplier. All it took was to get the two of them together, explain that they were the problem, and that I was going to make them part of the solution, or we would be out of business shortly.

During the meeting, they both were contrite, but they wanted to explain their sides, which irritated the hell out of me. I made it clear that it wasn't important what had caused the problem, which hadn't been there when I left just six months earlier. They had both let their egos nearly destroy what we had worked so hard to build.

After I finished my diatribe, to my surprise and delight, Mr. Lou apologized to John and me and asked if we could just go forward. John also apologized, and after he finished speaking, they shook hands and declared it was done. I thanked them for making things right between the two of them, but I suggested Mr. Lou should speak to the employees and communicate his vision for the company going forward. He arranged for a meeting to be held the next morning, and he did a beautiful job of establishing where the company was going, with the employees' help.

I went out to our customers to let them know that a short-term issue in the plant had been rectified, and they could expect better service than before. I was gratified that nearly all of them committed to purchasing from Bonded Motors when they needed a rebuilt engine.

I was able to generate enough sales to get Bonded back to a point where we were making money again, which alleviated a lot of Mr. Lou's stress, secured my job, and made the employees feel better. Furthermore, our family was able to take three-day weekends to the Pismo Beach area, go camping with the kids and their grandparents, and even go to Disneyland.

Nevertheless, leaving the beautiful Arroyo Grande and

Pismo Beach area and the friends they had made was very difficult for our children. The younger two had made friends in our neighborhood, and there was a beautiful park across the street where they could spend the day playing with no worries. They could also walk to school with their friends. Dena attended Judkins junior high in Pismo Beach, which was located on a hill with a beautiful view of the ocean. She had developed many friendships, and at that age it was traumatic to leave such an idyllic situation.

In LA we were able to lease a nice home up in Chino Hills, an upper-middle-class area with a low crime rate, which made Jane happy. The younger two children adapted quickly, as there was a nice park with lots of playground equipment close by and kids their age to play with. Dena was having a difficult time, as there were few kids her age in the area.

During this time we went to a family gathering. Dena's favorite uncle was also there. Lester was an expert horseman, having been around the horses all his life. He asked if she'd like to learn how to ride, and she was ecstatic. So, we took her down to where her uncle stabled his horses. After Lester showed her how to saddle a horse, put on the bridle and reins, he put a lunge line on a horse and took him out in the middle of the arena. He showed Dena how to get the horse to walk in circles to warm up.

After a few minutes of walking the horse, Lester showed Dena how to move the horse to a faster gait and then to another gait and then slowed the horse back down to a walk. Then he took off the lunge line and had Dena walk the horse around the arena as she held onto the reins. Then Lester called her to bring the horse over to him. After taking a few minutes to point out a few things, he helped her onto the horse and then walked it to the far end of the arena while holding the bridle. Then he stepped away, and Dena started walking the horse by herself in a circle as if he were on the lunge line. Lester called for her to reverse the horse without stopping. A few minutes later, he told her to pick up some speed. After watching to make sure she was okay, he came over to us and, to my surprise, said Dena was a natural horsewoman.

He gave her several more lessons, then he showed us a gentle, well-trained, pretty quarter horse filly that was stabled where his horses were. The guy who owned it wanted to get rid of it, and Lester said I could buy the horse and rigging for very little. After discussing it with Jane, I told him I would talk to the guy the next time we were there for Dena's lesson.

For some reason, the filly's owner was very bitter. He told me that he would sell the filly and everything that went with it with the provision that I moved it out of the area within two weeks. We told the guy we would have it out within a week, and just like that, we were horse owners.

Lester had a friend in Lake Elsinore where we could stable the horse. On weekends we would load everyone up so Dena could ride the horse. The man who owned the stables had things that kept the younger children busy. I was ecstatic because everyone was happy, and it didn't cost me a lot of money.

In early June, Jane's sister and husband and their two kids, who were about the same age as our two girls, came for dinner. During our conversation, my brother-in-law mentioned that they had been considering going to Kansas after the Fourth of July for a family reunion. Jane was very interested, as it had been years since she'd been back to Kansas to see her aunts and uncles, most of whom were successful farmers. Everyone thought it would be a great idea to travel together and do some sightseeing along the way. Before the evening was over, we had put a temporary itinerary together acknowledging that we could make changes as we went along, but we agreed that we would leave on July 6 and spend three days in Kansas for the family reunion.

We had just gotten settled from our move to Chino Hills, Jane had found a church we could attend, the younger kids had made friends, and our oldest was happy with her horse. She had also made some friends at church. Now we were planning a nice vacation that had everyone excited with thoughts of motel swimming pools sightseeing.

One Saturday we were in Lake Elsinore, so Dena could ride. The younger ones had made friends with the stable owner's kids and were having a great time playing with some of the farm animals.

The stable owner approached me and said we were about to have a visitor who wanted to talk to me about a beautiful Arabian stallion that he was taking to shows and which had been doing well. He said he thought very highly of the guy, but I was on my own if he wanted to talk about the stallion.

The man and his wife came over and introduced themselves as Richard and Jan Orbaker. They were very friendly. Richard was the businessperson, and Jan was the horse trainer. "I have an opportunity I'd like to discuss with you," Richard said after we'd introduced ourselves. "We found a pure Polish Arabian stallion out in the desert that we purchased. We've been showing him, and he's doing quite well. However, my mobile home business has taken a downturn, and I'm running out of money, so we've had to quit showing him, which has hurt our opportunity to promote him. His breeding fee is five thousand dollars per mare, but his sire Muzulmanin, a well-known stallion that was bred in Poland and imported to the United States in 1961, received fifteen thousand per breeding, and I have proof of papers. If we could continue to show him and promote him, his breeding fee could easily go to ten thousand dollars."

That got my attention. After further discussion Jane and I made an appointment to meet Richard the next afternoon. We would take our kids for lunch in Redlands and then go out to the Center at Green Spot in Mentone Beach, just outside of Redlands.

It was a beautiful drive down a gravel road lined with orange trees that opened up to a beautiful horse training center with gleaming white buildings and gorgeous landscaping, including roses and other flowers of assorted colors. Richard and Jan greeted us, then took us down to the corral. There stood the purebred Polish Arabian stallion, whose name was Muzan. He was short in stature, but he was beautiful, a gleaming chestnut with a white blaze down his nose, four white stockings, and a black mane and tail. Jan got on him and took him from a walk through to a trot, a cantor, and a gallop. He was beautiful and majestic when in motion. With his head tucked, everything about him was so picturesque, and his tail flowed like a fountain.

After Jan had worked him out, she rode over to us. "Dena, how would you like to ride him?" she asked. For Dena, that was just about the greatest thing she had ever heard. As for me, I was thinking this was a high-spirited stallion, and our daughter had only been riding for a short period on a gentle filly.

When I mentioned my concern to Jan, she smiled. "Don't worry about it," she said. "Dena will do fine."

She talked with Dena, then handed her the reins and told her to walk him around until she got comfortable. A few minutes later, Dena smiled at the trainer, who nodded to indicate it was fine for Dena to take the next step. Before I knew it, she was sitting in the saddle. Jan told Den to take him for a walk around the arena until she got comfortable, then to go into a trot. I was a beautiful sight. Dena had been practicing with her uncle, and Jan was impressed with her horsemanship.

Once we returned home, we discussed whether or not we should purchase the horse. It was quite a discussion because we were thinking about buying a horse, but we still didn't own a home. We would have to spend money to stable and feed the horse and take him to shows, which was more than I had expected, but I thought we could handle it, so we made a deal. Just before the Fourth of July, we signed a contract that made us half-owners of Muzan. We would pay the bills, and the breeding fee would be ours.

Shortly thereafter, in September, Richard and Jan took Muzan to Vancouver, British Columbia, for the Canadian nationals. They called us to say he had made it into the top ten, which was quite an honor.

When they returned home, we all went out to the Center at Green Spot and had a big party. I didn't realize I was footing the bill, but a good time was had by all. With the top-ten finish that Muzan had achieved in Vancouver, everybody was telling us how great he was. And so, every weekend after that, we'd go out to the Center at Green Spot so that Dena could ride Muzan. Things looked exciting as the season progressed. In January it would be breeding season. In February we would start showing Muzan in Pomona for another round of shows.

The following December, Richard and Jan called, asking Jane and me to visit without Dena. That made me uneasy, as I sensed something was wrong. Sure enough, when we got there, they explained that Muzan, being an older horse, had developed the equine equivalent of arthritis in his hind legs. If we continued to show him and promote him in the show ring, his hind legs could break down, and he needed his hind legs for breeding. So, we had to take him out of the show arena, then find another way to promote him for breeding. When we returned home and told Dena, she was heartbroken, but at least she still had her filly down in Lake Elsinore.

After the first of the year, Jan called and asked us to bring Dena to the stable, so she could play with Muzan but that she couldn't ride him. However, she added that with her natural ability, Dena was going to be a good horsewoman. So, every Saturday we went to the Center at Green Spot. On Sundays, we had family day.

To our surprise, Richard and Jan called again at the end of February, saying they would like us to bring to Dena in for a meeting. When we got there, they were beaming with good news. The vet had been out, and after an inspection declared that Muzan had been healed. He called it a miracle. That meant we could take him to some shows, and Dena would be able to ride him again.

It was a joyous time. Dena was making great strides as a rider. Then at the end of March, they decided to take Muzan to a show in Pomona. Everyone was excited. The kids' grandparents came down from their home on Lake Folsom, and we took them out to watch Dena ride. They were very impressed with Muzan and with Dena's riding skills. When they found out that we had to buy Dena a special English pleasure riding suit for $1,500 and that it had to come from Scottsdale, Arizona, they said they didn't want to have an argument, but they wanted to buy it for her. They certainly wouldn't get an argument from me! I had just spent about $1,000 on an English pleasure saddle and all the rigging that went with it.

The suit arrived just in time for the show in Pomona. Jan entered Dena and her in the Pro-Am class, which meant Jan would ride professionally, and Dena would ride as an amateur. Excitement filled the air.

It was Dena's first show, and she was extremely nervous. Unfortunately, things went horribly wrong. She had the horse in the wrong gait, couldn't get him to go where he was supposed to go, and blew a stirrup. There she was, one foot in a stirrup and the other foot hanging off the side.

After her ride, I went over to talk to her. She was crying, but I said I wouldn't tolerate that. "Hey, you made a mistake. Suck it up, and let's go again." Jan told me that I should probably leave and let them work things out because Dena was her student, and I was just her father. *Yeah,* I thought, *but I'm also the one who's paying the bill.* Jan made it very clear that if I continued, I could take Dena and go home.

The next day they had the Pro-Am class. Out of fifteen horses, they won Show Champion Pro-Am rider, and Dena did a beautiful job.

Following the success at the Pomona show, we decided to

promote Muzan in different shows around Southern California. I did my due diligence and learned that the Arabian horse industry was ablaze, and the Scottsdale, Arizona, show was the premier event in the country, with some Arabian stallions selling for millions. Their foals sold for thousands of dollars when they were born. We decided it would be a good place to take Muzan and promote him. Unfortunately, just before the Scottsdale show, he had problems with his legs and went lame again. He would not be able to perform in the show, but we decided to take him anyway, just for promotion. We had already paid for a stall, and people could come by and look at him. We also had promotional material printed up and hoped the show would bring in big bucks.

I had read all about Scottsdale. It was known for its spa resorts and renowned golf courses, including the TPC Scottsdale. It was obvious that it was going to be an expensive time for us during the three or four days that we would be there for the show.

We got off the freeway at Bell Road, which would take us to Paradise Park where the horse show was being held. As we drove along Bell Road, I was amazed at how ritzy it was. The motels and restaurants were beautiful, and as we got closer to Paradise Park we saw the magnificent Arabian horse farms for the big-time breeders. The farms advertised stallions selling for millions and had breeding fees of ten thousand dollars and up. We were told the average price at the auction for an Arabian horse was nearly $400,000. Needless to say, by the time we got to Paradise Park I was intimidated and excited that we could get some breeding fees if Muzan did well.

When we got to Scottsdale, we found it had been raining,

which was unusual for the area. As a result, the grounds were muddy and mucky. Unfortunately, when they unloaded Muzan off the trailer, the ramp was wet, and there was manure on it, which caused his hind legs to slip, and he slid down on his haunches. When he got up, he was angry, as if he were thinking, "How dare you let me fall like that?" He got up and stomped around and brayed and whinnied, totally indignant.

Jan told Dena to take Muzan by the reins and take him for a walk but not to ride him. "We don't want people to see him limping," she said.

When Dena was gone longer than expected, I became concerned and went to Jan. "Do I need to go find Dena?" I asked.

"Buddy, you leave that girl alone," she replied. "She knows what she's doing, and I wouldn't be a bit surprised if she's riding the horse when she comes back."

Sure enough, not long afterward, Dena rode up on Muzan, a big smile on her face. Muzan was trotting, not limping.

With Muzan back on his feet, Jan decided she would ride him in the native costume class. It was a flashy class with about forty horses and riders dressed as if they were in the Arabian desert. Muzan was selected in the top ten. We had quite a party afterward, and we actually got a breeding out of it. So, it was another miracle for the old horse.

After the Scottsdale show, we entered Muzan in shows all the way from Lancaster, California, to Las Vegas. Every place he went, he was either show champion or reserve to the champion.

Dena was doing well with him as a junior rider too. One of the shows she rode in was in Las Vegas. It was a big show because Wayne Newton's horses were there. He even had a horse entered with his junior rider, competing against Dena and Muzan and about twenty other horses. Muzan was named as show champion, with Wayne Newton's horse reserve to the champion. Being a good sport, Wayne came over and visited with us, then he leaned over and gave Dena a kiss on the cheek. I don't think she washed her face for a month.

After that was Santa Barbara, the most prestigious show on the West Coast. Wayne Newton's horse would be there, as would a horse that belonged to Kenny Rogers. All the movie stars had horses as a tax write off. It was a lot of fun competing against them.

When we got to Santa Barbara, once again I was in awe. The classes were to be held in a beautiful stadium at the Earl Warren fairground. The atmosphere was electric. The horses were beautiful and in their prime. It was intimidating to think that Muzan, at fourteen years old, was the grandpa of the show, but he was feeling good.

On the day of the English pleasure class, Jan was excited. "I'm feeling really good about what we're doing here," she said as they entered the arena.

Nearly forty horses were performing at the different gaits near the rail. After a couple of times around, the judge who was standing in the middle of the arena, called the riders to line up their horses side by side. Then she walked down the row of horses and dismissed those that weren't performing up to her standard. She dismissed twenty horses, but Muzan was still there.

She directed the riders to start at a trot and then transition to a canter. After several more rounds, she called them to the center, lined them up, and dismissed ten more horses. Muzan was still there, which meant he was guaranteed yet another top-ten finish.

The judge sent the remaining ten horses around again, starting them at a walk, then moving to a trot and then a gallop, which brought the crowd to their feet as they cheered, whistled, and applauded. She instructed them to go around three times, then called them into the center, arranged them side by side, and dismissed five more horses. Muzan was still there, meaning he would be awarded a top-five finish, which was outstanding considering the magnificent stallions he was competing against. We were breathless with excitement at what we had just witnessed from our old boy.

The judge walked down the line of the remaining five stallions, inspecting them. She told the riders they could relax their stallions, then sent her judging card to the announcer. The crowd grew quiet with anticipation. We had tears in our eyes, so proud of our stallion, who had outdone himself.

Then the announcer thanked everyone for their participation, droning on and on while the crowd grew restless, wanting to know which horse was the show champion. Finally, in the finest voice he could muster, he announced the winner. "Now that the judge's card has been verified, your reserve to the champion is number 415." While the crowd applauded, the horse chosen for reserve to the champion went to the center of the ring and received the plaque and the ribbon. As I watched, I felt that any of the top five could have been show champion, and I would be pleased with any outcome.

After the presentation to the reserve to the champion, a drum roll reverberated through the loudspeakers. "Now for the moment we've all been waiting for: your Santa Barbara English pleasure show champion stallion is . . . number 495. That was Muzan's number! He was the show champion stallion!

As the crowd gave him a standing ovation and music played, Muzan perked up in the lineup and brayed, clearly enjoying himself. We were crying and laughing. I was excited because I figured in a big show like that, there'd be big prize money which would help pay for our trip. When we got the envelope for the prize money, however, it was a grand total of $275 which I gave to Jan. I hoped we would at least get a breeding or two. Meanwhile, the big-time trainers yelled at the judge and called her names because she had picked our little, old horse over their million-dollar stallions.

When we got home, I was very appreciative, so I wrote a note to the judge, who was from Albuquerque, New Mexico, thanking her for naming our horse as English pleasure show champion. To my surprise, she sent a note back, saying, "Mr. Mercer, your horse was the only true English pleasure horse in that class."

After Santa Barbara, we went to some smaller shows, which were a lot of fun. Our younger kids liked the trips because of the motel pools and the chance to play with other kids at the arena while Dena showed Muzan.

As the season wound down, we did everything we could to promote Muzan, but we weren't getting any breedings. I was concerned, but I couldn't fault Richard or Jan. They were presenting Muzan in the finest fashion at the best shows. He was always an outstanding horse, and he was often named show champion, but he wasn't getting breedings. Nobody could figure out why, so we didn't know what we should change.

I had a serious conversation with our partner, who originally owned Muzan, saying that without the breedings, we couldn't continue showing him.

"Buddy, I've been wanting to talk to you about an opportunity without making any trouble for the Orbakers. I have a young lady down in Ramona. Her name is Timmi. She's a little different, but she loves horses. She takes good care of them, and she presents them properly in shows. I'd like you to think about taking Muzan down there."

After Jane and I talked about it, we checked it out, discovering that stalls and training cost about half as much as at the Center at Green Spot. By then we had enough ribbons and plaques to cover an entire wall, but we still hadn't won enough money to purchase a cup of coffee from Starbucks. So, we agreed to go down the following Saturday and take a look, as we had to do something different.

When we got to Timmi's training facilities, they were magnificent, located in the mountains just outside of San Diego near the quaint, little town of Ramona. Meeting Timmi herself was a shock. She was a gorgeous twenty-year-old who resembled a young Elizabeth Taylor with Snow White's black hair and pale skin. When we arrived, she was running around like a chicken with her head cut off. She had quadruple booked the appointment time, so she was trying to go between all of us.

"I'm so sorry," she said when she came over to us, "but I really want to have your horse, Muzan. I love that horse. I've loved him for a long time, and I'll do everything I can to make him a winner and get you some breedings."

When she left to see other clients, my partner, Richard, turned to me. "I told you she's a little different, but she'll take care of Muzan, and she'll present him properly. What have you got to lose?"

The following day was Sunday. After church, when I got home, and to my surprise, I had a message on my phone from Timmi. She apologized again for not being able to spend more time with us, then asked if I could come back down on Monday to visit with her. My first thought was how I was going to manage that, seeing as I had a company to run. Then I remembered she was close to San Diego, and we were looking to expand into that area, so I'd go down and visit with her, then call on some auto parts stores in San Diego. On my way back, I would stop in Temecula and Corona and make a day of it.

The next morning, on my way down I called on customers in Lake Elsinore, then went up to Ramona for our 10:00 meeting. This time, Timmie was Johnny on the spot. As a matter of fact, when I arrived, she was sitting at a picnic table, reading a book. I thought that was kind of cool. And when I walked up, to my shock and surprise, I realized she was reading *Atlas Shrugged* by Ayn Rand. I told her I had read it in the eighth grade.

"Oh, my God," she said. "It's so good. If we had more people like that in this world, we could get along much better. I agreed with her, but I wanted to talk about Muzan and the possibility of her taking him over as the trainer. That's when she got deadly serious.

"Buddy, I've loved that horse ever since he's been in the arena. He's a strong-hearted horse, and he's beautiful. I would love to have him in my stables. You know I'm going to take extra good care of him."

"Let's go look at your stables and see what they're lacking," I said. The next thing I knew, she grabbed my hand, and we were off to the barn.

She had about fifteen horses in the stables, which was pretty good for one young lady. She said she was breaking some that weren't in show training. The stalls looked clean and well kept, and it looked like the situation would be workable for us. She knew he was an older horse, so she wouldn't overtrain him, and we would be allowed to come down anytime to play with him and keep him company. It would be a lot less formal than the Center at Green Spot. After the appointment, I called my partner and said we should do it.

The next day, I went to the Center at Green Spot and told Richard and Jan about my plans, explaining that I had to do it because I was running out of money, and we weren't getting breedings. I didn't blame them, but I couldn't afford to keep him down there. I thought they would be upset, but they agreed. In fact, they felt bad because they couldn't figure out why he wasn't getting any breedings either. His sire had bred a lot of mares, and his foals had had a lot of success in the show arena.

A week later, we transported Muzan down to Timmi's place. Once he arrived, Timmi called me, as excited as a little kid. "You have got to come down here! He's so happy. He's playing and having a good time."

I decided to have another sales day in the San Diego area and went down without an appointment to find out what went on if Timmi didn't know I was coming. I was very happy when I arrived to find her in the stalls, cleaning them. She had a stall boy, but she was helping him.

"So, you clean the stalls too," I said.

"I am a trainer, believe it or not so let's not get snotty about things" she replied jokingly.

She finished cleaning the stall, then took me to Muzan. He was excited and having a good time, which was all that mattered to me.

She invited me to her condo to discuss my plans. It was a top-notch place, very expensive, but when we went inside, it looked like a thirteen-year-old lived there. Clothes were all over the floor, the sink was filled with dishes—it was a mess. She apologized, saying she wasn't expecting company that day.

"Is this how you live every day?" I asked.

"I do what I have to do," she replied. "I have fifteen horses in my stable, and I take good care of all of them."

"How in the heck do you afford this place?" I asked.

"Oh, my daddy has some pull," she replied, "and I get a little bit of a reduced rate."

When I heard her say "my daddy," I thought she was referring to a sugar daddy, but that was okay with me.

She was smart and creative in the way she did business, and I felt really good about what she would be able to do with Muzan.

After a couple of visits down to Ramona to see Timmi and Muzan, we had an in-depth discussion. She loved to discuss life and the things she had done.

"How do you really afford to live in this condo?" I asked her one day. "This training facility must cost a lot of money too."

"How do you think I can afford it?" she asked.

"I don't know, but didn't you tell me you have a sugar daddy?"

She broke into laughter.

"Timmi, with all the guys you have calling you and your 'boyfriend' with the red Ferrari, or so he's called, it wouldn't shock me to learn that you were a high-class call girl."

I thought I was going to get slapped, but she just laughed hysterically. "Buddy, I have fifteen horses in training, and I have a line of clothing with my sister in New York. Last year I paid taxes on $102,000 in income."

That set me back a bit. I realized she was deeper and more introspective than I had imagined.

We spent quite a bit of time with the horses. Everybody wanted to think we were having an affair, but I was married, and I had a good life with a great wife and three kids. After being around her for a while, I didn't understand how a forty-year-old guy would ever want to have a twenty-year-old girl-friend because it was all bubble gum and giggles.

Suddenly, Timmi became very pensive and quiet, studying me. When she spoke, it was as if she were an older person, each word measured. "Buddy, I want to speak to you confidentially and from my heart because I want you to know exactly who I am and what I'm feeling. I don't want to scare you, but I've become very fond of you, not in a sexual way but in a way that I don't understand. I like having you around. It feels good because you're honest, trustworthy, and absolute. You remind me of Hank Reardon in Atlas Shrugged. I know that may scare you, but I need that stability, and you have what I'm looking for. We're not going to be a love type of thing. I understand you're married, and you want to stay married. What I want is to be able to be around and draw from you and see what happens."

She went on to tell me about her life growing up. Her father was a multi-millionaire developer who owned approximately half of Azusa, including numerous strip malls and businesses. He lived in Bel Air, with Ronald Reagan's residence on one side and Merv Griffin's on the other. He had thoroughbred horses, and he wanted her to become a thoroughbred trainer, but she loved Arabians, so that's what she was going to do.

Despite her family's wealth, she had had a troubled childhood. She left home when she was thirteen and moved in with a horse trainer who was gay. They became great friends and slept in the same bed, her in her footsie pajamas. He taught her how to be a horse trainer, and he was one of the best trainers on the West Coast, helping her to become one of the better horse trainers, especially at her age. When it came time for her to start training on her own, he helped her to develop her stable with some of his horses because he had more horses than he needed.

After she finished expressing her thoughts, we sat quietly, and she appeared to be waiting for a response. I told Timmi that this was one of the most straightforward conversations I had ever had with a woman. "I appreciate that you respect my marriage and aren't trying to change anything," I said. "I really enjoy your company because you're creative and you're dynamic. I'm in a situation at Bonded Motors where I'm trying to pull the company out of bankruptcy, and there's a lot of stress and pressure. I handle it well, but to have somebody with your energy would be helpful to me. I'm going to let my wife and family know that you're going to become part of our family."

"That makes me feel good too," she said, "because I really like Dena. She has a lot of potential, and I'd like to help her become a trainer, if she wants to."

That suited me fine. I could just see the two of them in the

Arabian horse world. Timmi was gorgeous, Dena was quite attractive too.

I got a call from Richard at the Center at Green Spot who said they had a horse that we had seen at Santa Barbara. The owner had received an offer of $25,000 for the horse but declined, believing she could secure somewhere between $50,000 and $60,000 for it. Unfortunately, her husband left her, and she was unable to finance her horses and was in danger of losing them. Richard told me I could buy the horse for $2,000. I talked to Jane about it, and we decided to buy the horse. We put him in a couple shows, and some individuals from Texas offered us $20,000 for him, which was a great profit.

Timmi continued training Dena and showing Muzan, and she did quite well with him. Dena also grew in confidence as a rider and as a trainer.

Then Timmi had the idea of creating a doggy baby book. It was just like a baby book for a child, including locks of fur, paw prints, shot schedules, and other key events. We put it all together and then took it to a publisher in San Diego. We didn't sell a lot, but at least we could say we were published authors.

I also had a song that I was writing, and our youngest daughter, my baby girl, really liked it. We put the lyrics together, and through Timmi's contacts, we went to a studio in the house where Richie Valens recorded "La Bamba" in the San Fernando Valley. We were introduced to the producer and the engineer who was going to put our lyrics to music, which he did in an hour. Three young ladies also came in to record our song. Despite all that, there was no charge. I don't know how Timmi got the deal, but we recorded the song. It didn't go anywhere, but at least we could say we had a song recorded in a famous studio.

One day Timmi decided it was time for me to meet an Academy Award-winning actor. She didn't tell me what we were doing. She just asked me to pick her up and said we were going to Hollywood, that she had somebody she wanted me to meet. When we got to Hollywood, we went up to an office. It wasn't anything fancy, but there was a lot of security. In fact, they had us go into a room that used infrared lights to check us for guns. Once that was done, we went into the office, and I found myself face to face with Jon Voight, who had won an Academy Award for his performance in the movie *Midnight Cowboy*.

What does this have to do with me? I wondered.

"Buddy, I've heard so much about you," he said. "You have a wonderful story. I really wanted to meet you."

We had a fine conversation. Then they had lunch brought in. I didn't really know how to act in there because those people were a whole lot different from me. But we made it through.

"Timmi, how in the world and why in the world did you do that?" I asked once we were outside.

"He wanted to meet you, and I wanted him to meet you," she replied. "You need to get used to this because you're going to be meeting a lot of people."

I had no idea what she was talking about, but shortly thereafter she called me again. "Hey, Buddy, we're going to go get a strawberry colonic," she said.

That sounds cool, I thought. I didn't have anything else to do, so I asked her where we were going to get it. She just laughed. "Buddy, a strawberry colonic is like an enema."

"Oh my god, count me out," I said.

Her father had box seats at Santa Anita, so we got to see a race featuring the great thoroughbred, John Henry. When we got there, to my surprise in the seats next to her father's were Mickey Rooney, Vince Edwards, and Dick Van Patton, all well-known movie stars. They all greeted Timmi and asked her to sit with them. I couldn't believe everybody knew her so well.

The race was enjoyable. Those guys were betting big time, and Timmi was running around, having a ball.

"Oh, I forgot to tell you," she said at one point. "My daddy wants you to come over, so he can meet you." That meant going up to Bel Air where all the big shots lived.

When we drove up the hill to his house, I looked down and saw seven cars. All of them were European, from the limousine up front to the Rolls Royce to the Jaguar to the Porsche. But the last car in the line was a fancy Jeep Wagoneer. When I asked her what that one was for, she said, "Ask my daddy."

Her father was straight out of New York, probably with the mafia, and he talked just like one of them.

"Explain to me why you have the Jeep when you have all those other fancy cars," I said after we'd been introduced.

"Oh, my wife don't like for me to have the dogs riding in her European car, so I got that Jeep for me and the dogs."

A few days later, I got a call from his secretary. He wanted to meet me in Azusa at a restaurant in one of his strip malls, so he could buy me lunch. That scared the heck out of me because I didn't know why he wanted to see me, but I agreed to meet him.

While we ate, he talked to me about a property in Latigo Canyon in Malibu. He wanted Timmy to start a training center out there for thoroughbreds. "But that hard-headed little thing don't want to do thoroughbreds," he said. "She's stuck with those Arabian show horses, and there's no money in that. Thoroughbreds are where it's at. What do you think about it?"

"Well, the only thing I've got is an Arabian."

"You know, Buddy," he replied, "I like you, and my daughter likes you too, so I think you ought to think about marrying my daughter."

After I caught my breath, I told him I was happily married. "I've got a wife and three kids, and I'm rooted where I am."

"Well, that's a shame," he said, "because you marry my daughter, and you'll never work again except to help her with the horses, and you can be a man of leisure. Don't worry about your wife and kids. We can take care of them, put them in a better house than you got them in now. We can send your kids to the finest colleges. You ought to think about it."

Boy, I thought, *if I ever told Jane about this, it would be the end of it.* I told him I wouldn't even think about it, that it wasn't in my line of sight. He smiled and said that was the kind of guy he thought I was, but it was worth a try.

I was working a lot of hours, trying to get Bonded ready to file an IPO, so my time for the horses was limited, and I hadn't seen Timmi for about a month. One day she called, telling me she had met a guy and wanted me to go to lunch with them, so I agreed to meet them the next day. Before she hung up, she also told me that he owned Morgan Creek production and had a couple of movies in theaters. He had also produced Bryan Adams and a couple of other singers. The guy was big time.

We met for lunch the next day, and he was a pleasure, down to earth with a great sense of humor. Lunch went so well that I stayed longer than I had expected, so I had to work late that night.

The next morning, Timmi called to see what I thought about him. I told her I thought he was great, but I couldn't talk, so she hung up without saying goodbye.

A couple of weeks later, she called to tell me that she had moved in with him. His home was located on Queens Road, an upscale area just above Hollywood Boulevard. She said the trainer whom she had lived with had moved the horses she had been working with back to his stables, but she assured me that Muzan was in one of the finest stables in an upscale area of Hollywood, and she played with him every day.

Timmi called me again one afternoon, asking me to come over. When I arrived, she and the guy from Morgan Creek told me they were going to Las Vegas for a week or two. He had hidden a lot of cash in different places throughout the house, and he wanted to show me where it was so that if they needed money, they could call me, and I could get it to them. I told them no way because if something happened to that money, it would be a mess, and I wasn't going to take that chance.

"I can understand that," he said, "but we trust you implicitly."

"I'm sorry," I replied, "but I can't help you with that."

About a month later, they called again, asking me to come over. This time he told me he had a 1987 DeTomaso sports car that wanted to give to me, so his ex-wife couldn't get it. I was stunned, but once again, I had to decline the offer.

Shortly thereafter, Timmi called and asked me if we could go to lunch.

"Buddy, what do you think of this guy?" she asked once we had sat down.

"He's a great guy," I replied.

"Do you think it'd be okay if I married him?"

"You've got to be kidding," I said. "But do what you want to do. He's a good guy. Get married, and have a good time."

Needless to say, I did not belong in this crowd, but I got an invite to go with them to the Finer Affair, one of the hottest restaurants in West LA. When we went inside, I knew I was out of my league because it was fancy with a maître de and everything. The cheapest thing on the menu was a salad named after Timmi's daddy, and it was nearly $75.00.

Suddenly, the house lights dimmed, the spotlight shone on the door, and in walked Jon Voight wearing a top hat and cape. A drum roll started, and he spun the cape off, then flipped his hat off. He launched into a quick soliloquy, then he joined us for dinner. I was supposed to be having a good time, but all I could think was, *Get 'em out of here.*

When I saw the bill, it was over $1,200 for four people. Needless to say, that was my last trip with Timmi and those people.

A short time later I decided to retire Muzan, who was nineteen years old. It was a difficult decision because everybody loved him, but it was time that he went out in style. We found a stable down in the Lake Elsinore area. The owner had kids who loved Muzan, and he could enjoy his last days out. Plus, they had some mares that he could breed, which he enjoyed doing.

I got an invitation to Timmi's wedding, which was to be held in the Bel Air Hotel. I showed it to Jane, and we agreed that we would pray for them, but we didn't want to go.

. . .

OUR two younger kids wanted to play AYSO youth soccer, so we signed them up and took them to soccer practice two evenings a week and to games on Saturdays. I didn't know the first thing about soccer, but I found out there are very few rules to it, and I could read the rulebook and learn all about it, so I could help my kids as they progressed.

Soon, it soon became apparent to me that AYSO soccer was intense, the parents yelling at the kids. They had referees who wore black shorts and black shirts, and they were pretty full of themselves, running up and down and controlling the game as they blew their whistles.

The regional vice president was a tall, good-looking guy with blonde hair. When he ran up and down the field while reffing, his hair never got out of place. But he was a wise guy and condescending, looking down his nose at people.

One day toward the end of the season, I knew enough about soccer that I made a couple of comments about his refereeing. He came over and gave me what he called a red card. He said I had to leave the field and that if I ever did that again, I wouldn't be allowed back on the field.

At the start of next season, some people suggested that I become a soccer coach. They liked me, they knew I had experience working with people, and they wanted me to coach their kids. So, I went to one of the coaches' meetings to sign up.

When I walked in, the guy who had given me the red card took one look at me and asked what I was doing there. I told him I was going to be a coach.

"I'm sorry," he said, "but you didn't attend the coaches' clinics, and you don't have a coaches badge, so you won't be able to coach this year."

I knew that AYSO was a volunteer organization, so I went to the headquarters in Hawthorne and told them I was having a problem with one of the regional vice presidents. When they asked what was going on, I told them politics was ruining a game that was supposed to be fun for the kids. The woman in charge laughed.

"It's got to be region sixty-seven, Chino. Do we have a problem there?"

"He told me I can't coach because I don't have a C badge."

"Sir, you don't need a C badge," she replied.

"Okay, then what can I do to make things right?"

"We have a coaches' clinic for the next four days over in Pasadena," she replied. "It starts at seven o'clock in the morning, and it ends at noon. If you want to learn about coaching and refereeing, I suggest you go because it's an excellent clinic with excellent teachers."

I took the course, and I was glad I did because I learned a lot.

One night they had another coaches' meeting, and I attended. The regional VP came in and he said, "I told you, you weren't welcome here because you don't have a C badge."

I held up my newly acquired badge. "Actually, I do have a C badge," I said. He took one look at it and then shook his head.

"That's not from Chino."

"Look, partner," I replied, "I talked to the people down at AYSO headquarters in Hawthorne. They don't really care for region 67 and the political games that are played out here, so I think I'll coach."

Once they agreed I could become a coach, we held a draft. There were fifteen kids on every team, and all the kids had to play. We were allowed to draft eight, and they gave us seven. So, I went and did my homework about kids who had played before, anything that I could do to get the better kids. When the time came, I had fifteen kids, but when we got together for our first practice, I was mortified because I had never done anything like that before. So, I decided I was going to do it my way.

As the kids kicked the ball around, I went to address the fifteen sets of parents. "I'm here as a volunteer," I said, "and I'm here to teach what I know about soccer. I don't know everything, but the main thing I'm going to teach these kids is how to have fun. They're going to learn the rules of soccer, and we're going to play for fun. You folks are the parents, so you're not allowed to coach. All I want to hear from you is 'Go, little Johnny! Run, little Johnny.' But I don't want to hear you coaching, and you will not yell at the referees. We're just going to have fun." With that all cleared up, I went to talk to the kids.

The first thing we did was have a pizza party, which I paid for, and everybody got to know each other. The kids started playing games right there in the pizza parlor, and they had a good time getting to know one another.

The next weekend, we started practicing. I had some ideas that would make it more fun. I talked to a couple of guys who were excellent soccer players but who were not involved and asked them if they would show me some things I could do for the kids. They thought that was a great idea, and they were eager to help out.

During one game, a player from the opposing team got past one of the least athletic players on our team, Brian, and scored a goal. His dad was a six-foot-four, 250-pound cop from Chino, and he yelled at Brian. When halftime came, he went over and grabbed Brian by his jersey and shook him. I went over and confronted him.

"I told you when we started that this sort of behavior wasn't going to be tolerated," I said. "Now, if you want to stand up and act like a man, you stand there, but don't you ever do that again."

To my surprise, Brian's father started crying. "I'm so sorry," he said, going on to explain that he and his wife were in divorce court, and his nerves were on edge, but all he wanted to do was create a good experience for his son. From then on, he was a real supporter.

The father of one of my players was an alcoholic, and sometimes kids would go to school and find him lying on the ground, drunk. Come soccer day, he would show up, but he wouldn't stand with the team or the parents. He'd be down at the far end on his own. His son was always looking for him.

We started winning, and having a great time.. Everybody made fun of me because of the different things that I did, but we kept on winning and winning, going 12–0 for the regular season. Then we were into playoffs, including districts and regionals. If we did really well, we would get to go to the Rose Bowl and play on New Year's Day weekend. Even though we were winning, it was getting old. We had started in August, but by March, with all the games and practices, it was very tiring.

Toward the end of the season, one of the coaches who had made fun of me approached me. "Buddy, I want to apologize for what I said. You've earned my respect. I've coached for years, and I've never had what you've had—a winning team. But more than that, the parents like you." That really shocked me. Then the regional vice president, the referee with whom I had a problem early on, gave us the award for the best boys' team in the region.

Despite the team's stellar play, we wound up one game away from going to the Rose Bowl. When the final game ended, everybody was crying. I looked over and saw the alcoholic father who had gotten sober. I nominated him as my team's daddy. He was there for every game with his son. One of the moms had gotten hooked on drugs, but we had helped her get clean. As for the big cop from Chino, he and his wife got back together. It was a happy family situation.

One of the boys was raised by his grandpa, who raised fighting cocks and was quite a character. When the season ended and everyone was hugging, he came over to me and said, "I want everybody to go to Vince's Spaghetti, and I'll buy dinner for everybody." I just wanted to go home, but it turned out to be a great experience.

After that, I really got involved in soccer. I coached for the next ten years, including the select team. They didn't call it all-stars, but it was the all-star boys, and we traveled all over, from Salt Lake City to Phoenix, Sacramento, San Diego, and into Colorado. Our teams did well, and it was a real joy and honor for me to have been selected to coach these teams and be associated with their parents.

After I quit and we moved away, I returned to the area and was sitting in a restaurant when a tall, hairy-legged, wooly guy came up to me. "Hey, Coach, do you remember me?"

Our baby girl, Stacey Ann, decided she wanted to play softball. It surprised me because she had never been very athletic and was much more at home on the couch. But she wanted to play softball, so we signed her up and got her started. To my surprise, she turned out to be a fantastic player. She started playing first base because she was tall and could stretch out. She enjoyed it and was doing really well. When the season ended, she said, "I want to play soccer." That also surprised me because soccer's a whole different game with lots of running, but I backed my kids up no matter what.

Stacey's coach was a tall, blond-haired man whom we affectionately called Big Bird. At the first practice, I told the coach, "This girl has a lot of good things going for her, but I don't know about her athletic ability."

"Well, I'm the coach here," he replied, "so why don't you let me find out what I believe? I've been around this for eight or ten years, and I think I can pick the good ones."

At the next practice, I didn't see Stacey out with the other girls, so I asked Big Bird where she was.

"Oh, she's in the goal box," he replied.

"What does that mean?"

"She is going to be my goalkeeper."

"Whoa. That's a heavy-duty position," I replied.

He shrugged. "You've got a heavy-duty daughter. She can handle it."

After several practices, we went to Stacey's first game. It was against a team from Ontario, and they had a hot shot all-star named Pippi. She had pig tails hanging down on both sides, and she was good. She had played soccer for many years and was very aggressive.

Stacey was in goal, and when Pippi got a breakaway, Stacey went out to confront her, just like she was supposed to do, then slid down and grabbed the ball. Pippi leaped into the air and came down on Stacey's side on her knees, knocking the wind out of Stacey. That raised my ire, and I started to say something, but the coach shut me down.

"No, no, no. You don't say anything. Stacey will take care of it. I promise you." I looked out at the field and saw my daughter wiping her tears away as she caught her breath.

Later in the game, Pippi got another breakaway. Instead of going out and sliding like she was taught to do, Stacey stuck her arm out and clotheslined that little girl. Pippi's feet went out from under her, and she landed on her back, knocking the wind out of her.

Pippi's mother was so incensed that the referee had to go to the sideline to warn her not to be so verbally aggressive.

Coach Big Bird walked over to me. "I told you, Buddy. Your daughter is going to make a hell of a goalkeeper."

I'm proud to say that the further she went, the better she got, eventually becoming an all-star.

One time Stacey's team was playing at a tournament in La Puente, and they were poised to win. Stacey was stopping everything, leaping from side to side, stopping balls that were over her head, and diving into the dirt. She was having a great time. Then one of the other team's players sent a flat roller off her foot toward the goal. The ball was heading straight toward Stacey, not at any speed, just rolling. To my surprise, instead of going down on one knee, she bent over at the waist to pick it up, and it went right between her hands and her legs! She looked between her legs just as the ball went into the goal box. Stacey stood up and looked at the coach, and he looked at her, then she started giggling. As for the rest of the game, she was tremendous.

At the end of the season, the top two teams played, and the opposing goalkeeper was Stacey's best friend. The game ended in a shootout. That's where the goalkeepers go one on one with the shooter from the goal line or thereabouts. Each team got to choose five players, and each one of them took a shot. The team with the most goals would be declared the winner.

During the final round, one of Stacey's teammates took a shot, and the opposing goalkeeper got a piece of it, but the ball rolled into the corner for a goal. Stacey's team was up by one goal. Now it was time for the opposing team to take their final shot against Stacey. It was a difficult shot that she had to dive for. She tipped it, and it went into the top of the goal.

"Okay," I said. "That's good."

Both teams were hugging each other and crying, and everybody was happy, including the coaches, which confused me.

"Stacey, could you have not batted that ball out?" I asked once we got home.

"It's better that it ended the way it did," she said. I agreed, and I knew then that I had a winner. She went on to letter in cross country as a freshman. To me, someone who runs cross country for no reason at all has a lot of guts, especially because she hated running. But she wanted to get a letter, and she succeeded.

Our son, Brent, started playing soccer when he was six. I think he only played because he enjoyed being with the guys. He was more of a computer guy, always tinkering with something. But he stuck it out, and we were proud of him. They won trophies, had pizza parties, and had fun, which was the most important thing.

To my surprise, after a few years of playing soccer, he came in one day and said, "Dad, I want to play football."

All I could think was, *You didn't like soccer, and now you want to play football?* But if that's what he wanted to do, we would let him.

He was kind of out of shape, but he worked hard, and he dropped weight. He was beginning to change from a little boy into a grown-up boy, and he was looking good.

I went to one of his football practices one day. His coaches were rough, treating these eleven- to twelve-year-old boys like they were college seniors. I talked to some of the other dads about that.

"Oh, you must be a soccer guy," one of them said. "In soccer, everybody gets to play, and you pamper them, and all they do is run up and down and have fun. But this is serious stuff. Your boy is out there, and he's going to have an opportunity."

At that moment, one of the coaches whacked my son on the helmet with his hand. I was about to go out there and talk to him about that, but the dad with whom I was talking grabbed my arm. "Don't do it," he said. "Your boy wants to play football. Let him work it out his own way."

"Okay," I replied.

When we got to the car after practice, Brent said, "Dad, I don't like football."

"It's okay, son," I replied. "I saw what happened out there today, and if you want to—"

"I know," he said. "I know I can quit. But I don't want to quit. I want to finish playing this year."

"I'm all for you," I said.

He continued playing, and after a few practices, he got put

into a position at tackle where the quarterback's best friend played. The team had a clique of players who had played together for quite some time. During an offense versus defense scrimmage, the other players started making it rough on Brent. During one play, he tackled one of the guys and laid him out, then got up and returned to his position. The next time, I guess he went in and nailed the quarterback, because all of a sudden, he was playing football.

We had the pleasure of going down to El Centro for a game. It was either called the Vegetable Bowl or the Garbage Bowl. I'm not sure, but we had a good time watching it. When we came back, they were going to have the end-of-season football banquet. Brent wasn't sure he wanted to go, but we wound up going together. To our surprise, he won the award for most improved player.

When his name was announced, he looked up at me. "I really don't want to go up there. I don't want that trophy."

"You do what you want to do," I replied. A moment later, he walked up there, shook hands with the coach, but left the trophy behind. I was very proud of our young son. He had gained a lot from that football season, and it proved what a man he was going to become.

9

COMING BACK TO JESUS

It was normal at Bonded for business to slow down in the fall through the Christmas season and into February, at which time money would start to flow again, and the business would rebound. Unfortunately, in September 1988, Bonded began to slow down, but the business did not rebound as usual in the spring. Hence, my commissions continued to shrink.

I cut out all extra expenses, but our personal finances were tanking. With Jane working, however, we would be able to make it. Regrettably, I forgot one thing. We had sold a horse that year, which put us in a higher tax bracket. I came home and found Jane crying. When I asked what was wrong, she handed me an envelope that our accountant had sent. When I opened it, on an otherwise blank sheet of paper, there were teardrops. Written in block letters was "I AM SO SORRY." We owed the IRS $9,000. We were able to do some creative financing, which alleviated the immediate crisis, then continued with our lives.

Between my work at Bonded Motors and soccer, I was extremely busy, and Jane and I were growing distant from each other. Everything was falling apart. One day she wanted to talk to me about our problems, but even after we talked, nothing really changed. Then she asked if we could try going to church, and out of desperation, I agreed.

We started attending First Baptist Church in Chino, which seemed to brighten the mood, but I wasn't sure how it was going to help in the long run, even though I was of the mind that, yes, there was a God, and He loved us. The pastor, a kind, humble, gentle man, spoke quietly of the Father's love for us, but I could not relate to what a father's love meant. The best part for me was the pastor's uncanny ability to give the benediction exactly at 12:00 p.m. At 12:01, I would have our car out front, pick up Jane and the kids, and get to Tony's Spunky Steer, our favorite restaurant, before the crowd.

At the end of 1989, Brent asked if he could start attending Living Waters Church where his friends went, to which we quickly agreed. However, Jane, our youngest daughter Stacey, and I continued attending First Baptist. Brent often asked us to come to Living Waters, but I declined, telling him we were happy at First Baptist. Besides, I coached the all-star soccer team, and we had tournaments all over, often on weekends, which meant that sometimes I had to miss church.

On Sunday, January 20, 1990, I had everything prepared for the Super Bowl game party, but then at 1:10 p.m., our phone rang. I heard Jane say hello, followed by silence. Then she screamed for me to come to the phone. The voice on the other end of the line identified himself as a captain with the Ontario Fire Department. He said that Brent, who had been out to lunch with the youth, had a seizure and was being transported by ambulance to the hospital in San Antonio. He assured me it was just a precaution, as Brent was doing just fine.

My mind was blank until Jane and I made it to the hospital, just as the ambulance arrived. They pulled Brent out on a gurney, his head held by restraints. I stood there paralyzed, not hearing any noise until a man identified himself as Pastor Dave Culp. He said he was the youth pastor, which didn't mean a thing to me. Finally, I regained control of my emotions and turned to see if Jane was okay, but I couldn't see her. I nearly panicked again until I saw her standing with several ladies surrounding her.

"Father God, we ask right now that you give this lady peace and strength," one of them prayed.

I looked for Brent again and saw that he too was surrounded. A bunch of kids were crying out for Jesus Christ to bleed on him. That made no sense to me, but it was comforting to know he was loved. Then Pastor Dave came back and put his arm around me, speaking like he was from another world because his words made no sense to me.

I followed Brent until they said I could go no further. Then a big, tall guy came over and identified himself as Ray, an usher at Living Waters. He began to speak to me about Brent, but I was in no mood for conversation. A doctor came over and told me that Brent would be just fine. He advised me to take Jane home because we would not be able to see Brent, as they would be running tests and then would want him to sleep.

On the way home, Jane and I talked about how Brent was fifteen and had never been seriously injured or even seriously ill, so this had to be some kind of fluke. I took Jane home, but then I went back to the hospital to make sure everything was okay.

They were in the midst of telling me that Brent was sleeping and that I should go back to be with my wife when I heard a familiar voice behind me. When I turned around, I saw it was Pastor Dave and Ray.

"Sir, why don't you go home?" Pastor Dave said. "Your boy is in the Lord's hands, and we'll be here with him." They gave me a hug, then I went to my car where my emotions all tumbled out, for no one had ever shown me such sincere kindness.

When I called Brent's room the next morning at 6:00, he said, "Hey, Dad, can you stop at John's Restaurant and order three hamburgers, three orders of fries, a Coke, and two cups of coffee? We're hungry." I couldn't believe it. Those men had spent the night with our son.

When Jane and I went to pick Brent up, we asked what had caused the seizure. The doctor smiled. "We did all the tests that come with a seizure but could find nothing wrong. We gave him some anti-seizure medicine, so he will be okay for now, but take him to his regular doctor for further tests."

Brent told me that it would only be right if we went to Living Waters, so we could hear Pastor Duke preach and meet all of Brent's friends.

"You know I'm coaching the AYSO all-star traveling soccer team," I replied. "We usually make it to the tournament finals. As a matter of fact, we're playing in a tournament in Mission Viejo, and I'm sure we will be in the finals. If by chance we don't make it, I give you my word we'll be at Living Waters." He just smiled and told me he loved me.

The next weekend we played in the single-elimination tournament in Mission Viejo and on Friday afternoon, we beat one of the better teams quite handily. When I got home, I told Jane that I was sure we would be playing on Sunday because the team we were playing on Saturday morning we had beaten before. I drove back to Mission Viejo early on Saturday morning to watch the best team in the tournament win their game easily, but I noticed some weaknesses we could exploit.

Later, it was time for our game, so I went to warm the boys up to prepare them for the game. The match kind of went like expected with no scores in the first half. The second half was normally when our boys came to life and scored several goals, as the other team would get tired. To my surprise, the other team upped their game, and neither team scored a goal in the third quarter.

"Okay boys," I said once the third quarter ended, "this is where you give it all you have and run away with this game."

They did give it their all, but the other team matched them stride for stride, with everyone in attendance on their feet, cheering both teams on. Then midway through the fourth quarter, one of their players took a long, arching shot from near midfield that hit the goal post and ricocheted into the net. My boys fought their hardest and got several shots on goal, but couldn't put the ball in the net, so we lost 1–0.

When I got home, Brent was out playing with his remote-controlled car. He greeted me with a big smile. "I guess you're going to Living Waters tomorrow."

Later, when I asked him what kind of church it was, he replied, "It's a Christian church. Why?"

"Is it one of those holy roller churches?" I asked.

"I don't know. I ain't never rolled, so I'll see you there."

I talked to Jane later and asked if she had ever been to a holy roller church. When she said that she had not, I told her, "Those people get crazy, so we'll sit in the back row. Be ready to leave when the craziness starts."

The next morning when we entered the church parking lot, the church sign caught my attention, including the pastor's name, Alvin "Duke" Downs. I knew two other guys named Duke, and they were both slick-haired hustlers. *Oh well*, I thought. *I did make the boy a promise.*

When we walked in, Brent met us at the front door and introduced us to almost everybody. We were early since I wanted to get a seat in the back near the door. Once we were seated, I reminded Jane that when people started getting crazy, we were gone. She just smiled and patted my hand.

The musicians came in and started playing songs I remembered from my childhood. Then an elderly lady went to the platform, asked us to stand, and began to pray for the Holy Spirit to have His way. As soon as she said "amen," she led us in singing "I'll Fly Away." Then, without stopping, she took off on a song I didn't recognize. All the while, everyone was singing, clapping, and raising their hands. I looked over at Jane and nearly choked, for she was singing with her eyes closed. I knew she was enjoying it, but I was determined that when it got crazy, we were leaving no matter what.

After the worship service, a pretty, blonde-haired lady went up on the platform and sang another song I had never heard before, but a pleasant sensation came over me, making me feel very strange.

When Pastor Dave went up to the pulpit, he made some announcements and then opened his Bible and began to read about bringing our money into the storehouse. He said a few words about tithing 10 percent. I turned to Jane and smirked, about to say all they wanted was our money, but to my surprise, she was digging in her purse for money to put in the bucket.

Then it was showtime for Pastor Duke, and he was up to it, yelling that Satan was after us for all our evil ways. It took me right back to when I went to the altar as a child. Then he kicked into high gear and was all over drinking, fighting, and not being able to control our tempers, which made me think it was time for us to leave.

Suddenly he stopped, lowered his head, and mumbled something in what sounded like another language. Then he said some words that I did understand and which I will never forget. "There's someone in here who is nervous about the way we worship and praise our God, but you will go to a soccer game and get . . ." He paused for what seemed like an eternity to me. "That had to be for somebody in here. I have never been to a soccer game in my life."

I was angry, as I thought Brent had snitched me out. As soon as we were dismissed, I headed straight to my son, who was sitting up front with the youth, and grabbed his arm. "Boy, that was dirty, snitching me out to Pastor Duke," I said. He gave me a strange look.

"Dad, I hardly ever speak to Pastor Duke."

I knew Brent didn't lie, so I headed down front where the pastor was talking to Ray and another big guy named Wes. I tapped him on the shoulder, and when he turned around, I said, "What was that crack regarding soccer all about?"

He smiled. "I don't have a clue. I've never been to a soccer game." Then he looked me in the eyes. "Sir, if that was for you,

you can't get mad at me because I'm just the newsboy. You now have a choice. You can go to the altar and change your life, or you can walk out the door and split hell wide open. I have told you the truth, so your blood is not on my hands."

I nearly ran up the aisle to get Jane and take her to the car, so I could get away from that place. When she asked what was wrong, I told her exactly what had happened and said I would never go back there. However, all afternoon I was troubled in ways I had never been troubled before, so back to church we went, and that night I headed to the altar, even before Pastor Duke gave the altar call. I was crying like a baby, and as the saying goes, "I left it all on the altar." "Repent then and turn to God so that your sins may be wiped out" (Acts 3:19).

We began to attend Living Waters twice on Sunday and on Wednesday night, and I started reading my Bible, wanting to understand all of it. God's word says His ways are higher than our ways. Through all this, I began to understand that God loves me personally, especially after letting John 3:16 sink into my inner being: "For God so loved the world that he gave his only begotten Son that whoever believes in him shall not perish but have everlasting life." I wanted everything to change at once, but I realized that everything happens according to God's perfect timing.

Bonded Motors was in deep financial trouble due to poor management. Arthur the owner who had taken over for his father had hired a general manager named Gerry who professed to be a Christian, but he continually lied, was prejudiced according to people's skin color, and had a haughty attitude. Everyone despised him, but since I was out in the field, calling on customers, I had very little contact with him.

One day when I went into the plant to pick up supplies, Gerry yelled at me because, according to him, everything was my fault. Previously, that would have been enough for me to bust him in the face, but to my surprise I just said, "I'm sorry you're having a bad day, but you should rejoice that God loves you." That really set him off. So, I just walked away.

Arthur's son, Seth, came over to ask if I was okay. He wanted to know why I hadn't hit Gerry. I laughed and told him I was acting with the love of Jesus. He shook his head in reply and walked away, but then came back and said, "We need to do something to run him off."

I laughed and asked what he had in mind. Then to my surprise, I said, "Seth, be patient, for I have a feeling he'll be gone soon."

"I hope you're right," Seth replied, "but my father said Gerry will be here for another year."

The next week, I had to go into the plant to meet a customer. Before I got to my office, Seth asked me to follow him. When we got outside, he gave me a strange look. "Buddy, have you been talking to my father?"

"No, why?"

"I talked to my father early this morning, and he told me he's firing Gerry today."

"I guess my Father knows more than your father," I replied.

Just then, Gerry walked past us to his car, and we never saw him again.

One Sunday a few weeks later, Pastor Dave read out of the book of Malachi 3:8 about God robbers, saying if we don't tithe, God cannot bless us. I thought, *God when I get money, You get yours.*

After church on the way home Jane said, "Buddy, we have to start tithing our ten percent."

"We're going broke, Jane," I replied, "and that ten percent will just get us there quicker." There are times when a guy knows when to shut up, and this was one of them. I didn't say another word about it, and you will see throughout the rest of this book that she was right.

About two weeks after Arthur fired Gerry, Arthur called me to his office. When I arrived, our accountant, Peter, was sitting at a table. When I joined them, Arthur's next words blew me away. "Buddy, we are in serious trouble, and we think you're the guy we need as general manager." I just sat there staring at him. Then I asked how soon they needed an answer. "As soon as possible," he replied.

"I think the Titanic has hit the iceberg and is sinking," I said as I stood up. "You guys are tossing me the captain's hat while you're running for the lifeboat."

As I turned, I heard Arthur say to Peter, "Well, that went well, didn't it? Maybe he'll think about it."

I left work and I headed to the church, asking the secretary if Pastor Duke was available. I guess he heard me because he stuck his head out of his office door and told me to come in. I told him what had happened at Bonded and how the company was going down the tubes. I had no idea how, as general manager, I could get it back to being a viable business. I had barely graduated from high school.

"Buddy, I don't have an answer," he said, "but I know a God that can give you the answer. Let's pray and ask Him to guide you in the way you should go." When he finished praying, he said, "Now we'll wait for God to give you an answer."

I thanked him for his time, then walked out of his office thinking, *Well, that was a waste of time.* God had never shown me anything. I figured that, as always, I would have to take care of things myself, so I called Bonded and told the receptionist to let Arthur know I wouldn't be back until Monday. I wrestled all weekend with the direction I should go and finally decided I wouldn't take the job because I would be in way over my head.

On Sunday morning, we went to church and then to lunch where I told Jane that I had decided I wouldn't take the job. I asked if she had any thoughts. "I don't know," she replied, "but I think we ought to pray and wait to see if God is going to give you direction."

That evening after church, Pastor Duke asked if I had a minute to talk. We walked out into the hall where it was quiet. "I believe God wants you to take the job for a reason we won't understand," he said, "but if you step out in faith and seek His will, He will open doors you would never be able to open on your own. Right now, I want to pray and ask for guidance for you." Boy, did he pray, asking God to give me wisdom, to give me Holy Ghost boldness, and most of all, for God to give me patience to wait on Him.

On the way home, I told Jane what had happened. When she asked what I was going to do I said, "What *can* I do? I ain't gonna argue with God and the pastor." I thought of all the times I needed God but wound up having to do things my way, but now I was supposed to trust Him in this life-changing situation. *Oh well,* I thought. *My back is against the wall, so I can't turn back now.*

The next morning on the way to the plant, I felt more confident because I had done a good job when I ran the little plant in San Luis Obispo, especially the way I had handled problems with customers and how they only wanted to talk to me. I thought that if I did things the way I know to, I would probably be successful.

Soon, though, the nagging fear crept back in. My mind took me back to the lowest, most devastating period of my life on the streets of LA. I saw my mother and grandparents praying for me, and I cried out to God for mercy. Then I pictured the young man at the mission who helped me get ready for my trip, the lady at the employment office who sent me to a job where they weren't expecting me, the night I met my wife to be, and Lela at the bank on the day we needed the car loan. Our prayers for the opportunity to live in the Pismo Area had been answered too. Then there was the miraculous way we were led to Living Waters where I asked Jesus to come into my life. During all this I had no control. Then I became aware that God had opened the door for me to come off the streets, and from that day forward He had made a way when the situation seemed impossible. The only thing I had to do was step through each door as God opened it. He had just opened another door and was extending His hand to guide me on a new journey.

When I arrived at the plant, I was late. I went straight to Arthur's office. As I opened the door, I was filled with an indescribable feeling of confidence. Arthur and Peter were so deep in conversation that, for a second, they barely noticed me. When they finally did, there was hostility in Arthur's voice. "Where the hell have you been? You didn't show up Friday, you didn't call, and now you come strolling in late."

"Last week you asked if I would take over as general manager," I said as I sat down. "Is the offer still open?" When they both nodded, I continued. "I'm willing to take the position but only on my terms which I will lay out, pulling no punches. This company is on the edge of bankruptcy. Arthur, since you have a personal loan locking everything up, including your house, you are at risk of losing everything. Over the weekend, I realized the company's troubles were created by poor management, for which you are both culpable. Arthur, as the owner, you have created a hostile environment where there is no trust in management. The plant is filthy, and there are girly pictures all over the walls. Peter, you have allowed the company's overhead to skyrocket. The inventories are out of whack, and customers are leaving due to our poor quality work." I stopped and stared at them, waiting for a response but none was forthcoming, so I continued. "It will take a miracle to turn this place around. I'm going to lay out the steps required, some of which will be painful. These steps have been burned into my heart, and you both know what they are, but if you need them on paper, take notes.

"Number one, since the plant is in disarray, I will terminate the current plant manager. I already have a replacement in mind. Unfortunately, the next step is very painful for me, but we will be laying off sixty employees, and the three of us will be taking pay cuts. Next, we will put a freeze on all purchases. Vendors have overloaded us with product. Finally, Arthur, because you're the flashpoint for these issues, it is imperative that you take a ninety-day vacation."

I stopped and waited for a reaction. When it came, it left me stunned.

"Who gave you this plan?" Arthur asked. "You're not capable of creating this yourself."

I just smiled. "I'm not at liberty to divulge that information at this point, but when the time is right, you will be unable to deny the answer. The question before you is this: will you accept my terms? If so, I will accept the position of general manager. I expect an answer within the hour. I'm going to my office to await your decision."

As I headed to my office, I was amazed at what I had said, for it truly was beyond what I knew. I never would have asked Arthur to take a ninety-day vacation. Then I recalled Pastor Duke praying for God to give me His wisdom and Holy Ghost boldness.

When I got to my office, I closed the door and thanked God for what he had done, leaving me in awe. I don't know how long I was lost in my thoughts before the phone rang. It was the receptionist, telling me to return to Arthur's office.

When I walked in and sat down, he and Peter looked at me as if I were an alien. I waited for one of them to tell me what they had decided, but they made no effort to start a conversation. I just sat and stared. I thought I had made my case, and now it was up to them because they had called me in. Several moments passed in silence, so I pushed my chair back and started to get up. Then Arthur finally spoke. "We asked you to take over as general manager and are certain that you are right for the position, but would you share who you've been talking to regarding what course of action you feel compelled to take?"

"I told you that I'm not prepared to divulge that information right now. I'm waiting on your decision and see no need for further conversation."

"We've agreed that the terms you've laid out are exactly what's needed," Peter said, "but can you give us more details?"

"If you commit to having me as general manager according to the terms I laid out, I will be more than happy to give you a simple plan in writing three days from now. But so far you have not made that commitment."

"Why three days?" Arthur asked.

"As soon as you make the commitment, we will meet with the supervisors and let them know I'll be general manager," I said. "Since there's a lot of hostility toward upper-level management, the three of us will answer their questions openly and honestly, as painful as it may be. Tomorrow, we will invite all the employees to a brief meeting and let them know the direction I'll be taking the company. We will also announce that Arthur will be gone for ninety days and answer their questions. On the third day, I will have had a conversation with the man I intend to promote to plant manager. Then I will terminate the current plant manager. During those three days, I will have formulated the simple plan that I will be using to go forward. This should be sufficient to quell your curiosity."

They were both silent for a moment, and then Arthur spoke. "You have the commitment you've requested. Even though I won't be here, I demand to be kept in the loop with written reports."

Without hesitation, I stood up and extended my hand. "A handshake will consummate the deal as far as I'm concerned, but if that's not satisfactory for both of you, then this has all been in vain." They both stood, and we shook hands. "I'm going to lunch," I said. "I have sales work to do prior to my meeting with the supervisors, which I will hold at four o'clock."

In January 1992, I became general manager of Bonded, overseeing all operations and sales, but in my mind, I was under God's will.

The person I had in mind to be plant manager was an African American man named James from the worst part of South LA. He was an ex-gangbanger with a teardrop below his eye, but he had worked at Bonded for over ten years. He had been very helpful to me in incidents when I had an engine with a warranty problem. I called him up to my office and told him what had transpired, including that I was now the general manager, that I would be firing the plant manager shortly, and that I wanted to promote him to plant manager. He responded with a glare. "Mr. B, if you are dissing me, I'll cut you." I told him I wasn't sure what dissing meant, but my offer was serious. He stood and stared at me for a while longer, his veins bulging. "You better be for real," he declared. Then he turned and stormed out of my office, leaving me alone to think, *That went well, didn't it?*

A short time later, he returned to my office. "I'll be plant manager if I can pick my assistant," he said. I told him he could do whatever he wanted because it would reflect on him, but there was no money to go along with the title. He laughed, then went out the door. A few minutes later, he came back in with a Hispanic fellow named José whom everyone called Joe, who was a former gangbanger out of East LA. I agreed to having Joe become the assistant plant manager. Then I thanked them and told them to keep our conversation confidential until the following morning.

Then I went to terminate Larry, the current plant manager, as it had been revealed to me that he was prejudiced and a bigot. I called him into my office and told him that, effective immediately, his job at Bonded was over. He gave me an incredulous look. "You can't fire me," he said. "You don't have the authority. Arthur hired me, so he's the only one who can fire me." I told him that I was now general manager. "I have sent Arthur home for a ninety-day leave of absence. He is no longer on the premises. Larry, remember the day you asked me what I thought of Arthur? When I asked you what you meant, you told me that you didn't trust the Jew boy with your money. Then you called him a 'kike.' At that point, I realized you were a despicable bigot. I don't want you to be on these premises any longer. I have seventy-two hours after termination to get you your final paycheck, so I'll walk you to your car now."

Before we met with the supervisors, I spent time alone in my office, praying for God to give me the words He would have me say. At the meeting, the supervisors poured out their venom regarding their feelings toward Arthur and Peter. They felt they had been mistreated. When things calmed down, I announced that Arthur would be away from the company for a few months. Then I told them I was now general manager.

"What are you going to do to us?" one of the most vocal guys asked, his voice full of derision.

I smiled. "I will make no promises except that I will treat you all with respect as long as you treat me the same way. I will be honest with you about everything, and I expect the same from you. My office door will always be open. I will arrive at work each day before you, and I will leave after you. We are in trouble, and my job is on the line, just like yours." We did not announce the change in plant managers.

The next morning, we announced to the rest of the employees that I would be the general manager, effective immediately. I also told them that Arthur was taking a leave of absence and that I had fired the plant manager, which was greeted with shouts, whistles, and applause, but I did not mention James or Jose. Then I answered a few questions and assured them they would know more soon.

That evening when I got into my car, I found a note threatening me, but it was unsigned. The next morning, I called another employee meeting and held up the note. "I have your message here saying you're going to hurt me or worse, but you failed to sign it, so that makes you a coward. Now, I will be in my office all day, so if you want to whip me, come on up. Let's talk, then we can go out and fight if you have the guts."

After that I introduced James as the new plant manager and asked him to say a few words. He did a great job, explaining that the company was in trouble, but we were going to do everything possible to fix it, and we needed everyone's help. Then he introduced José as the assistant plant manager and told them to go to work

That afternoon one of the guys came into my office. "I wrote the note, and I'm truly sorry," he said. "Please forgive me, as I really need a job." Much to his surprise and mine, I stood up, walked around to where he was standing, and gave him a hug and said.

"Thank you. You'll have a job here as long as I do. Now, say nothing to anyone about this, and go back to work."

I walked outside of the building and started laughing. "God, I know you're here because on my own I would have whipped him and then fired him."

A major low point occurred about a week or so later when we laid off the sixty men. The hard part was that they had done nothing wrong; they were just victims of bad management. About thirty days after I took over, our vendors demanded a meeting to find out how I was going to turn things around. The morning of the meeting, I was in my office, praying when my new plant manager walked in. James stood staring at me, his eyes wide.

"Mr. B, are you a praying man?"

"Yes sir," I replied.

The meeting was very contentious because the vendors stood to lose a lot of money. "We have started the turnaround," I said, "but I won't make any promises. Please remember that none of you have received an insufficient check from this company. You all have let Bonded Motors get behind and owe you for one simple reason—greed. Many of you have loaded us up with your product, and now you want promises that we'll correct this immediately. I won't make that promise, but if you work with us and let us return the overstock, you stand a good chance to not only get the money owed to you now, but when we grow, I promise you this: you will grow with us."

The vendors asked Peter, our accountant, and I to step outside while they discussed how they were going to proceed.

"How do you know Bonded has never written one of these vendors an insufficient check?" Peter asked once we were outside.

"Remember when you and Arthur wanted to know who helped me with the plan I gave you guys? Well, the same guy let me know there were no bad checks."

The vendors called us back in and told us something had happened in that room that no one could explain, and they all agreed to work with us.

Arthur, the owner, returned from his "enforced vacation" and was working hard to gain the respect from the employees which made my job easier and my life much better.

I was in the back of the plant when James told me that a couple of guys up front wanted to talk to me, and they didn't look friendly.

When I arrived, I realized one of the guys, who was wearing a suit, was from the bank, and the other guy, who was wearing a flashy shirt unbuttoned to the chest with gold chains hanging around his neck, was probably the liquidator in case we went bankrupt. The guy in the suit started to introduce himself, but I interrupted him, saying they needed to speak to the owner and the accountant. I directed them to Arthur's office and then headed back to what I was doing before I was called up front to meet them.

A little while later the guy in the suit came to where I was and asked if he could talk to me somewhere quiet. As we walked up to my office, I felt confident with what I was saying even though I didn't have a clue about our financial situation with the bank. When we got to my office, I told him that I had just taken over as general manager, but I knew we were in trouble with the bank to the tune of probably a million dollars or a million and a half in yearly sales. I also said I found it ridiculous that the bank would allow that to happen. While I couldn't prevent a shutdown, I warned that it would be costly for them, and I had a solution to avoid it.

He stood and stared at me like I was from another world. Then he cleared his throat and asked if he could see the plan. I explained that I had not had time to formulate the plan on paper, but if he gave me ninety days, I would provide him with a plan complete with numbers to back everything up. I also told him that our vendors had agreed to work with us and that I was going to lay off several employees to reduce our overhead.

The guy gave me a strange smile. "I can't believe this. I'm responsible for this account, and you want me to go back to the bank and tell management I'm giving you ninety days to present us with a plan that's in your head. This is way beyond protocol for this situation, but it's just crazy enough to be believable. I'm going to accept your proposal with the caveat that I get a weekly report of what's transpiring. Then I expect you to be at my bank in ninety days with your comprehensive plan."

Ninety days later I was at the bank with the improvements we had made and a comprehensive operating plan for the future, to which the bank readily agreed.

One day I was taking a walk through the plant when James came up to me with a big smile. "Do you see anything different?" he asked. I looked around and saw all the girly pictures were gone. I didn't say a word; I just gave him a big hug right there in front of everybody. By the end of the year, the plant was operating more efficiently, and inventory was under control, but the quality of our engines was not improving quickly enough.

On a late spring day in 1993, a guy walked into my office, closed the door, and introduced himself as Richard Funk. "I've heard you have good things happening here," he said, "and I'd like to see if I can help you out." He was the foremost engine rebuilding guru in the United States, sought out by all the major engine rebuilders, where he could name his price for consulting. He had been the general manager for Thomas Engineering in Tacoma, the most respected company in the US. I knew that Arthur had offered him big money several times, but Richard would never even consider working at Bonded Motors in the past.

I stood up, shook his hand. "Mr. Funk, we can't afford the money you deserve, but you can have my position. This company is at a point where we need your expertise."

"Let's talk awhile and see what we can work out," he replied, smiling. We talked at length about what was going on in the engine rebuilding world and then he said, "Buddy, what you have succeeded in doing here is the talk of the industry. I had to come see for myself. I hope it doesn't offend you, but I took a tour of your plant before I came in to speak with you and have found the rumors to be true. This place is bright and clean, the employees are smiling and friendly, and the improvement is astounding. I really believe I can help you."

Then he laid out what he would be doing and the salary he would accept in return, without hesitation, I asked when he wanted to start.

"What about right now?" he said, laughing. From there, he laid out the things we needed to do immediately, which were simple and would not cost much. "Why don't you start with what I have given you? I'll be back in two weeks to see how you're doing."

I was still blown away by what had just transpired when Arthur came into my office and sat down. "I understand Richard Funk was here," he said. "Mind telling me what transpired?" I laid it all out to him, from Richard hearing rumors regarding what was going on at Bonded to him wanting to be a part of it.

Late into our conversation, my phone rang. It was Richard.

"Buddy, I forgot to ask where you go to church. Can you give me the address?"

"We go to Living Waters in Chino on the corner of Ramona and Eucalyptus," I replied.

The next weeks were great as James incorporated Richard's suggestions, which had made an immediate difference in quality and productivity. When Richard returned two weeks later, he was greeted by James and a couple of supervisors who were excited to show him what they had done. When Richard made it to my office, he was smiling from ear to ear. "Buddy, I didn't tell you everything. Prior to my first visit, during prayer time I felt in my spirit that I should come and help. I know Arthur isn't a believer, but I don't think he'll mind if we do good things. I have to go to Phoenix this week, but my wife and I will be at your church this Sunday, and we'd like to take you and your wife to lunch."

The plant began to operate at a higher level of efficiency. The quality of our product was better than ever. Employee morale was exceptional, and sales began to pick up. In January, I was promoted again, this time to vice president of operations and chief operating officer. Then in early August 1994, I received an unexpected phone call from a guy named Jake Forester who was vice-president of merchandising for Pep Boys in Philadelphia. "Buddy," he said, "your company has been servicing our stores in the southwest and doing a good job. I'm calling to see if you could provide engines for our warehouses to stock in Texas, Arizona, Colorado, Nevada, and California. We want to provide better service to our customers and continue the service you're giving us now."

I nearly screamed "yes," but instead I did my best to maintain my cool. "I'm sure we can do that. How many engines are we talking about for the warehouses? How soon do they need to be in stock?"

"There will be a total of one thousand engines," Jake replied. "We want to roll out the program on January first, so the engines will need to be in the warehouses before Christmas. We will pay for the product when it arrives at the warehouses. Buddy, I want you to know the other VPs here recommended we go with a company out of Phoenix, but Bonded Motors kept coming back to me."

"I certainly want to thank you for giving me a call," I replied. "Though I'm sure we can do this with no problem, I need to speak to my plant manager. I'll call you in the morning to confirm."

When I hung up the phone, I began to sob. This was an answer to our prayers for more business. I quickly regained my composure and paged James and Richard. When they came to my office, I closed the door, told them about my conversation, and waited for their reactions. Sure enough, their response was similar to mine. Then we linked hands and thanked God for His blessings.

I called Jacob the next morning at 6:00 LA time with Richard Funk and James in my office. I asked Jacob if I could put him on speaker mode, so we could all be on the same page, then I repeated our conversation from the previous day. When I finished, I asked when we would get our first purchase order, so that we could start completing the job. "If you look at the fax machine, it will be coming through momentarily," he said. We went to the office and, sure enough, there were several purchase orders on the fax machine, each for a different warehouse, totaling one thousand engines. We made extra copies, so that we could leave one set on Arthur's desk and another on Peter's desk. We were ecstatic. This would allow us to repay our past debts to our vendors. James increased production, and we shipped engines to the last warehouse in the middle of December.

In early summer of 1995, Bonded Motors' entire operation was performing at maximum efficiency. Our warranty rate was below 4 percent while the industry average was over 9 percent. Our overhead was at an all-time low, sales were rising, and profits were climbing. Arthur called James, Richard, and me into his office where he and Peter were waiting. He told us we had done a marvelous job and was ecstatic with our progress. "Bonded Motors is operating so well that we caught the eye of an investment group who saw an article in Forbes magazine," he said. "They want to talk to us about doing an initial public offering that, if successful, will make us all a lot of money." An initial public offering, or IPO, means selling shares of stock to the public on a stock exchange.

When we left his office, we were all troubled with the feeling that greed was taking over. But Arthur was the owner, and it was our responsibility to maintain the operation at the current level or better, which we did for the rest of the year.

In February 1996, the people from the investment group came to Bonded Motors to meet with Arthur, Peter, and me regarding the IPO. They were nice people, and they told us that we had a great story to tell. The group assured us that the IPO would be successful, which would make us all a lot of money.

I felt very uncomfortable when they asked what I thought about the idea. The only thing I could say was, "It's Arthur's company, and if it's his wish, I will honor my commitment." One of them noticed that I didn't appear to be too happy about the idea and said as much. "I have no issue with the IPO," I replied. "It's the greed that comes with it that bothers me. By the grace of God, we've taken this company from near bankruptcy to where we are today. We have some terrific employees who deserve the credit. What will this do for them? But at this point, I'll do what's right for the company."

The next step in the process was an independent audited inventory, which was detailed and meticulous and a real pain to do. We were doing it under the watchful eye of our big-eight accounting firm, KPMG Peat Marwick. I hired some outside help to assist us, and they had to pass certain qualifications. Four young people were hired, two guys and two girls. One of the girls was kind of out of place. She looked like somebody with an upper-middle-class background with the way she dressed and the way she presented herself. The rest of them were rather common and ordinary, which didn't make any difference to me. It was not how they looked that was important, but she seemed out of place.

The audit was extensive, lasting for five or six days. At the end of it, Arthur came to me and said, "I'd like that girl to stay around. She seems to be somebody we could use."

I called her into my office and asked if she would like to stay on with us because we had a job opening, and we felt that she could fill the position. As we talked, she impressed me with how bright, cheerful, and forward-thinking she was. "I'm not supposed to ask how old you are," I said. "But how old are you?"

She laughed. "I'm twenty years old."

"Well, congratulations, twenty-year-old young lady; you

have a job here with us. We're going to put you to work in the parts department after you finish doing inventory for us. There are some things that I want to do there. When you come into work from now on, you probably don't want to wear those fancy clothes because it's going to be a little grubby."

"Is there something wrong with what I'm wearing?" she asked.

"Nope," I replied, "but you're gonna be working around dirty stuff. But wear whatever; just be ready to work."

I gave her a couple of days to finish her inventory work. When she came to work in the parts department, she was dressed in more appropriate apparel. With little instruction required, she went to work. Everybody was impressed with what she was doing. After she completed the job in the parts department, I told her we were going to take the company public, and I had additional work that I needed for her to do. I also told her that I was going to give her a raise because she was going to be answering the phone for me and doing some secretarial work, but she wasn't going to be a secretary. She was going to be like a Girl Friday who could be used anywhere. She was very appreciative and agreed to work anywhere she was needed. It didn't take long for her to prove that she was worth the raise.

One day I was sitting at my desk eating lunch when she asked if she could talk to me. She was concerned about her future with her job and asked if she could get on permanently. I told her that as far as I was concerned, as long as she continued to perform like she had, she would have a job.

She continued working for us, and after about four or five weeks, we had formed a relationship where we could laugh and joke with each other. She had a twenty-year-old look, but she had a much older attitude about things. One day a parts guy came up and asked if she had any Rolaids in the first-aid box.

"You don't look old enough to need Rolaids," she said. When he asked her what she meant, she said, "Well, Buddy eats Rolaids, but he's old."

"Thanks a lot, girl," I retorted.

"Did I say something wrong?" she asked. I could tell right then that her comments were innocent. We continued joking back and forth like that for weeks. Eventually, whenever I'd have lunch at my desk, she'd come in and chat.

One day she asked if I could take her home. She lived in Azusa Hills just off the I-60 freeway, which was on my way home because I lived in Chino Hills. "My boyfriend's supposed to pick me up, but his car broke down," she said. "So, if I could get a ride, I would appreciate it."

On the way to her place, I turned to her and said, "Girl, I got to tell you something. You're an amazing person. You're only twenty, but you have the mind of a much older person, and you dress nice. There's something going on."

"My background is awful," she replied. "I'll talk to you about it because I need to get it out. I've been molested, and I've been treated awful by my cousins who have used me in an awful way. My uncle was a homosexual and had AIDS, and he just passed away not long ago. That's why I'm with the guy that I'm with now. I want to make a fresh start of my life."

"Whoa, that's a rough road," I said.

"Have you noticed?" she asked.

"I recently noticed when you go to a restaurant you take

quite a while," I said. "And when you come out, you're wiping the door handle."

"You're perceptive," she replied. "That's a sign of somebody who's been molested. I'm going to therapy to try to get past it. My mother hasn't been a good mother, and we don't get along. I'm really thankful for this job, Buddy. You've helped me to feel like I'm valuable for who I am and not for my body like all the other guys."

The next morning when I picked her up on my way into the plant, as we had agreed, she was bubblier than ever. She thanked me for letting her tell me about her awful life and not judging her. I had some things that I wanted to tell her about my past and what God had done for me, but I couldn't get the words out. She continued to tell me of her hopes and dreams, so I just kept quiet and listened all the way into the plant.

It didn't take long for rumors to start that we were having an affair. Later that day, Arthur came into my office and told me that I should get rid of the girl. He was concerned about a sexual harassment lawsuit. I told him not to worry and assured him that I would not file a sexual harassment claim. He stormed out of my office, calling me a vile name. I had kind of expected something like that, but I have always believed that people are going to think whatever they want to.

The girl came into my office, troubled about the rumor and what it could do to me. I assured her that I wasn't worried and that she should just go to work and forget it. Sure enough, the rumor died within a couple of days.

Not long after that, she did something that blew my mind. She handed me a piece of paper and a pen and said, "Do me a favor and write my name on this." Without questioning her, I did as she asked. "Okay, now wad it up and throw it in that trash can," she said.

"What the heck are you trying to get at?" I asked.

"Just do it," she replied. "Buddy, that's what I'm concerned about. That's what you do to people. When you get tired of them, you just throw them away.. You haven't talked to your mother in years. II'm afraid you're just going to wind me up and throw me away when I leave here."

I stood there in stone silence and then nodded. "Okay. You got my attention."

On a different day, she came into my office and started crying, which was out of character for her. When I finally got her calmed down, she told me she had been offered a great job at a doggie daycare center.

"That's wonderful," I said without thinking, which was the wrong response. Then it hit me that she would be leaving her foundation at Bonded Motors. We talked for quite a while until I convinced her that she was getting a chance to do something that she really wanted to do because she loved animals. She took the job and was extremely happy doing what she loved. Eventually, the owner told her that she was going to open another center and wanted her to manage the first one.

We stayed in touch by phone and an occasional lunch. She left her boyfriend and was living alone in Santa Monica, where she was dating a new young man who worked as a stockbroker. A few months later, he asked her to marry him. She wanted me to meet him and see what I thought of him. "Just bring him by the plant," I said.

When she did, we sat down and had a talk. He was a bright, well-educated young man with his eye on the ball. As a stockbroker, he was already making a lot of money. It didn't surprise me that they were together, even though her background was way below that. "You know what?" I told her. "I think this is the man for you. You guys make a beautiful couple, and it ought to be." She started crying, big tears rolling down her face. "I thought you'd say that" she said. "It means a lot to me."

In April 1996, Bonded Motors became the only engine rebuilder ever to do a successful IPO, opening at 5 7/8 on the Nasdaq. It did make me a lot of money. I had taken out a loan on our home for $100,000 and was able to buy 100,000 shares at $1 per share. Instantly, those shares were worth $587,000. Me, a homeless skid row bum, was over halfway to becoming a millionaire.

When I told Jane about the IPO, she asked how I felt about it. I didn't really know because my emotions were jumbled. The money would allow us to do things for our family that we couldn't have done previously. We would be able to give more to God's work too, but somehow I felt empty inside. At that moment I really missed my mom. She would have been proud of her son.

In July 1997, I was sitting in my office, working on a sales report. At about 9:00, I felt in my spirit to sell 50,000 shares, which were selling at $10 a share. I called our CIO and told him what I wanted to do. He said he would start on it right away.

Just before 11:00, the receptionist called and said the CEO and CFO wanted me to report to Arthur's office right away. When I walked in, I realized they were angry.

"How dare you sell your stocks without conferring with us for Bonded Motors too. At that moment, the receptionist stuck her head in the door and said our SEC attorney was on the phone. He wanted to speak with me immediately, so I picked up the phone right there in the office.

"Hello, Michael, how are you?" I asked.

"Well, not as rich as you," he replied. "You just sold your fifty thousand shares for ten dollars a share making you a half millionaire. Congratulations. The stocks were marked, but the mark was lifted for your sale. How do you want the money, by wire transfer to your bank or a check?" I remained quiet because I was in shock, and I had an audience. "Make up your mind how you want this to be handled, and give me a call," Michael continued. "Your sale has been completed so, again, congratulations."

Without saying a word to those in the room, I returned to my office and called Richard Funk at our plant in Macon, Georgia, where he was helping to straighten out some problems. The receptionist said he wasn't available, so I left a message for him to call me. Meanwhile, I called Jane to get our routing number for the wire transfer, and for a moment, I felt good. I knew the stocks had been released to sell by the hand of God. Just then my phone notified me I had a call waiting, so I told Jane I would call her later. It was Richard calling me back. When I told him about the situation, he was quiet for a few moments. Then he said he would call back when he gathered some more information and knew what was going on.

About an hour later, he called and said he had just spoken with our SEC attorney who told him that he would not be able to sell his stocks until the end of the year. So, he had called his personal attorney, and somehow he had also gotten his stock released and was selling 50,000 shares too. Then he warned me that we had to be careful with Arthur and Peter.

For the rest of the year, I was out of the plant on sales business, so I didn't have to deal with what was going on in the plant. Early in 1998, Bonded Motors landed the Genuine Parts/NAPA account. It was trouble from the moment we started selling to them. They were very demanding and created a lot of animosity in a plant that had been operating so well just a year earlier.

Just after Christmas, Richard called and asked if I could meet him but not to let anyone know. I was in Nashville, so it was no problem to get a puddle jumper to Atlanta, rent a car, and be in Macon that evening.

"I don't know everything that's going on yet," he told me when we met at a nearby Holiday Inn, "but I know enough to know that I'm through at Bonded. I'll be flying home tomorrow. Greed has taken over, Buddy, just as we thought. There are going to be big changes at Bonded, probably starting in April. I'm selling all the stock I can, and I hope I can collect the money I have coming." When I asked what was happening, he said, "I really can't tell you everything, but it looks like they're going to try to blame me for the troubles they're having with NAPA."

"What do you want me to do?" I asked, incredulously.

"I think it would be good if you show up at the Macon plant," he replied. "Tell them I asked you to take my meeting with NAPA tomorrow morning. I have an emergency and must go home." He said he was going to see his attorney and that he would let me know afterwards what was really happening.

The next morning, I met the NAPA guys. They seemed okay, but they were concerned that Richard wasn't there. After they left, I didn't talk to anyone else at the plant, just made a reservation for a flight home.

After the first of the year, I got a call from a small operation in Portland who wanted me to come talk to them about helping them with their operation. When I told Jane, she was quiet for a moment. "When we were on vacation in 1973 in Oregon," she said, "I prayed that God would open the door for us to move to the Northwest."

I was stunned. "Ain't God good?" I said.

On February 1, Arthur stormed into my office and demanded to know what was happening. When I asked what he meant, he went ballistic, saying I was helping to bankrupt Bonded after all he had done for me. He also accused me of convincing Richard to quit. I sat and listened for a bit, but then I stood up and told him that I was quitting too and that if he didn't get out of my way, I would knock him on his backside. Little did he know I had already accepted a position at Portland Motor Company.

In the afternoon, I headed home. When I got there, I called Richard to tell him what had transpired. "Buddy, there's something bad going on there, but I can't get a complete answer. Just be careful when you go back tomorrow."

The next day I went in, made the obligatory public announcement to the employees, told James and the supervisors goodbye, wished them well, then left without looking back.

The following year in April, the creditors forced Bonded Motors into bankruptcy, but a company from Philadelphia bought the equipment. I called the owner, whom I knew well, and gave him a list of the men I thought he should hire, including James as plant manager, which he did.

10

THE GREAT NORTHWEST

IT AMAZED us that a prayer request from 1973 was being answered in a miraculous way in 1999. At the time, I saw God's hand removed from Bonded Motors due to greed. He opened the door for us to go to the Northwest, as Jane had prayed some twenty-six years earlier. With a new job in Portland, we found a house in the picturesque little town of La Center, Washington, only fourteen miles away. It was on a cul-de-sac nestled on a hill surrounded by tall evergreen trees, overlooking the beautiful Lewis River Valley. It also had a magnificent view of Mount Hood, the Three Sisters (Mount Rainier, Mount Adams, and Mount St. Helens) and farther away, Mount Jefferson. The move allowed Jane to retire, and Brent relocated with us.

We found a church, Mountain View Christian Center, that we believed God had led us to. It was a large complex that housed not only a sanctuary that could seat five hundred but also offices, rooms for classes, and a large kitchen. A two-story addition had a gymnasium and classrooms for a school with about two hundred children from kindergarten through sixth grade. The facility was located in the country on twenty acres of grassland and, as the name implied, had a beautiful view of the Cascade mountains. It was a beautiful, serene setting.

Sure enough, a phone call to Richard Funk who lived in Tacoma, only ninety miles away, confirmed our feelings. I called him to let him know what had transpired regarding the position I had accepted and the home we had purchased in La Center. He was very interested, as he knew the area, and told me he thought we had done well. He was more interested to see if we had found a church to attend. When I told him about our decision with Mountain View Christian Center, he was over-joyed and began to weep and laugh at the same time.

"Buddy," Richard said, "we've been praying you would find that church, but we didn't want to say anything, for we wanted you to be led by God to go there. We know the pastor well because he was our two kids' youth pastor in Tacoma. He's been at that church now for about six or seven years and is a true man of God." We were so happy with our decision to move to the Northwest and felt it was an answer to prayer.

Shortly after we moved there, the twenty-year-old girl that I had met at Bonded Motors called. "Buddy, we're gonna get married," she said. "I'd like you to walk me down the aisle." That caused my breath to catch.

"My God, it would be an honor," I said.

"Will you do it?" she asked.

"I would be honored, but you have an uncle who means more to you than anybody. I think it would be perfect if he walked you down the aisle."

She started crying. "I knew you would say that, but I was praying that you wouldn't."

"You can stop right there," I said. "Janie and I will be there. We'll be sitting on your side as kinfolk."

When she came down the aisle for her wedding, she was beautiful. Her groom was a good-looking guy too. It was a great wedding, exactly what she deserved. I have prayed for her over the years, and from what I've heard, she's still doing well. They had a couple of kids, and she became a businesswoman. I'm thankful that God gave me an opportunity to influence someone for the good for a change.

My job in Portland was going well. Jane was elated with the home we had purchased, and when I went out of town on sales calls, she went with me. These trips covered the states of Oregon, Idaho, and Montana, so we were basically on an extended vacation.

Then came the horrible day of the attack on America on September 11, 2001. Things began to change over which I had no control. Business slowed down across the Northwest, and my salary took a hit. Jane went back to work, so things worked out financially, but we were not as free to travel.

During Christmas 2001, we decided not to go to California to be with our family but instead to stay at home and have our own Christmas. This did not sit well with our daughters and their families. Our daughters were quite vociferous when showing displeasure with our decision, but we reiterated that we were not coming. They did not give up easily, however. When the phone rang about an hour after our announcement, it was our three-year-old granddaughter. "Gampa, can you pease come to my house for Christmas? Pease?" That did it; we were going to California.

On Christmas Eve morning, we left La Center at 2:30 a.m., planning to be in Chino at about 6:00 that evening, but "the best laid plans of mice and men often go awry." Our plans did exactly that because our brand-new car's power steering belt broke in Lodi, California, and as the song goes, "We Are Stuck in Lodi Again." Unfortunately, on Christmas Eve there was nothing open, so we got a motel and planned to get a rental the next morning. We would leave our car in Lodi to get repaired and pick it up on the return trip.

On Christmas morning, I found out that the nearest rental car available was at the Sacramento Airport, some fifty miles away. Not to be deterred, I would get a taxi. But no taxis were available on Christmas morning. On a bulletin board at the motel, I spotted a handwritten card that had the word "taxi" on it with a phone number. I called the number, but I was not comforted by the voice on the other end of the line.

"What the hell do you want?" the person asked.

"A cab," I replied, stunned and rather sheepish.

"Do you have cash?"

"Yes sir," I replied, then told him where I was.

I went to our room and told Jane about the situation. "You have to pray, for this doesn't sound too promising," I said.

When the guy showed up, it was even worse than I expected. The checkered black-and-white car was about ten years old with the word "taxi" handwritten on the side. And when I got in, things hit rock bottom. The guy was unshaven, his eyes were bloodshot, and his breath reeked of alcohol. But our granddaughter was waiting, so away we went.

We had just gotten on the highway when the car started backfiring, stalling, and nearly dying. The driver would curse, then away we would go. I prayed for God to do something because I was so uncomfortable. What God did was nothing short of miraculous. The driver looked over at me and said, "I know you're a Bible thumper, dying to preach to me, but I don't want to hear it, so don't even start."

When I replied, it was hard to believe it was me. "Man, I'm not wanting to preach to you, but I am praying we get to the airport. I have a little granddaughter who wants to see her grandma and me. So, if you could just shut up and drive. I'll pay you, and you'll never see me again. But I feel for you because I've been where you are. There ain't no time lonelier than Christmas. I was homeless for a time, found out my mom died, and I didn't get to see her, but I know I will soon. On the other hand, I now have a wife who loves me."

It got quiet. After a few moments, he spoke. "How were you able to get off the streets?" That opened the door, and I proceeded to tell him how God had miraculously lifted me off the streets. I explained that God is no respecter of persons; what He had done for me, He could do for anyone. When I stopped talking, I looked over at the driver and saw tears rolling down his unshaven face. *Now is the time to let him know about Jesus,* I thought, but I couldn't speak, so we just drove in silence apart from the car sputtering and backfiring.

When we made it to the airport, I pulled out my money, but he pushed it away. "Sir, I don't know what just happened, but when you called, I was in dark despair. I was sure I would take my own life because I had lost everything—my home, my wife, and my kids. I haven't seen or talked to my mother for over six months. But when I get back, I'm going to change everything. I just pray they'll forgive me."

"Sir, I know that God has forgiven you, and I believe He will work strongly in your family, for He loves you, and He loves families."

We got out of the car, and the next thing I knew we were hugging and crying, not caring who was watching. Then I handed him more money than the meter showed and told him I had just had the best Christmas ever.

"Sir, because God put you in my life, I will see the rest of the day, and I will see my mother," he said. God's ways are higher than our ways.

The morning of Monday, March 7, 2002, was bitterly cold with freezing rain falling, but I had to get to the post office because I had a certified letter that needed to be picked up right away. At the post office, I saw a few friends already in line, so we chatted about the weather and why we were there on such an unpleasant day.

When my turn came, I realized the certified letter was from Brownwood Medicine Center in Texas, a place unfamiliar to me, but since it was addressed to me, I opened it. When I saw the heading, every emotion inside me exploded. I could hardly breathe. It was from my half-brother, Dr. Jim Mercer, whom I had not had any contact with for thirty-seven years. The first sentence said, "I can't divulge how I obtained your address, but I do believe it was arranged by God." As I unfolded the letter, I saw a picture that included Jim, his wife, their two kids, and an older lady whom I didn't recognize at first. Then it dawned on me. It was my mother, and apparently, she was alive.

That made no sense. I was certain my mother had passed

away in 1977 from a heart attack. I thought someone was playing a horrible joke on me. But then the letter explained that they had received notice of my death, and my mother figured she would never see me again until the next life. When I read those words, I lost it. Reality set in. My mama was alive.

When I regained my composure, I read the rest of the letter. It said my mom was in relatively good health, but she had gone through quadruple bypass surgery. My stepdad and other half-brother both died of cancer. Jim also wrote about his life and brought me up to date regarding his family. Then said he had not told our mother that he had located me. He didn't know if I wanted to be in contact with them. If not, he said I should just let him know, and he would never contact me again.

I drove to Mountain View Christian Center to see our pastor. I needed help. When I got to the church, the pastor's secretary took one look at me and said, "Buddy, are you okay? You look as though you have seen a ghost."

"I think you hit the nail on the head," I replied, smiling.

She took me to the pastor's office, where he greeted me warmly. Without a word, I dropped the letter and the picture on his desk. He started reading the letter and then stopped, tears filling his eyes as he shook his head. "Buddy, this is huge. God has given you a miracle." The secretary stuck her head in to see if we were okay, so I handed her the letter. When she read it, she started crying too.

"Praise God," she said.

We prayed, thanking God for his goodness and mercy. Then I went home to wait for Jane.

When she arrived, I handed the letter and picture to her and then waited for her response. She read the letter and then stared at the picture for a few moments. Then she leaped to her feet and danced across the living room, crying and shouting, "Hallelujah!"

With her encouragement, I wrote back to Jim, letting him know everything that had transpired with my life. I also included a picture of my family. I concluded the letter by telling him that if he wished to continue what God had put together, he should call me the following Wednesday evening.

Jim did just that. The conversation felt stunted at first, but then Jim started shouting. "I have a nephew, nieces, and a sister-in-law, and my brother is alive again!"

The following Sunday, our phone rang, and Jim asked me to hang on a minute, then I heard, "Is this Buddy, my son?"

"Yes, ma'am," I replied. "Mom, we're going to buy you an airline ticket, so you can fly up and spend some time here with us. We want to catch up on everything, and you can see the beauty of the Pacific Northwest."

"Well, no, I don't think you need to do that," she replied.

"I don't think you understand!" I replied. "We're going to fly you up here, so we can spend some time together."

"Don't argue with your mother!" she said in a voice that only mothers can project. Instantly, I felt like I was six years old again.

"Yes, mama," I replied. Boy, it's so true; a mother is always your mother, no matter what.

Later, I learned that she had some health problems that made her feel uncomfortable flying. So, Jane and I flew to San Antonio, Texas, the following weekend. We rented a car and drove to Bryan, Texas, where my cousin Beth Van Cleave and her husband Horace, also known as Buddy, lived. They welcomed us to spend the night with them, bringing us up to speed on everything that had occurred in the family since I left. We didn't stop talking until nearly 2:00 a.m.

The next morning, we drove to Brownwood, Texas, where I was reunited with Jim and his wife, Carolyn, whom I remembered from my days in Eldorado. After a brief visit, we drove to Eldorado. Jim and I traveled together, so he could inform me about the events that occurred while I was away.

When we pulled into my mom's driveway, I spotted her standing on the back steps. It became very emotional, a true Kodak moment, with everyone laughing and crying. My mom held out her arms as I approached. "Oh, my son!"

"Mama!" I replied, overcome with emotion. Then, without warning, she slapped me.

"Boy, I have waited nearly forty years for that. Now give me a hug." Once again, she proved a mother is always a mother. She gave me a huge hug, then she grabbed Jane and did the same.

For the next four days, my mom and Jane were inseparable. I had brought along two VHS tapes, one featuring Channel Nine's news story on Bonded Motors' success, and another of our twenty-fifth wedding vow renewal. It surprised me that Mom was more enthralled with the renewal of our vows than she was with the other. She watched it every day we were there.

That Christmas, we couldn't go to Texas, but something unexpected happened that amazed me. We sent Mom a nice gift that Jane had picked out early to make sure she received it for Christmas. We called to make sure she got it, then agreed to talk on Christmas Day. On the Saturday before Christmas while working at home at around 4:00 p.m., I felt compelled to send my mother another gift, though it seemed illogical. We had already sent her a gift, and it was already 6:00 p.m. in Texas. Since the next day was Christmas Eve, there was no way to make it happen. But the prompting got stronger, so I started making phone calls. The only store still open was Hickory Farms, which again made no sense, but I thought, *Okay, no problem.* They were located in Abilene, Texas, which was near my brother's home in Brownwood, so I hoped something good would happen.

When the lady answered the phone, she told me that I had reached the Hickory Farms in San Angelo, Texas, which is only forty miles from Eldorado where my mother lived. I told the lady about my dilemma. She was very nice, but she said they were closing and would not be open again until the Tuesday after Christmas, which proved what I was expecting was true. Just then, another lady came on the phone.

"What seems to be your problem, cowboy?" she asked in a jovial voice. I was surprised and told her not to worry; everything was okay. She laughed. "Let me be the judge of that. Now, what do you need?" So, I told her how my mother and I had been separated but eventually reunited by chance. I also shared how I had been prompted to try to send another gift. I paused, waiting for her response. To my surprise, I heard her crying. "Give me your phone number, and don't you dare leave your house," she said once she regained her composure.

About twenty minutes later, my phone rang. "Okay I found a couple of Christmas cards your mama will love, so give me her phone number and your credit card number, and she'll be taken care of," she said.

Afterward, I told Jane what had transpired. It was all so

strange, but I felt peace come over me, and that night I slept well.

The next morning when the phone rang, Jane answered it. I could tell it was my mother. Jane became very emotional, then she handed me the phone and told me to talk to my mother, who was also very emotional. When I finally got my mother calmed down, she said, "Buddy, I just got the most wonderful gift. The pretty lady that delivered it and her beautiful little girl were precious."

"Hickory Farms isn't that great," I replied, "but it was the best I could do."

"Boy," she shot back, "it wasn't just the Hickory Farms but a beautiful glass angel and a five-pound box of See's Candy." I was stunned beyond belief. I told her I loved her and wished her a Merry Christmas. Then I hung up, pondering what I had just heard. I realized the lady had driven forty miles to get the gifts to my mom. As Paul Harvey the newscaster would say, "And now for the rest of the story!"

Later, my phone rang again. It was the lady from Hickory Farms. "You just listen because I'm an emotional wreck," she said. "I want to share with you my own story, while I can. My name is Sarah Thompson. I remember you and your family from high school. Thank you for being obedient to the prompting that had to come from God because it has melted my cold heart. My fiancé was killed in an oilfield accident in September. We buried him in the Eldorado cemetery, and I turned my back on God and my parents. I had even considered suicide. Since you shared your story with me, I have taken my little six-year-old daughter to the cemetery, so she could put flowers on her father's grave and tell him how much she misses him. I also called my parents to let them know that I'm coming home for Christmas. She wished me a Merry Christmas and then hung up, leaving me to my own emotions.

My mom was seventy-eight at the time. She regained her health and finally came to our place for a visit. Later that year, Jane and I, Jim and his wife, and their married kids all met in Ontario, California, where my mother got to meet my kids and their families. We had four wonderful years with my mom before the Lord called her home.

As for how Jim made the initial connection, all I can do is report what happened. You decide why.

In January 2002, my mother went before the church in Eldorado, Texas, where I attended as a child. She told the congregation that she had a son who had been killed in an oilfield accident in the Gulf of Mexico. She said his body was never found, but God told her that her son was alive. She asked the church to pray that if her boy were alive, God would bring him home, so she could see him before she passed away.

In early February, Jane's sister, Judy, needed a doctor. She lived in Cisco, Texas, with her husband, Eddie. She was referred to Dr. Jim Mercer in Brownwood. When Judy and Eddie walked into the doctor's office, Eddie took one look at Jim and said, "You have a brother who lives on the left coast don't you?"

"I had a brother," Jim replied, "but he died many years ago."

"He ain't dead," Eddie said. "He's alive and kicking out on the west coast."

"Sir," Jim said, "I hope you understand that I would need proof of what you're telling me."

When Judy and Eddie went back to the doctor in late February, they brought the family genealogy with them. It showed Vida's maiden name of Prestage, her marriage to Glen Jacobs, their son, born Glen Roy Jacobs Jr., and the adoption papers showing Buddy Roy Mercer. They laid the papers on Jim's desk, who promptly passed out from shock. After he was revived, Eddie said, "That ought to be enough proof to get your attention." Pretty miraculous, right? If it can't be explained in the natural, then it appears to be supernatural. Thank you, Jesus!

During the time we were in Washington, we were heavily involved with Mountain View Christian Center. Jane and I sang in the choir, I taught Sunday School, Jane was involved with the lady's group, and we led a Tuesday night Bible study from our home. We had been accepted by the church members and enjoyed fellowshipping after church every Sunday evening at McDonalds, of all places.

Unfortunately, in churches there is always dissension of some kind, but Jane and I had stayed out of church politics. We believed we were guided by God's Word and our own beliefs. Things went wonderfully until February 2004 when it came time for deacon elections, and the pastor called to see if I would allow him to nominate me for a deacon position. The board thought my background in business and leadership would be an asset to the church. I asked to call him back later, so I could speak to Jane about it. We agreed that I was not a good fit. Also, the fact that I had been divorced put me at odds with the church's by-laws. I called the pastor and said that although I was honored to be considered, after praying over the situation, I had to decline. After I hung up, I laughed, telling Jane how much I appreciated her support because I wasn't good at dealing with political situations.

Later that evening, I received a call from one of the retiring deacons whom I respected deeply. After a bit of small talk, he told me that, during prayer, the Spirit had shared something that he was to tell me. He said there were things on the horizon that would be troubling for the church, and I should allow my name to stand for election and let the congregation decide with their votes. When I asked him to elaborate, he said, "Buddy, we have built a relationship based on mutual respect, trust, and a love for the Lord. I know in my spirit you were brought to this church for such a time as this, and I am asking you to trust me with my request because I have no firsthand knowledge of what's going to happen." I was humbled and could not turn him down, so I allowed my name to stand. The election was held the following Wednesday evening, and I was elected unanimously.

It didn't take long for the trouble to which he had alluded to manifest itself. One Sunday morning before church, the church pianist gave me a hug and told me that she was very happy that I had been elected. Then she handed me a sealed envelope. I handed it to Jane, thinking it was probably a letter of congratulations. Later when she opened it and read it, the look on her face told me the trouble had already started. The letter requested that we remove the pastor. The reasons given were not even worthy of a reprimand, never mind a removal. I put the letter away to wait for the first deacons' meeting, which was a month away. I figured her complaints would just disappear by then.

The following week I went to the church early one morning to visit with the maintenance man regarding some repairs for which he needed financial approval. I was on my way out when the bookkeeper, a lady in her fifties with whom I had spent some time regarding church finances, called me into her office. When she closed the door behind us, I protested. Males and females never met alone behind closed doors, but she was crying, and she told me to just sit down and listen because we had a problem that she could only trust me with.

After she regained her composure, she informed me that the principal who had been hired a few months back had come into her office under the pretense of going over the school's finances. He told her how nice she looked. Then he told her that she looked stressed and walked behind her chair. He began rubbing her shoulders, sliding his hands down onto her breasts. When she protested, he apologized and left. As she told me this, she was trembling and started crying again. "Buddy, I know you well and have ultimate trust in you, so I need to tell you about three other ladies who are teachers in the school who have similar if not more horrendous stories. Please listen, and when I'm done, we can talk." When she finished sharing her story, she appeared calmer, even smiling. "Welcome to the deacon board," she said.

I was stunned, but I knew this problem had to be addressed. I told her that we needed to bring this to the pastor. After all, he was the head of the church, and he needed to be apprised of the issue. She shook her head. Then she told me that the four women *had* gone to the pastor with their stories. He told them he would take it to the Lord in prayer, then did nothing.

I thought of every avenue we could go down, but each time she assured me that I was the only one they felt they could trust. It was obvious that this had to be dealt with immediately. If word of the abuse got out to the public, along with the news that the church had done nothing about it, all hell would break loose. I thanked her for making me aware of the issue, then asked if she and the other ladies could give me a couple of days to develop a plan.

I left her office in turmoil, not knowing which way to turn. All the people that I could think of had already been approached. Then a plan unfolded in my spirit. I went home and called the lady who had talked to me and asked her to get me a copy of the principal's resume. As soon as I had it, I called his previous employers, asking them to speak to me candidly and in confidence. The responses I got over the phone were beyond hideous. Each person I spoke to was afraid of the guy because when they terminated him, he threatened to sue them. By early afternoon, I realized no one from our deacon board or the school board had bothered to check on the guy's background. Either that or they didn't know how to do a background check.

It became clear that I had to call the man who had persuaded me to become a deacon. At that point, he was the only person I could trust. After I told him what had transpired, he said he would meet me at the church after 5:00 when everyone was gone. He would bring another former deacon that we could trust, so we could devise a plan.

Once we got to the church, we prayed for wisdom. Then we discussed what I had been told, concluding that we needed to call the deacons and ask them to meet at the church at 6:30. All we told them was that we had a problem that needed to be handled but we did not divulge any details.

To my surprise, they all showed up. When they saw the former deacons with me, the mood became very somber. After praying again for wisdom and swearing them to secrecy, I shared a portion of what I had heard about the recently hired principal because I wasn't sure if they could be trusted. My concern was confirmed when one of the men basically called me a liar. Even though he didn't know who had told me these things, he had decided that someone just wanted to get rid of the principal.

I asked the two men who were with me to step out into the hall for a quick conversation to determine our next move. At that point, it was clear that we needed to call the pastor, tell him what was taking place, and ask him to chair the meeting. When I shared the situation with him and asked him to come meet with us, he said that since I had knowledge of the problem, I should handle things on my own and then report back to him. I was stunned, and the two former deacons were nearly in tears. They had worked with him for years, and now he wasn't willing to do the things the head of the church should do.

Shortly afterward, with no explanation, the pastor submitted a letter of resignation. It was a horrible turn of events, as we had no assistant pastor. I formed a committee to begin a search for a pastor to fill that position. Amazingly, in short order we found two viable candidates.

When we stepped back into the room where the deacons were waiting, I told them I would call the principal to ask him to come down, so he could share his side, and we could get to the bottom of things. When he arrived, I told him that some accusations had been made regarding his character that we needed to clear up. During the investigation, he would take a paid week off, but he could tell no one. He readily agreed.

After he left, I told the deacons that the church depended on our integrity and swore them to silence regarding what had been revealed. They all agreed that it would remain in confidence, then we prayed for guidance, wisdom, and clarity.

The next morning, I went to the church school. When I entered the office, I was met with stony silence until the school secretary called me a bastard and stormed out, along with a couple of the teachers. Apparently, the principal had called several of the school employees as soon as he left the meeting with the deacons and said we were firing him. The deacon who had called me a liar also called some of his friends. The church and the school were in total disarray, so we closed the school for the remainder of the week, then arranged for a meeting with the church congregation the following Sunday afternoon to discuss the school's future. To my surprise, the congregation was in favor of closing the school, but I believed if we closed the school, evil would win. After I shared this belief, one of the teachers informed the congregation that she needed the job and that it was part of the church's ministries.

A retired deacon who had the respect of the entire congregation stood up and said he recommended that we keep the school open with the stipulation I take on the role of substitute principal to support the teachers and maintain control with the kids. While the congregation discussed the suggestion, he asked me to step out into the hall with him. I was astounded to find the principal's four accusers waiting outside for us. The ladies said they would help me run the school until we could hire a new principal. Their only stipulation was that no one could know they were the ones the principal had harassed.

When we returned to the meeting, the retired deacon called for prayer. Afterward, he asked that any who opposed his suggestion stand to vote in the negative. Everyone remained seated.

The next day, after a sleepless though prayerful night, I returned to the school. Since the pastor had resigned, it fell on me to meet with the students' parents to tell them what was going on. I told them that anyone who wanted to take their kids out of the school would be allowed to do so with a full refund. During the contentious meeting, I answered every question I could regarding the school's direction, when we would hire another principal, and so on. I refused to discuss anything regarding the principal except to say no concerns about children were involved.

"Anyone who wants to remove their children, please do so now," I said once I finished answering their questions. To my relief, no one did.

During this time of turmoil, the deacon board elected me to fill the pulpit, as I had a background in teaching God's Word. This was very uncomfortable for me, as the church was divided and on the verge of a split. I prayed for God to take control. To my relief, His Holy Spirit took charge, bringing peace and unity to most members. The troublemakers either repented or left.

By the power of God, the pastor search committee brought a young pastor in for a tryout a few Sundays later. In what can only be termed a move of the Holy Spirit, after the candidate spoke on Sunday morning, one of the members stood and asked that we vote to make him our pastor. The young candidate was elected by unanimous approval by a church that just a short time earlier had been on the verge of a split. Pastor Mark, his wife, and their two children were excited. They were given a tearful release from the church where he was currently pastoring, making him available to take the position two Sundays later.

In August 2008, we felt compelled to move back to California. Jane was missing the kids and grandkids, our financial situation was deteriorating, and we had gone through a serious church upheaval. One night during a Bible study, we had an indepth discussion with our dear friends, Dave and Ellen Kimmitt. We laid out our difficulties, as it was apparent we would be leaving the Northwest. It was a difficult evening, but the Bible says, "And ye shall know the truth, and the truth shall make you free." Sometime later, we were able to go back to the Northwest and visit them at their "cabin," a beautiful home with a great view of the Hood Canal.

Shortly thereafter, Jane called our baby girl to let her know we would be coming back to California. The following Sunday I went to church. I had prepared our letter of resignation for Pastor Mark, as I was serving as a deacon, and Jane was employed as the church bookkeeper. Instead, I put the letter in my pocket because Jane wasn't feeling well that day and wasn't with me. I thought I would wait until Monday. But during Pastor Mark's sermon, he noted that there was going to be a stirring in the church. "I really don't want to go into detail," he said, "but some who will be taking on more responsibilities here at the church, and others will be called to move far away to serve in ministries elsewhere."

Jane felt better later in the day, so we went to church that evening. Afterward, I handed Pastor Mark our letter. "Oh no!" he said. "It's not you guys who are going far away, is it?" He began to tear up, but he hugged us and said, "I'm sure it's God's will."

11

HOA JANITORIAL

WHEN WE GOT TO CALIFORNIA, the jobs we had been promised were no longer available. Because our finances were dwindling, we stayed with our kids as we looked for employment. Our son-in-law worked as a property manager. One day he asked if I would do some janitorial work at one of his properties. I had a good laugh because that was my first job when I got off the streets. In December 2008, in the middle of the Great Recession, I started doing janitorial work at a property in Chino. A little while later, I received a call from a property manager with another firm who wanted me to take care of a property for her. By March 2009, we were servicing a total of five properties, so we started HOA Janitorial as a sole proprietorship.

In April, I found a young lady who was familiar with the condominium/homeowner's association industry who wanted to help us grow our business on a commission basis, which was fine with me. By the middle of May, we were servicing eight properties. Jane and I were extremely happy because we were making enough money that we could catch up on things. Then the young woman who had helped us delivered surprising news. "Buddy, you don't need me anymore, so I'll be leaving. The properties you have picked up have not been through my efforts. It's almost miraculous because we're in the middle of a recession. Other janitorial companies are closing or going broke, and you're growing."

By the middle of 2010, we were servicing nineteen properties. Since I was doing all the physical labor by myself and Jane was doing the bookkeeping, we had little to no overhead, so our finances were improving greatly. This allowed us to move into a nice apartment complex.

We were attending church in La Habra, where the pastor was a young man who had sung at our twenty-fifth wedding vow renewal. One Sunday, we met Jack and Roberta Pierce, who from all appearances were doing well financially. On a Sunday night after church, they asked if we wanted to go to Denny's to get a bite to eat. As we talked, I let them know we were doing well. Even though we had struggled because of the recession, God was providing a way. They told us how they had an employment agency that used to have multiple offices but which was now down to just one office, and they were fighting to survive. By the time we left Denny's at about midnight, we knew God had put us together to weather the storm. We grew to love them dearly. On the way home, Jane and I talked about what had just transpired, and then it hit me. God had kept us in great health throughout all our troubles. If I had gotten sick or injured or the car broke down, we would have been in serious trouble. So, we praised God right there in the car.

Through a divine inclination, God had moved us back to

Living Waters, where Pastor Duke was still leading the church. At a Sunday evening service in August 2014, he announced that he was taking a leap of faith by opening a home where men could live to get their lives together whether they were just out of prison, bound by drugs or alcohol, or just needed help. I knew HOA Janitorial could be a vehicle for him to use and that it could also be a benefit to us. After service, I told Pastor Duke what I was thinking.

The following week, he and I met to work out plans to go forward with the home. By next Monday, men from the home were doing work for HOA Janitorial, which another prayer answered.

Our business continued to grow. In 2017, it became evident that we needed dependable help. It was becoming more than I could handle and still maintain the quality of service that I had developed. One Sunday after church, a guy came up to me and introduced himself as Phil, saying he needed a job. For some reason, his words struck me wrong. "Get in line," I said, then I got in my car and drove away.

The next week I had another meeting with Pastor Duke regarding the men's home. During the conversation, he mentioned the guy who had approached me. Phil was living near the church, and every morning, rain or shine, he rode a bicycle some six or seven miles to work. Pastor Duke convinced me that it might be worth my time to talk to him. The following Sunday, I told Phil that I would give him an opportunity, but it would only be part time, to which he readily agreed. All he wanted was a chance to prove himself. I told him to be ready the next morning when I would pick him up and give him the opportunity he requested.

The next morning, Phil was ready and waiting, as promised. We had about an hour's drive to the property. As we talked, it became apparent to me that Phil's background was eerily similar to mine, right down to being homeless and on the streets. He had no car and very little money. By the time the day was done, I was convinced God had given me a man who deserved an opportunity. I talked to Jane who said that we needed to pray about the situation. After we sought God's guidance, Jane was adamant that we give him a chance. We had an extra car that he could use, and we purchased the equipment he would need to provide janitorial service to some of our properties. We gave him money for gas and some on-the-job training, and in no time at all, he was up and running. Things looked great because Phil had the job he wanted, and I was able to do my work and manage the company.

Phil did well until he developed a highly contagious disease called MRSA, which put him in the hospital and prevented him from returning to work for a month or so. We were heartbroken, as everything was going so well. Now he was in critical condition, no one was available to oversee his properties. Then I was reminded that before Phil started, I was doing all the work myself. Since it would only be for a month or so, I could handle it on my own. That would also allow me to continue to pay him his regular wage.

When he regained his health, he returned to work. After a while, he was able to buy his own vehicle and move into an apartment. He even repaid us for the equipment we had purchased for him, and he moved into an apartment. He hasn't looked back.

Today, Phil is married and driving a new truck. He attends

church regularly and even heads up a street ministry. He makes over six figures annually with his own company. With HOA Janitorial Consultants Inc., God allowed us to add three more independent contractors. They now have their own janitorial businesses and are making good money. God put these men together with us. They are church attenders who pay their tithes and are blessed in many ways. We were blessed with these men who provided great service for our company and allowed Jane and I to move into semi-retirement.

In June 2018, I developed a weakness in my legs and did a face plant one morning while jogging. I went to my family doctor about it. He's a great doctor, but he has a grumpy demeanor. When he entered the examination room, he took one look at my bloodwork and said, "What the hell?" Then he looked at me and said, "Get the hell out of my office, and go straight to the rheumatologist next door. You're in trouble."

When I entered the rheumatologist's clinic, the doctor had been notified and was waiting for me. After looking at my bloodwork and doing an examination, he said, "You have elevated inflammation, and we need to put you on steroids immediately. I'll be ordering a couple of tests to see what is causing this inflammation, so we can see what we're dealing with." I took the steroids as directed, and the next day, I was well enough that I could do my business as usual, but I was still weaker than normal.

Over the subsequent weeks, I endured blood tests and X-rays, but the results showed nothing. Then they ordered an MRI of my lungs. After the doctor got the results, he asked me to come to his office ASAP. When Jane and I got to the clinic, they asked Jane to go to the waiting room while the doctor checked me out. He started using medical terms I didn't understand, so I told him to use English.

"It isn't pretty," he said. "I believe you may have cancer, but I need the results of some other tests that I've ordered, and they won't be available for a few days."

"Well, what did the doctor say?" Jane asked when I returned to the waiting room.

"He thinks I may have cancer," I replied, "but he needs the results of the other tests to confirm it."

Jane stared at me for a few moments. "The Holy Spirit said you don't have cancer," she said, "so let's go to lunch."

Not only did we go to lunch, but we also packed the car and took a road trip. We started in Yosemite National Park, then went to the old mining ghost town of Bodie. After we spent a day or so in Mammoth, it dawned on me that I had better check with the doctor. I made an appointment for the next day.

When I got to the clinic, I sensed a problem because everyone was being way too nice. I was taken to the room to wait for the doctor, which normally took quite a while. To my surprise, the door opened, and in walked a young, attractive, but very apprehensive woman. She introduced herself as the doctor's assistant. "I'm so sorry," she said. "You don't have cancer." I couldn't help laughing as I replied.

"It's okay. I know you're trying to say I don't have cancer, and you're sorry I was misdiagnosed. But where's the doctor?" Before she could answer I added, "I'm sorry you had to be the one to tell me, but if we could set this aside, that would be great. What about my inflammation problem?"

"Thank you for your kindness and understanding," she replied. "You still have the inflammation issue, but it's much better, so I'll give you a prescription for a lower dosage of the steroids."

I thought about that for a moment. "What happens if I choose not to take the steroids?"

"Oh, Mr. Mercer, don't do that, or you'll get worse," she said.

I smiled. "Okay. Give me the prescription, and I'll get out of here."

When I got to my car, I felt that I didn't need the prescription. God would take care of the inflammation, just like he had apparently taken care of the cancer. So, I took the prescription home, put it in my desk drawer, and to this date, I haven't had any more inflammation problems, nor have I had cancer.

12

LIFE EXCEEDS OUR EXPECTATIONS

SOME YEARS BEFORE, Jane and I enjoyed a chuckwagon dinner in Jackson Hole, Wyoming. After checking around, we found one in Red River, New Mexico. So, in July 2019, we decided to drive the 900 or so miles, stopping along the way at the Native American trading stores. We spent the night in Gallup, New Mexico, in Navajo country. The next day after breakfast and some shopping for Native American souvenirs, we drove straight through, stopping only in Taos, New Mexico, for some delicious Native American tacos. We arrived in Red River in the early afternoon, allowing time for some sightseeing. It is a beautiful area, loaded with history.

The chuckwagon dinner met and exceeded our expectations. The steaks and baked potatoes, cowboy red beans, and fluffy biscuits were delicious, and the big cinnamon rolls with sweet tea topped the meal off beautifully. The family-type entertainment was outstanding. They began with a moment of prayer, the Pledge of Allegiance, then all sorts of music on fiddles, washboards, guitars, banjos, piano, and harmonicas. We were in an area called Bobcat Pass, which is approximately ten thousand feet above sea level. The stars twinkling like millions of diamonds in the black New Mexico sky made the evening marvelous and magical. The next morning, we left Red River with a twinge of sadness but also looked forward to sleeping at home in our own bed.

For Christmas 2019, our youngest daughter, Stacey, invited us to go with her to Flagstaff, Arizona, where she had access to a beautiful time share. We planned to go to the Grand Canyon and then take her to the Blazing M Ranch, so she could experience a chuckwagon dinner. Once again, "The best laid plans of mice and men often go awry." Boy was that an understatement. We were late getting to Flagstaff, where the weather had turned extremely cold. Ice began forming on the roads, which made travel dangerous, so we missed our chuckwagon dinner. From Flagstaff, driving to Cottonwood would take an hour under normal driving conditions, but with the roads icing up, it would take significantly longer. Fortunately, the people at the Blazing M Ranch were gracious and allowed us to save our reservation for a later date.

The next morning dawned cloudy and cold, but the roads were okay for travel. We drove about one hundred miles to Meteor City where a meteor had crashed to Earth many years ago, creating a huge crater. It was quite an experience. We spent the rest of the day in the Painted Desert. It was stunning.

When we got back to the hotel, we were advised that a snowstorm was on the way, and we should put chains on our tires, which we did. The next morning it proved to be a prudent move, as snow was covering everything, and we had planned to go to the Grand Canyon for the day. It was a little concerning, but we decided to head out to Williams, where we would catch the train for the Grand Canyon. It was a beautiful drive, as the sun had broken through, and the freeway was mostly clear. Nevertheless, the chains were a blessing.

Once we got to Williams, we boarded the train for the Grand Canyon. Lo and behold, snow started falling. By the time we arrived at our destination, it was snowing so heavily we could hardly see into the canyon. Despite the snow, or more correctly, *because* of the snow, it was an amazing experience that few people will ever see.

The train ride back was in the dark. Unfortunately, when we got to our car in Williams, it was evident that we were facing a dangerous drive to the hotel in Flagstaff. Everything was covered with snow, and it continued to snow so heavily it was nearly impossible to drive. I don't know when I prayed more intensely for traveling mercies, which God gave us, and we made it safely, but a drive that took only thirty minutes under normal conditions took over two hours.

The next morning, we packed up, as it was Christmas Day, and our family was expecting us back home in the evening. The chains were still necessary as we left Flagstaff, but as we reached the lower elevation, the freeway was clear enough that I felt confident we could remove the chains to drive at a more normal speed. I pulled to the side, expecting to simply unhook the chains and drive off of them, as the instructions showed. However, something went wrong, and the chain on the right front wheel wrapped itself around the frame, making it impossible to drive. While I tried to loosen the chain, to no avail, Jane prayed for a miracle. It was Christmas Day, and nothing was open. Even AAA was of no help. It looked like we were not going to be home for Christmas dinner.

Suddenly, Stacey took off walking down the side of the road by herself. This concerned me, but she was clearly a girl on a mission. I was amazed when, about twenty minutes later, a pickup pulled up with Stacey in the passenger seat. A man got out, said good morning, and in ten minutes, had the chain off. When I offered him money, he smiled and said, "Miracles still happen. I just happened to be in the right spot when your daughter walked up and explained your predicament. I thank God that He put me in a spot where He could use me to help on this special day. Merry Christmas." Stacey explained that she had sensed that God would make a way if she took the first steps. Ain't God good? We made it home for a fantastic Christmas dinner with our family.

At the beginning of January 2020, it appeared that we were going to have a good year. Our janitorial company was doing very well. Jane and I seemed to be in good health and were fairly active for people in our seventies. So, we scheduled a cruise on the Mexican Riviera with our friends, Jack and Roberta, which we thoroughly enjoyed. When we got home, we discussed taking an Alaskan cruise later in the year and possibly even a trip to Ireland.

One morning, on the spur of the moment, we decided to drive to Palm Springs to have lunch and then browse the antique shops and thrift stores. When we got there, we decided to eat lunch first, so we could spend the afternoon shopping without interruption, which pleased Jane. Curiously, we bypassed our favorite restaurant and wound up at an open-air Mexican restaurant on the main street. It was out of place among the more elite restaurants. After we were seated and the lady came out to take our order, I asked if the restaurant was new to Palm Springs. She laughed and said, "We're new to *uptown* Palm Springs. As you can tell, we don't fit in with the other upscale eateries around here, but we're doing quite well. I believe you'll enjoy our style of food."

When the waitress brought our food, we bowed our heads and gave thanks for our many blessings. Little did I realize it, but the lady who had seated us was watching. As soon as we finished eating, she came to our table and asked how we enjoyed our food, then inquired about what brought us to Palm Springs. Jane told her about the shopping opportunities. It turned out she owned the restaurant and enjoyed meeting her customers. It was amazing how the conversation took off from there. The next thing I knew, I was sharing a bit of my story. When I got to the part about my mother and I being separated for years, tears streamed down the lady's face.

"We have a son whom we have not seen nor heard from for over six months," she said. "We have had an investigator try to find out where he is, but our son has just disappeared. I'm at my wits' end."

Our hearts broke for the lady, and we asked if we could pray for her, reminding her what God had done for my mom and me. "Please do," she said, so right there on the main street of Palm Springs, we had a prayer meeting.

About six weeks later, we returned to Palm Springs for the day. When it was lunchtime, we headed for our favorite restaurant but were instead prompted to return to the Mexican restaurant, even though it was not what we had really wanted to eat.

After we were seated, we both admitted to being somewhat relieved that the owner of the restaurant was not there, for we didn't know what had happened to her and her son. We enjoyed our lunch: the weather was gorgeous, the mariachi band was good, and the food was delicious.

Just then, the owner appeared out of nowhere and came over to our table. "You're the people who prayed for me and my son who was missing, aren't you?" she said. Then she blew us away when she asked if we would like to meet her son. She revealed that he had come home shortly after we prayed for them. He came over and hugged us, thanking us for our prayers. Even though he didn't believe in God when we prayed, he felt something tugging at his spirit, telling him to go home. God works in mysterious ways.

Our plans and dreams for travel came to a screeching halt in March of 2020, when the onset of COVID-19 made the whole world, as we knew it, stop. California was locked down, and fear gripped everyone. Fortunately for us, janitorial services were deemed essential services, so our guys could continue to work. They even made extra money because I found a disinfectant that we could use that was designed to kill the virus. Jane and I continued to live as normally as possible, but we were limited, as most places of entertainment were closed.

During the beginning of the pandemic, we went to a great Mediterranean restaurant and ordered our favorite meal. We were waiting to be served when Jane said, "I feel horrible. I'm getting chilled, and I have a headache." We thought she had the flu, so we headed home, taking our food with us.

The next morning, she felt somewhat better, but I called the doctor who requested that we come to an outdoor tent behind his office to get tested for COVID. When we arrived, we were met by a nurse who took blood samples. After a fifteen-minute wait, we were told our tests were negative, and we should go home, rest, drink plenty of fluids, and take Tylenol.

At about 4:00 p.m., things took a severe turn for the worse. Jane had developed a fever to go along with her other symptoms, and I was having a terrible time breathing. I called the doctor again. He told us to get to his outdoor office immediately. Another test confirmed we had COVID. He gave us a shot and some medicine.

We went back home, feeling somewhat better and relieved we were not being hospitalized. We began to pray and trust God for our healing. Jane recovered slowly and by the middle of the following week, she felt well enough to be up and around. I, on the other hand, was still having a hard time breathing. Our doctor came to our home and put me on a steroid regimen, which I took for the next six weeks because I didn't want to end up in the hospital. I had heard horror stories of elderly people going to the hospital where they were put on ventilators, and they stayed until they died.

As I began to improve, to the doctor's surprise, I started feeling well enough that Jane and I could go for walks. I quit taking the steroids and continued to improve.

On the first of September 2020, I woke up and had a terrible time breathing, so I went to the emergency room. I was diagnosed with pneumonia and was admitted to the hospital. The next day a young guy came into my room and introduced himself as Dr. Chan, a cardiologist. This confused me because I had been diagnosed with pneumonia, not a heart issue. He explained that the COVID virus had caused my heart to go into atrial fibrillation, also known as A-fib. This meant the upper chambers of my heart were beating irregularly and were out of sync with the lower chambers. He explained that he could give me medicine, which could take care of the problem. He also told me that he could perform a process which would shock my heart back into its regular rhythm. That sounded good to me, so that afternoon the procedure was performed. The next day, I was released with some medicine for pneumonia.

I began my morning gym routine again, and Jane walked with me in the afternoon, so we both got exercise to help us regain our health. It wasn't long before we started feeling really good, and I was back to a strenuous exercise schedule at the gym: thirty minutes on the treadmill, a weightlifting routine, and four two-minute planks, which are extremely demanding physically. Doing these exercises with no ill effects at seventy-seven years of age was pretty good.

In October 2020, while shopping one day, Jane felt awful and wanted to go home. This concerned me because she really enjoys shopping. Instead of going home, I took her to the emergency room. Because of the new pandemic protocols, I wasn't allowed to go in, so I went home and tried to stay busy. Our three kids kept me company on the phone, but as the day dragged on, I was more convinced that Jane had COVID again. At 11:30 that night, she called and confirmed my worst fears.

The next day, our daughter Dena, who was an RN at another hospital, called and told me to get to the hospital. She wanted me to get checked for COVID right away due to my previous heart problem. This did not sit well with me because I knew in my spirit that if I went, they would want to admit me.

But she was adamant, and she is quite strong willed, to put it nicely. I called Jane, and she agreed with Dena, so away I went.

When I got to emergency, they wheeled me past receiving and started running tests. I explained that I felt great and was just there for a checkup. I resolved not making a big deal and was trying to make that clear to the ER staff. The on-call cardiologist came in and in a very brusque manner told me to "knock it off," as they needed to run tests. Sure enough, they ran the tests and told me they wanted to keep me overnight. They said I had the flu and a slight case of pneumonia but no COVID. I gave up the fight and went along with their program. Jane and I spent the night in the same hospital, but we weren't allowed to see each other.

The next day, they told me that my heart had kicked back into A-fib, and I was retaining fluid, so they started me on something to remove the fluid. At that point, an ominous feeling overtook me. I called Jane, who was up on the COVID floor. "Move over," I said. "I bet I'll wind up on the COVID floor with you."

"I'll be here waiting for you," she joked back.

That afternoon a nurse came in and wanted to test me for COVID. She was insistent that it was a different test. "Is this the one where you go up the nostril to the brain and then turn left?" She just smiled and showed me the swab.

At about midnight, a guy came into the room, put my personal effects on my bed, then rolled me out of the room. He told me he was taking me to a better room with a more modern television. "Nope," I replied. "You're taking me to the COVID ward."

The next couple of days were very difficult. I was in room

317, and Jane was in 316. We were so close, but we might as well have been a world away because we still couldn't see each other, not even for a minute. We were on the phone constantly with each other, though, praying that God would heal us.

On the fourth day, Jane called. She was so excited because they had cleared her to go home. They could no longer find a trace of COVID in her. "Thank you, Jesus."

I was still at San Antonio hospital that evening when the head doctor appeared at my door and asked if I was up for a visitor. Without waiting for my response, he walked in, sat down and started talking about football. This puzzled me. After a conversation about football and my favorite sport, NASCAR, I said, "Okay, Doc. I know you're not here to talk about sports. You're checking for symptoms of COVID, aren't you?"

He chuckled. "You're correct. Your test showed you had COVID when we brought you up here, but all the tests we 've taken since show you're clear of COVID." He stood up, shook his head and smiled, then walked out of my room.

The next day, my favorite nurse came in, smiling. "Buddy, get dressed," she said. "You're going home." She gave me a hug, which was a no-no.

"Thank you, Jesus," I said.

Once at home, we were on a fourteen-day quarantine and not supposed to leave the house, but after three days, we had to get out, at least for a drive. As soon as the fourteen days were up, I called the hospital and asked the HR lady if we could bring some goodie baskets for all the employees on the third floor. She said it would be great. We were overjoyed because these were precious people who were risking their lives, working in the COVID ward.

We wanted to just drive up, unload the baskets, and leave because we didn't want to make a big deal about it, but when I called back, the HR lady asked if it would be alright to have three or four people meet us, so they could take the baskets to the COVID ward, which sounded reasonable.

Upon arriving at the hospital, we were met by the HR lady and a couple of hospital officials, who greeted us warmly. Then they stepped back, and we heard people clapping. When we looked around to see what was happening, we saw about twenty people from the COVID floor coming out the door clapping, laughing, crying, and even doing little impromptu dances. When I started to protest, the female cardiologist who had been so brusque with me in the beginning, grabbed me by the arm with tears in her eyes and said, "Buddy, you don't understand. These people are highly emotional because not many people have left the COVID ward in as good of shape as you and your wife did. Many have left in body bags, so shut up and let them enjoy your miracle."

"Thank you, Jesus," I said.

By January 2021, businesses had begun to open up with mask restrictions, but fear still gripped the nation. After much prayer, Jane and I decided to live our lives trusting God, as He had brought us through the pandemic so far. The Bible tells us that faith is greater than fear, so we also trusted God with HOA Janitorial. Our business continued to thrive, and the guys who worked with us also trusted God and saw their money grow.

In June 2021, churches reopened, and we attended services with other members of the congregation; however, the church environment had changed. The messages were more about not wearing a mask because if you wore a mask you didn't have as much faith as you should. The Bible states, "Work out your own salvation with fear and trembling," which means it should not be dictated by the pastor's belief, so we started looking for another church. After several weeks of trying different churches, we could find nothing that met our needs, so stayed home and enjoyed worshiping with the television ministries, reading our Bibles, and praying with each other.

Later in the year, one of the guys who worked with us called and said his truck had been broken into. All that was taken was a set of keys to one homeowner's association, which made no sense at the time. I dreaded making the phone call to the property manager. When keys went missing, it often meant they had to rekey the entire property.

It turns out the property manager and our youngest daughter, Stacey, had been great friends growing up, even attending church together. After a brief conversation, I told her about the keys, and I was blown away by her response. "This is interesting, Buddy, because I just had new keys made for the property, and one of them must have been for you. Come to my office and pick up a set."

We continued to talk for a bit, and I asked her where she was attending church. She told me the name and address and said she thought we would really enjoy the service. She added that her pastor, Doug Hefley, was a great guy and a man of God who really loved people. I thanked her for her time. Later, we found out from Stacey that it was the same church she had attended for a time, and she agreed that Pastor Doug was one of the good ones.

On Friday, November 13, 2021, the day before our forty-seventh wedding anniversary, Jane got very ill. Back to the hospital we went, where they admitted her with a gall bladder that had been attacked by COVID. They said it had to come out, so she spent our anniversary in the hospital while I was home alone. The surgery to remove the gall bladder was scheduled for the following Monday.

On Sunday morning, I felt compelled to attend church, feeling odd being there without Jane. I decided to check out the church that had been recommended to me. The small congregation held services in an industrial complex with a large, dimly lit sanctuary. I walked in without saying a word to anyone and sat at the back. For some reason, I felt completely safe. My worries went away, and I felt like I was at home.

The service started with praise and worship. Then Pastor Doug preached about how God is a healing God, which I was in complete agreement with. He went on to say that God can heal cancer, arthritis, broken bones, and gall bladders. Then he stopped and smiled. "I have never heard of a gall bladder being healed, but God just spoke to me and said He would heal gall bladders."

Huh, that's weird, I thought.

He started speaking again and then paused. After a few moments, he said words that stunned me to my core. "God just spoke to me. I'm to tell someone here that your loved one who's in San Antonio hospital will be just fine and will be released early next week." I sat there frozen for a moment, trying to process what I had just heard. Then I bolted to the nearest door to get to my car and my cell phone, so I could call Jane. When she answered, I maintained my composure long enough to tell her what I had just heard. Then we both burst into tears. We spoke of how God had worked in our lives so many times and were sure everything would be fine.

After our conversation, I went back inside, wondering who told the pastor about our situation. I didn't know anyone at that church, so he must have learned it elsewhere. I wasn't sure about prophesying like I had just heard. My thoughts were interrupted by Pastor Doug.

"Sir," he said. I looked up and realized he was staring at me. "Do I know you?" he asked. "Have we ever met? Have I ever spoken to you?" I shook my head because I couldn't find my voice to speak. "Sir, God spoke to me, saying you are where He wants you, and the troubles from your previous church will be wiped from your memory, leaving you with pleasant memories."

The following Sunday, Jane was not completely well, but she was determined to attend the new church, so she could hear Pastor Doug and maybe talk to him after the service. After a time of praise and worship, Pastor Doug introduced Pastor Dan Sherstad, who has a ministry of his own but serves as an associate pastor. He had been on an evangelistic trip in Wisconsin and arrived home late the night before. This left us a little disappointed, as we had come to hear from Pastor Doug, but we settled in to hear what Pastor Dan would bring us.

It didn't take long for us to realize we were in for a blessing, as Pastor Dan was dynamic. He had our attention from the beginning, but just as he got going he stopped, then looked at me and said the same words Pastor Doug had spoken the previous Sunday. "Sir, you in the blue sweater. Do I know you? Have I spoken to you?" When I shook my head, he continued. "Sir, that lady sitting next to you must be your wife. God just told me to tell you that you are in the church where he wants you, and the heartaches from your previous church will be wiped away, leaving you with pleasant memories while you serve Him here."

Jane and I looked at each other in amazement. "I know we're where we're supposed to be," she whispered.

We started attending services there regularly, and as the old saying goes, "This just keeps getting gooder and gooder."

In December 2021, I had an appointment with Dr. Chan, the cardiologist, to check on my A-fib issue. "I think we ought to perform an angiogram to check for any blockages," he said. "It's a simple one-day procedure." I told him that I had done a treadmill test with another cardiologist and passed with flying colors. He was adamant, but he said it was my choice. Jane, who was in the room with me, gave me a look that conveyed her thoughts without a word. What was I to do but tell him to make the appointment?

Just after Christmas I checked in for the angiogram and immediately regretted my decision. They handed me a gown and told me to let them know when I was ready. Then the technicians hooked me up with all sorts of things.

"I thought this was a simple procedure," I said.

"You won't feel a thing," one of them replied in a cheery voice.

Dr. Chan entered the room, chatting with the technicians, then he came to me. "Good morning, Mr. Mercer," he said. Then he explained what was going to happen and had the technicians give me a light anesthetic, which put me in the twilight zone.

Shortly thereafter, or so it seemed, Dr. Chan asked how I

was feeling. To my amazement, I was cognizant enough to have a conversation with him. I felt a bit hazy, but my mind became very clear when he said, "Everything is just fine, but we found you have three arteries with blockage. One is seventy percent blocked, one eighty percent blocked, and, unfortunately, the one we call the 'widow maker' is ninety percent blocked. We can have a conversation in my office next week to figure out how we need to proceed."

"Dr. Chan," I replied, "we have to go with doctor-patient privilege here, but I'll be sure to tell my wife tomorrow. Then we'll come to your office." He laughed, patted me on the shoulder, then left me to my thoughts.

Jane came to pick me up soon after and asked me how it went. I started to tell her what I thought she ought to know, but she laughed and said that Dr. Chan had called her to make sure she got the facts straight, not my story. I guess patient-doctor confidentiality doesn't apply when it comes to spouses.

The next week, we went to Dr. Chans' office to discuss the options, which included putting in three stints or triple bypass surgery. That sounded like a radical unnecessary option.

After our initial conversation, Jane's cell phone rang. It was our daughter, Dena, the registered nurse. Dr. Chan greeted her by her first name, which meant they had already been talking. I was trapped, as the three of them instantly killed my idea of delaying any actions. All three were very negative regarding stints and the fact that they didn't last long, leaving triple bypass surgery as the best option. After our conversation, I realized it wasn't the surgery that concerned me but the rehabilitation period. I had heard some horror stories, but the three of them said I would be fine. Easy for them to say!

The next week, Jane and our daughter Stacey, and I had a Zoom appointment with the surgeon who would be doing the procedure. He had a great reputation and a good sense of humor. When we were all on the call he said, "Buddy, I'm the 'slice and dice guy' who will be doing the procedure. After a conversation with Dr. Chan, I believe you'll be able to come through the surgery with flying colors. We'll be doing a lot of tests in the meantime before you and I meet."

I felt completely at ease with the surgeon, especially after his "slice and dice" comment. Dena, who was terrific with the technical stuff, spent a few minutes speaking to the surgeon, using words that were completely foreign to me. When did she get so smart? We all agreed I would have the triple bypass surgery whenever the surgeon could arrange for an operating room. Operating rooms were in short supply due to the COVID pandemic.

During the second week of January 2022 we received a call from the surgeon's office to say they had an operating room available on January 15. The day before the procedure, Stacey came to be with Jane during the surgery. She would stay with us for as long as needed post-surgery. This gave me great comfort because she is very strong mentally and emotionally and not given to drama. The evening before, we sat and chatted, then prayed that God would be with me during the surgery and that He would guide the surgeon through the procedure.

The following morning, I arrived at the facility at 5:30 a.m. After completing the check-in process, I was transferred to a pre-operative bed to await the procedure. Soon after, a couple of guys came in, put my clothes bag on the bed, and wheeled me down the hall. They were overly friendly, making lighthearted comments that had nothing to do with me or about what was happening.

When they wheeled me into a regular hospital room, I knew there was something wrong. I asked what was going on, but they said they were just the transporters and that a nurse would fill me in momentarily. In the meantime, they suggested I relax and stay calm, as everything would be okay. But that just made me angry. I wanted immediate answers.

Shortly thereafter, a nurse came in, looking a little apprehensive. "Good morning, Mr. Mercer," she said. "There have been some complications, and your surgery has been postponed. Just rest, and the doctor will be in shortly to explain what's happening."

"If the surgery has been postponed, then I'm going to get dressed and go home, and the doctor can explain it to me over the phone," I said. That didn't sit well with her.

"Please calm down," she said. "You need to stay here so we can run some tests to help straighten everything out."

By then I had been there about three hours, so I called Jane to let her know that the surgery had been postponed, but I didn't know why. That upset her, but she said, "Hon, God is in control. It will be okay. We'll have answers soon."

After we hung up, I prayed. *Father, you are the God of order, so I know you'll bring peace out of this chaos.* As soon I said "amen," a song we sang at church ran through my mind, including the lyrics "What have I to fear, what have I to dread, leaning on the everlasting arms?"

A few minutes later, Dena called. "Dad, I'll have some answers shortly," she said. "Just stay in bed, and let them do the tests they need. I understand why you're upset, but they put off the surgery for your own good. Now behave yourself, and quit giving the nurse a hard time."

A short time later, the charge nurse came into my room. "We know that this has been a difficult situation for you," she said, "but I don't have an answer yet. I don't want to say anything more, but I want to assure you that you're not in any danger. You're basically fine. At about one o'clock, four specialists and the surgeon will come in to give you all the facts, so please bear with us."

I laughed. "Boy, that is comforting," I said, "but what can I do?"

Shortly after 1:00, four specialists and the surgeon came into my room. I was confused because they got another doctor on the phone and began to discuss my case, using a term I had never heard before. That went on for about thirty minutes. Once they disconnected the call, the surgeon finally addressed me. "Buddy, I'm just the 'slice and dice' guy. These doctors are the ones trying to figure out what has transpired. Never before have I had a call at 5:30 a.m. to tell me that I must not do a surgery. Your body is a curious puzzle. They have come to conclusions that will allow us to do the surgery in a couple of weeks after you see the specialists in their offices. I can tell you now that you have a rare autoimmune blood condition called cold agglutinin. It's not life threatening, but it could have caused problems during the operation. Now that we're aware of it, we can overcome the issue with no problems. We want you to stay overnight, though, so we can monitor some of the procedures."

Later that day, Dr. Chan stepped into my room. "We've experienced some things that we don't have complete explanations for yet," he said. "However, it was very fortunate that a nurse saw your report and recognized the blood issue. Had she not called the surgeon to stop the operation, there could have been serious problems."

"I understand the problems with my blood," I replied, "but there are also issues with my kidneys, thyroid, and other organs. My question is, why didn't these issues show up on the lab reports before 5:30 this morning? If the nurse hadn't checked the reports, I could have wound up dead."

Dr. Chan paused before replying. "I don't want to put it quite that way, but yes, it could have looked very bad on the surgeon's resume."

During the next couple of weeks, many tests were run, all of which came back negative, leaving the doctors puzzled. But I just thank Jesus that a nurse listened to the Holy Spirit and cared enough to check on something that was not technically her responsibility.

When I was finally cleared for surgery, in March it went off without a hitch. When the anesthesiologist was putting me to sleep, I felt someone on the operating table with me, and I knew it was the Lord. The surgery and rehab went so well that, with my doctor's permission, I attended church the following Sunday. I continued to rehab so that by the middle of June, life was pretty much back to normal. We were able to take trips to the Pismo Beach area, which was wonderful therapy. Walking on the beach every day was great for my continued healing.

13

STEPPING INTO NEW BUSINESS

THE REST of summer of 2022 passed quickly. I was feeling great, so Jane and I began to drive throughout California, antiquing and enjoying our time together. We knew that God was blessing us with additional time on Earth.

In the fall, I was feeling bored, so I started looking for a business we could run out of our home that required little labor, needed little to no inventory and did not involve purchasing a lot of equipment.

One day after a number of interesting conversations with other people, I mentioned the idea of starting an online janitorial supply store to Jane. She rolled her eyes, as if to say, "Here we go again."

"We don't have a clue how to do an e-commerce store," I said, "but God has always made a way for us through all of the years, so I'm going to pray that He'll help us one more time." And pray we did.

The following Tuesday evening, we went to Bible study,

which we enjoyed immensely. Pastor Doug was teaching. In the middle of the study, he stopped talking for a moment. "God just told me that someone here is contemplating starting a new business." He went on to say that whoever undertook the task should proceed, as it was likely to be successful. Jane and I smiled at each other as we recognized the confirmation.

"Thank you, Jesus!"

We asked our regular computer guy, John Jefferson, who lived in Oklahoma City, to set up an online store for us. After he had worked for some time, he told us that he wasn't happy with what he was able to do and needed some help. He's a Christian, so I said, "Hang on because God is in this with us, and I believe He'll make a way."

In early November, on the spur of the moment, Jane and I decided we needed to get away for the day, and we felt that a trip to Temecula, about an hour's drive from our home, would do the trick. One of our favorite restaurants is there, and it also has several antique stores we could check out.

We were led to a store called Granny's Attic that we had never heard of. During a conversation with one of the employees, I mentioned that we were building an e-commerce store, with little success. She laughed. "That's what my son does for a living, and I still have no idea how they work, so good luck."

"Ma'am, this isn't about luck," I replied. "I believe God has answered our prayers and guided us here to get acquainted with your son." She gave me his number, and after quite a conversation, Kelly Sanchez, who lived in San Diego, agreed to see if he could help us, with the caveat that he thought we were way in over our heads. I was adamant that we give it a try even though it was going to cost a chunk of money.

After the conversation, I arranged a phone call with John, Kelly, and another computer specialist. Several conversations later, they felt like they were on the right track, but several hurdles still had to be overcome to start the store. They finally got everything in order, and the store began to take shape, or so I thought. In December 2022, we named our company Adonai Cleaning Supplies. We started putting products in the store, but we ran into some technical problems, which slowed our progress.

I was beginning to lose patience. We were spending money, but we weren't making any progress with respect to opening the store. The computer guys were doing the best they could, but my spirit was troubled. I told Jane that I was ready to call it quits, terminate the guys, and just write off the expenses. She didn't disagree, but she also reminded me of God's confirmation that we would be successful, so she suggested that we continue to pray about it.

A couple of days later when I asked if she had any thoughts on how we should proceed, she suggested I talk to our local computer repair guy, Mark Ridley, to see if he could help us. He said he didn't do that type of work, but referred me to another guy, who referred me to yet a third guy. A couple of weeks passed, and things still were not progressing with the e-commerce store. I also hadn't heard from the third guy, so I was ready to drop the idea and move on to something else. Then the phone rang, and the voice on the other end said, "My name is Darnell Edwards. Are you the guy who's looking for help with an online store?" I started laughing, thinking it was all in God's timing.

Darnell told me how he had been involved in the Christian

music industry in Las Vegas. He had worked with some big names in that genre and also helped some unknown people get a start. He also stated that he had earned a substantial income and had a $2 million line of credit from the bank. However, due to some things that were out of his control, he had lost it all. He was falsely accused of doing drugs and making sexual advances by a woman as he helped to get her music career started. When this rumor got around the industry, his big-time clients dropped him. I contacted several individuals in the Las Vegas music industry who corroborated his account and informed me about his accuser's background. His story was compelling, but it was a lot for me to assimilate, so I arranged an in-person meeting.

Jane came with me to the meeting. He was forthright and sincere, and everything he said made sense. Four hours later, we had an agreement in principle. When we left the meeting, Jane seemed to be comfortable with Darnell. She was reminded that God had told us the business would be successful. She felt God had put Darnell in our lives for that purpose. I didn't disagree, but I needed some time to seek God's council.

The following Sunday, Jane and I attended church. As the service was concluding, Pastor Doug announced that he and Pastor Dan would be up front if anyone wanted prayer. I approached Pastor Dan and asked him to pray for wisdom and clarity regarding our business. After he prayed for my requests, he grabbed my arms, his eyes wide with excitement. "God just told me that your business is going to be more successful than you could think or hope. God is going to open the windows of heaven and pour out financial blessings beyond your wildest imagination." All I could think was, *Thank you, Jesus!*

When I got back to my seat, I told Jane what had taken place. She smiled and told me that she was sure that Darnell had been sent by God "for such a time as this."

Unfortunately, once Darnell started setting up the e-commerce stores, he informed me that after having looked at what the other guys had accomplished, he would basically have to start over. He assured me that while it would take additional time, he was up for the task. I thought that was strange, but I also remembered what John Jefferson and Kelly had discussed with me, so I chose not to follow up with them at that time.

We went to Tuesday night Bible study where. Pastor Doug was teaching, but partway through the study he stopped and asked Pastor Dan if he had something from the Lord. Pastor Dan stood up and began moving around the room, prophesying over different people in a mighty way. Jane and I sat there, enjoying the prophesies, as it meant God was working in our Bible study. That changed when Pastor Dan came up behind us, put his hands on our shoulders, and whooped. "God is reminding you about what He promised you," he said. "Your business is going to produce a financial windfall that will blow you away. He's sending a man to help you be successful. He also wants you to know that the person He's sending is a broken human being who has taken a fall, and God is going to restore him. This will all happen so quickly that people will see it as a miracle. They will come to Jesus as their Lord and Savior because of it." When Pastor Dan stopped, Jane and I were laughing, crying, and shouting. We wanted to testify because no one but us knew that Darnell was already at work, doing what we needed to be successful. Then Pastor Dan said, "God said you are greatly blessed and highly favored." We had never felt so humbled.

The next time we saw Darnell, we told him about what happened at Bible study and what God had said about wanting to restore him. He looked at us in disbelief. "Are you serious? That really happened?" We told him about the different prophecies that had been spoken over us and how they had all played out. Then I asked if he would like to go to church with us the next Sunday, and he was quick to agree.

When we arrived at church with Darnelle, we found our seats and waited for worship to begin. Some friends came by to say hello, so I introduced them to Darnell and chatted for a minute. Then the worship team began to play, so we joined in.

After the worship service, Pastor Dan went to the platform to speak. On the way, he stopped and asked, "Buddy, do I know the fellow next to you?" When I shook my head, he continued. "I don't believe I have ever spoken to you before, but I know God has told me . . ." At that point, I wasn't listening to Pastor Dan anymore. I was watching Darnell. He was standing, listening intently to the prophecy. As soon as the prophecy ended and Pastor Dan began his sermon, Darnell sat down, gave me a quizzical look, and asked if I had told Pastor Dan about him. I just smiled and shook my head.

After the sermon was over, Pastor Doug invited anyone who needed prayer to come to the front. I watched with interest as Darnell joined the line for prayer. When Pastor Doug prayed for Darnell, then he spoke to him in a serious manner, which I surmised was some sort of prophetic message. Pastor Doug moved on to another person, but Darnell continued to stand there.

At that point, Pastor Dan moved across the front and went directly to Darnell, praying for him. Then he also spoke to him with a prophetic attitude as if God were speaking through him. When he was finished, he gave Darnell a hug and then moved on. Darnell stood motionless, as if in a trance.

When he finally came back to where we were seated, he looked at me and shook his head. "This is crazy. Pastor Doug told me things that I have never shared with anyone. Then Pastor Dan told me the same thing, and he didn't even talk to Pastor Doug beforehand. I've never witnessed anything like it before."

Darnell had been working diligently on Adonai Cleaning Supplies but had reached a point where we needed to put up some more money for him to continue. He needed to go to Las Vegas to meet with his team for marketing, advertising, and social media, which was important, but money was tight. I was concerned as to why he had to go to Las Vegas when we could do a Zoom call, but I also realized that meeting face-to-face with people is important.

The following Tuesday night, we went to Bible study. Pastor Doug taught the lesson, and as always, it was great. After Bible study, we had some lighthearted banter with him, then we asked him to pray for our business, as we were concerned about the future.

"I started praying for your business," he said, "but I just heard God say, 'Stop.'" That rattled my timbers, as all we had been hearing was "go, go, go." Pastor Doug must have seen the surprise in my eyes because he smiled and said, "You and Jane have been obedient, but now is the time to pause. Get everything that's disturbing you out on the table. I'm sure Darnell will be happy to put everything into perspective."

The next week when Darnell returned from Las Vegas, we met with him in our home. The meeting went great, and we were able to address all of our concerns. After the meeting, we felt confident about the direction of the business. *Truly, God is not the author of confusion but of peace and order,* I thought.

Darnell and I visited the bank to complete a money transfer. When we got there, we were confronted by a long line. Normally, I would have gone back later rather than wait, but we needed to do the transfer.

As we stood there, I noticed the line growing behind us, and people were getting quite irritable due to the lengthy wait. Darnell and I talked quietly regarding the money he needed and what he was doing with it. While we were talking, I noticed the young man standing in front of us with his restless four- or five-year-old daughter. He appeared to be preoccupied with keeping her in line, but he turned to us and said, "The Holy Spirit just told me to tell you guys that the business you're starting is going to be a huge success. God is going to open up the windows of heaven and pour out a blessing, more than you will be able to receive." He smiled, and we shook hands as another teller opened a window. He and his daughter went to take care of his business, leaving Darnell and I stunned at what had just transpired.

As we continued to wait, I glanced at the man and his daughter, and he motioned for me to approach him. "Sir, God just told me that you have had heart surgery," he said as I walked up, "and he wants me to lay hands on your chest. He wants to touch you." What could I say? I stood there while he laid his hands on my chest and prayed for healing in my heart. As he prayed, I felt a warm glow in my chest. I was overwhelmed and somewhat concerned because he was speaking loudly, and people in line were watching.

After his prayer, the man walked away without another word, leaving Darnell and I in front of the teller, who was smiling. I asked her if she knew the guy. "Yes, I know him casually as a bank client, and he's a great guy," she said. Then I asked if she had heard what he told us. "I didn't hear his words," she replied, "but I heard through the Spirit that your business is going to be a success, and God has blessed you with your heart issue."

By the time Darnell and I finished our business, to my surprise the people who were in line behind us had gone from being irritable and grumpy to smiling. On our way out, some of them told us to have a nice day.

When Darnell and I got outside the bank, we laughed at what had happened inside. It was surreal. It just proves that "Where the Spirit of the Lord is, there is liberty."

Later on Darnell wanted to have a meeting to discuss another opportunity that could be very lucrative. We were impressed by what he shared with us and agreed to get involved and. He showed us some of the big-name people he had worked with in his previous entertainment business in Las Vegas. Then he introduced a couple of newcomers whom he had worked with who did very well with him. Apparently, they had done *too* well because they had decided that they no longer needed him. It turned out to be disastrous for them because they were no longer in the music industry.

Darnell proposed that we continue with our online store for

antiques and one for home goods which were beginning to show signs that they could turn a profit in a couple of months, but he also wanted us to branch out into the entertainment industry which he was very familiar. However, it would take some time to get everything in place, along with extra financing. Even though our finances were okay, we told him we needed to pray for God's wisdom and direction for how to proceed. We also asked God to intervene with our financial situation.

A couple of days later, Jane and I were on our way to a friend's home for lunch when I received a call from a lending company in the Bay area. It was an unfamiliar bank inquiring whether our business could make use of a hundred thousand dollars. Without thinking, I hung up, assuming it was a scam. However, the person called me right back.

"Please don't hang up," he said before I could speak. "I have good news for you. Based on my research, your janitorial company meets the qualifications for a small business loan at a competitive interest rate. Please give me a minute." How could I say no? I knew such loans from the government were available.

During our conversation, I questioned the legitimacy of his company, how he had gotten my company's information, and how he could offer me a $100,000 loan without more information. He was very professional, and he answered each of my questions to my satisfaction. Then he asked if I was interested in the loan and, if so, if I would answer a couple of questions, so he could find out what he could offer me for sure. I spent another ten minutes answering his questions. Then he told me to enjoy my lunch, and he would get back to me in a couple of hours. After I hung up, Jane reminded me that we had prayed a few days earlier for God to intervene regarding our financial situation.

A couple of hours later when we were on our way home from lunch, the guy from the lending company called back, as promised. He asked a couple more questions, which I answered to his satisfaction. Then he asked me to hold for a few minutes. When he came back on the line, he said, "Mr. Mercer, I have you qualified for one hundred and fifty thousand dollars at the rate we discussed. How does that sound?" I was speechless, wondering if I had heard him right.

"It sounds good to me," I said once I regained my composure. "But I want to speak to my CPA, and I'll get back to you shortly."

After I hung up, I pulled to the side of the road, where Jane and I said a quick prayer, thanking God for his intervention. Then I called our CPA, who was blown away at the sequence of events. After I got his okay, I called the guy at the lending company and told him we were good to go. Fourteen days later, we were funded.

Once we heard from the lender everything was secure, we met Darnell. To our amazement, he had a proposal in hand for our entertainment venture. The proposal was more than I had expected, but he explained the extra costs, which appeared reasonable, so I approved it. Then I asked what had possessed him to prepare a plan when we weren't sure we were going to proceed with the venture. He smiled and said, "The way things have been going, I felt sure God would provide."

Darnell went to work on the entertainment venture right away, and in a couple of weeks, he had artists lined up who were already performing that he could sign. They were unhappy with their current agents' agreements, which would mean less expenses and maybe a quicker return on our money. He asked if we could get together for breakfast, so he could show us his agreements with the artists and their promotional material.

The first artist was a pretty girl in her early twenties who was a country-and-western performer. When he played her video on his phone, she sparkled. The next was a handsome young African American man who sounded like Michael Bublé. We were satisfied with Darnell's presentation and agreed that he should proceed.

With a renewed sense of excitement, I decided to open more online stores one for elegant jewelry, one for Indian artifacts and one for automobile parts, three of them were beginning to show life but were not yet profitable. The others were not catching on, costing money for advertising and keeping them current. We had assumed it would take five to six months for these stores to become profitable, but we had underestimated the cost to maintain them. Therefore, we decided that any store not generating a profit by August would be closed.

The entertainment venture did not progress as anticipated. The young African American man we had signed began using drugs and became unreliable. When Darnell confronted him about it, the young man became violent, threatened Darnell, and stormed out, never to be seen again. Unfortunately, monies were owed to third parties that we were not aware of regarding the singer. Also, the young country-and-western singer couldn't get out of her contract with her agent until August, so there was no money coming in from her either. Meanwhile, money was still going out for Darnell's expenses and other operating costs.

In early fall I was becoming concerned because we were burning through money at a higher rate than I had expected. At that point, I pulled the plug on three of the online stores, the three that I had expected to be the most profitable. They sold vintage items, such as *Gone with the Wind*-type hurricane lamps, Waterford crystal, and Thomas Kinkade artwork, which we had purchased recently for what appeared to be great prices. For whatever reason, the market for these items had disappeared. Even after closing the stores, we were still paying for overhead.

Shortly afterwards our debt was mounting at an alarming rate, with seemingly no way out. During Tuesday night Bible study, Pastor Doug said God told him we shouldn't worry about our debt because God would handle it. I could not wrap my head around that because the Bible says, "The rich rule over the poor, the borrower is a slave to the lender" (Prov 22:7) and "The wicked person borrows and does not repay" (Ps 37:21.) Later that evening, Pastor Dan said to us, "Buddy and Jane, God said you shouldn't worry about the debt, as God will take care of it in His time." I didn't understand, but I couldn't argue with God, for He had been so faithful.

The next Sunday, our worship leader, Tim, a talented young musician who played the keyboard for worship, brought his saxophone instead. When he started playing "Amazing Grace," the anointing was upon him. Members who were normally reserved, stood and raised their hands, clapping and praising God. I noticed Darnell sitting transfixed as if in a faraway place in his mind or spirit. It was a glorious moment.

As soon as the pastor finished his message, Darnell walked to where Tim was putting his instruments away and spoke to him. I saw Tim smile and nod.

When Darnell made it back to where we were standing, he was trembling with excitement. "I know your musical background," he said. "You recognize that we have just heard a saxophone played like very few can play it. I spoke to Tim, and he was blown away that I offered him the opportunity to have a professional demo done at no cost to him. It's going to cost us about two hundred bucks, but I think you'll agree that that will be cheap for what we can do with it." The next week, Tim went into a studio to record a track. When I got my hands on the recording, I was overjoyed with the results.

Darnell contacted me to inform me that he had received a call from a well-known composer who had listened to Tim's demo. He had requested a meeting with Darnell to discuss Tim and the possibility of getting him in one of the best studios in Hollywood with an award-winning engineer and producers. The composer was a Christian, and he believed that God had put everything together. He was willing to come to the studio on the day of Tim's appointment at no charge. It would only cost us studio time, which we would receive at a reduced rate. Even at a lower rate, it was still expensive, but I felt like it was an opportunity that we couldn't pass up.

We received an invitation to go to the studio the day that Tim recorded, so Jane and I drove to Torrance to be a part of the event. Jane was excited, as was I, never in my wildest dreams having imagined I would experience such a thing.

When we got to the studio, Darnell introduced us to the composer, who was a very down-to-earth guy. We also met the engineer/producer. When we entered the recording area, we were overwhelmed by all the equipment and the entire setup. On the other side of the glass into the recording room, Tim was warming up with his saxophone. I looked at Jane, who was in awe, tears rolling down her cheeks.

When everything was set up, we sat just outside the recording studio where Tim would be playing, along with the composer. The engineer was at his control board. And to my amazement, professional photographers were on hand to take photos of Tim for promotional material. It was a professional, elite operation.

When the engineer was ready, he told Tim to start playing at his convenience. To my astonishment, the composer stood up and said, "I feel the Lord in this place. I would like to pray for a blessing over this event." After he finished praying, he told the engineer to proceed.

Once Tim started playing, it was like time was nonexistent. The engineer was watching the equipment, then he turned to the composer with a huge smile and nodded.

"Move over, Kenny G," the composer said.

After the session ended, Tim came out to give his wife a hug, not even noticing that everyone in the room was giving him a standing ovation.

Later that week, the composer met with Darnell and Tim to discuss Tim's future, which included an engagement on a Carnival Cruise ship. It meant we would start receiving some money in December. It wouldn't be a lot, but at least something would be coming in.

Several days after the recording session, Darnell contacted me with a proposal to create a Christmas video featuring Tim playing the saxophone. I told him I was interested, but we were beginning to use the SBA loan to pay our other debt, which was not good. I told him that he needed to get back to me immediately with all the costs and when the video would be ready to sell.

"I understand your position and your concerns," he said, "so I have a proposal with all the costs, including my charge for producing the video. I'll email it to you now for your approval or any suggestions you may have."

The completion date for the video was mid-November, which was important to make it in time for the Christmas sales. After confirming everything was in order, Jane and I prayed for wisdom. I knew that we were in trouble, but I hoped that after this video, the drain on our finances would start to slow down, so I told Darnell to proceed.

He called toward the end of October to tell me that the video shoot would take place on Halloween, and he invited me to watch the shoot. It took place at a church in Baldy Mountain village. It was a wonderful setting, and getting to see our video being made was very exciting.

The shoot was on a Sunday. We had asked Darnell if he was going to attend church, which began at 1:30 p.m., and he told us he was, but when we arrived, we were concerned, as Darnell wasn't there. About thirty minutes after the service started, he finally arrived. I sensed a problem when he walked to where we were sitting and started talking to me during the sermon, disturbing the service, telling me that he would be leaving early for the video shoot. Then he got up and walked to the other side of the church, disrupting the service yet again.

Pastor Doug stopped speaking for a moment. "No, Darnell, don't take another step. You have disrupted the moving of the Holy Spirit three times, so I'm going to ask an usher to walk you out."

An usher behind Darnell stepped up and asked him to leave. Darnell resisted, so the usher took him by the arm and escorted him out of the building.

After the service, Pastor Doug came to our car in tears. "I love you guys," he said. "I have never had to do what I did today. I know Darnell is your friend and associate, but I can't have anyone disrupt the moving of the Holy Spirit." Jane and I assured him that as far as we were concerned, he handled the situation perfectly.

When we arrived at the video shoot at about 4:00 p.m., it had already begun. They were shooting the outdoor scenes, which looked good to us. Darnell met us with a cheery greeting, as if nothing had happened at church. I decided to let things go until after the video was completed.

Later in the evening, Darnell became quite angry because things weren't going to his liking. He started threatening that if things weren't done his way he would shut the shoot down. I brought Tim, the director, the production manager, and Darnell together and clarified that I was funding the shoot, and they were responsible for ensuring it proceeded effectively. After about thirty minutes, they came to an agreement, and the shoot finished that night at about 11:00.

During the holidays, I got very busy with my janitorial company, making sure it was operating at the highest level of quality, as it was our primary source of income. I spent time in the field with the independent contractors at each of the properties. Communication with the tenants at the properties was important, as they provided information about any issues that required attention. In addition, I visited each of the property management companies and spent time with the property managers to take care of any issues that the homeowner association board members might bring up. After spending two weeks in the field, I was relieved and gratified that our company set the standard for the other janitorial companies.

During this time, I trusted Darnell to ensure the video would be ready to make the Christmas playlists no later than November 15, and everything appeared to be on track. On November 15, he called and said there was a problem, but I shouldn't be concerned, as he could take care of the issue. It would necessitate him flying to Nashville, so he could meet with the executives of Broadcast Music, Inc (BMI). Apparently, something was wrong with our license.

He called me from Nashville the next afternoon and said the issue had been addressed, but it wouldn't be resolved for a couple of days. We would not make the initial playlist. In fact, we did not get on a playlist in time as was promised.. That meant all the other Christmas videos were already playing. I was furious and devastated at the turn of events because we were not going to make any money with the video.

Darnell did not come back home right away. He went to Missouri to visit his mother who was in poor health and to take care of some business. While he was gone, I started poking around and discovered that he had listed our video under his previous music business name. As a result, I was increasingly concerned, as his departure from our business offered no remedy or opportunity to recover any losses incurred.

When Darnell got back, I confronted him about the situation, and he admitted what he had done. He told us that his old business name had more power in the music industry than our business. While his statement was valid, his actions made me very uncomfortable, as he had overstepped his authority, but it was too late to do anything but hope for the best.

Things got even more complicated when the country-and-western singer got pregnant. When my frustration with our music venture hit an all-time high, I stumbled across the original version of the story you are reading, which I wrote in 2001. I found a copy of it in an old briefcase and showed it to a lady who was doing some work for us in the office. After she read it, she said, "I believe God wants this to be published. This story could encourage someone who needs it. God would be glorified by what He has done for you and your family. You know that if it's successful, you could use the money." I told her that I had made a couple of attempts to have it published over the years, but each time something went wrong, and finally I prayed for God to give me a sign that He wanted it published. She laughed and said, "I think God has been talking to your spirit, but you haven't been listening. I just told you what I felt in my spirit, but you want to tell me why God wouldn't want you to do it. You know that with your supervision, Darnell could help you get this story published." I couldn't argue with her.

That afternoon I went to my prayer closet, seeking God's wisdom. I knew this project would cost a lot of money, that our debt was growing, and it was certainly not a guaranteed success. I was reminded that God's word came forth in prophecy through two different men, saying He would take care of our debt. I contacted Darnell to tell him what had transpired and asked if he was interested in being involved in the book project. He said he would like to pick up a copy of the story. If it corresponded with what I had told him about my life, he would like to pursue it, and we could work out the financial arrangements as we went along.

He picked up a copy that afternoon, then called me a couple of hours later. He said he was doing an initial rewrite of the story, putting it in manuscript form, and would send it to several authors, publishers, and agents to get their feedback. That blew me away because all I had expected was his input on what he thought we could do with the story. He was way ahead of me, but he assured me what he was doing wouldn't cost me anything. If he got the response that he thought he would get, we could come to an agreement on his compensation. He also told me that he had the ability and the people to help with editing, publishing, and so forth, which would save money to help us get started.

Later in the week, Darnell called to say we needed to get an intellectual property attorney, hoping I would take the time to get him a few prospects he could interview. I assured him I would have a list that day. I made a few calls, without success. I was ready to give up, but I made one more call.

"I'm just heading out the door, so make it quick," the guy said. I was about to hang up, but instead I decided to make my pitch.

"I need an intellectual property attorney. I have a story ready to go. I'm desperate, so please don't hang up."

He laughed. "You have my attention but make it quick."

When I started telling him my story, I expected him to hurry me up at best or maybe even hang up on me, but he kept saying things like "Go on" and "Is this for real?" Finally, I stopped my story. "You said you were in a hurry. What else do you want to hear?"

"When can I get a copy of your story?" he asked.

As soon as we disconnected, I called Darnell and informed him that I had just spoken to Jay Baldino, summarizing our conversation. After a long pause, Darnell said, "I don't know how you got to talk to that guy. He's one of the top intellectual property attorneys around." I gave Darnell Jay's number, then went about my business.

Just after Christmas, Darnell wanted to meet, so he could give us an update on everything we had going, including some new artists that he was talking to, the headway Tim the saxophonist was making, and what was transpiring with my book. When we met, I was pleased to learn that Tim was booked for the month of January. Darnell was also talking to a young woman who sounded like Whitney Houston. The video that he showed us of her was amazing. He was also continuing to work on my story with Jay, the attorney.

In the second week of January 2023, Darnell called, sounding very excited. He and Jay had been in contact with Netflix and Lions Gate. They were interested in discussing a movie deal, as my uplifting story was exactly what Hollywood was looking for. That blew me away because the amount of money they were talking about was more than I could grasp. Even though it would be some time before we would see any of it, I had never even dreamed of receiving such an amount.

The next week, Darnell called again and told me to hang onto something because he had received a call from Jay, saying a well-known actor and his wife, an actress in her own rights, were interested in having a part in the movie and also investing some of their own money, up to $100,000, in exchange for a percentage of the profits. To top it all off, an actor in a hit television show wanted to discuss the possibility of him directing the project. Darnell said if we could put the deal together with these guys, it would give us a package to present to the studios when we started negotiations. All of this sounded wonderful, but with all the negotiations that had to take place, it would be a long time before money would start coming in, and our debt was still climbing.

During the first week of February, Jay called, saying he wanted to talk to me about financing the project ourselves. Jay thought that Darnell would be in negotiations with both studios for no more than three months. I told him that we had enough financing to carry us through but not much more, and our debt was mounting. I felt uneasy during our conversation, and I voiced my concern regarding Darnell's expenses. We were getting a lot of promises, but nothing was coming to fruition. Jay said he couldn't speak to the progress with the studios or the big-name actors because he wasn't involved in the negotiations.

Shortly after that conversation, I developed a sleep problem. I was having wild dreams, my body was restless, and I was snoring loudly. I would wake up after three or four hours, gasping for air. At first, I wrote it off as the stress I was feeling from our lack of success with our business ventures, but Jane was adamant that I go to a sleep apnea clinic. I was diagnosed with severe sleep apnea and was advised to see a pulmonologist. By the second week of February, I was having more serious problems, gaining weight at an alarming rate because my kidneys weren't functioning properly. I was also having problems staying awake during the day and not being able to think coherently.

On a Sunday morning as we got ready for church, I was distraught because my clothes no longer fit due to the weight gain. Undeterred, I proceeded to don athletic attire and appropriate footwear. Jane suggested that maybe we should go to the emergency room, but I convinced her that I would be okay, and we could deal with the issue after church.

Jane drove us to church, which was rare, because I was worried about falling asleep at the wheel. When we got there, I had difficulty walking from the parking lot to the church door because the sunlight was blinding me. Once inside, it was dark enough that I could see well enough to walk, but I was getting dizzy. I finally made it to a chair, where a couple of church members came over to pray for me, along with Jane. Seeing that I was in poor shape, Pastor Doug came to me and said, "Do whatever you need to do. Take your liberty, and don't be concerned about anything."

Shortly thereafter, the worship band started playing. The music was soothing to my mind, but I had a sudden, deep feeling inside that I had to get to the altar. I started to get off my chair, but I fell on my hands and knees and started crawling toward the altar. I felt Jane walking beside me, her hands on my back and shoulders as she prayed in tongues.

I looked toward the altar, where I saw a figure with a light shining from it, beckoning me to come just as I was and not to be concerned. In my mind, I heard Matthew 11:28, where Jesus says, "Come unto me, all ye that labor and are heavy laden and I will give you rest." I became aware that Pastor Doug was walking with us, also praying in tongues, which gave me a sense of security. I felt in my spirit that the whole congregation was praying for me.

When we got close to the altar, a peaceful feeling came over me. I tried to get up, but I was too weak.

"We have you, brother," Pastor Doug and another man said as they lifted me to my feet. I was shouting and praising the Lord. The figure and the light I had seen was gone, but the peaceful feeling was still with me. With Jane's help, I was able to walk back to my chair. Before we were seated, a brother looked at Jane, who nodded, then he helped us out to our car. Later that day, Jane demanded that we go to the emergency room, so we could find out what was going on, but by then I was feeling euphoric and didn't want to go.

When we got to the emergency room, it was crowded, as usual, meaning a long wait. Jane was highly concerned and spoke to someone regarding my condition. I was taken into a room to talk to a nurse. I told her that we were wasting her time because I was doing fine. She told me that she just wanted to ask me some questions. I agreed, but the first question annoyed me. She asked me what the date was. I don't worry about the date because I'm retired, which is what I told her.

"What year is it?" she asked. I had to think about that one, but I came up with "2043." The next question was easy. She asked who the president of the United States was.

"Ronald Reagan," I replied, my chest swelling with pride. Then she asked if I knew where I was. When I told her I was at the hospital, she smiled.

"Which one?"

When I told her it was San Angelo Mercy, she smiled again and asked me to relax while she and Jane stepped out to have a conversation. Upon their return, the nurse told me that they were going to admit me for observation, which made me angry. I felt I had answered her questions correctly, but she was more concerned about issues with my heart. I agreed for one reason: I saw the concern on Jane's face.

At this point, for the purpose of maintaining the honesty and integrity of this story, I must say that the anecdotes I convey going forward are composed of what Jane, Dena, and my pulmonologist recall as well as my own memories from when I was lucid.

I was taken to a bed in the emergency room, as all the hospital beds were full. That was fine with me because by then I was exhausted. I was also confused. After I had been in bed for a few minutes, a nurse entered the room. She had a wonderful, perky personality. I became somewhat alert and answered her questions as best as I could while she took notes. Shortly after she left, an older female doctor came in along with Jane and Dena. The doctor had the notes that the nurse had taken. She asked me the same questions, which I could not remember. Then she stepped out with Jane and Dena, returning a few minutes later to tell me what was going on. I was very tired and didn't really listen until Jane told the doctor that I was allergic to Ambien. That got my attention because I remembered a previous episode when I was given Ambien, which had created a problem for the hospital.

After Jane and Dena left for the night, a nurse came in and gave me something to help me sleep. I fell asleep and had vivid dreams. When I woke up, a couple of nurses were in the room, trying to calm me down. Apparently, I was living out part of my dreams in real life. The rest of the night went without incident.

The next day I slept off and on, waking up only briefly when it was time for shots or whatever other things the nurses did. I had no appetite, and I refused food until Jane insisted that I eat the food and drink the water and other fluids that they brought to me.

Later that evening, Dena came back with Jane. After conferring with the doctor, Dena was furious because my primary doctor had prescribed a derivative of Ambien, which had already been given to me. That explained my wild dreams the night before.

At that point I fell into a deep sleep, and my body, which had been retaining fluid due to congestive heart failure, became more unresponsive. The doctor ordered an ECG, which showed my heart rate had fallen to the low thirties, causing my lungs to fill with fluid. My lungs would not drain properly, which was causing pulmonary edema. This is a life-threatening issue that can cause death. Dena also became very concerned after consulting with the pulmonologist. He said if they couldn't get my lungs to drain, I would die. She called Brent and Stacey to let them know what was happening.

No longer able to stay in the room and watch, Jane kissed me on the cheek, then stepped out into the hall and prayed for God to intercede. She asked Him to drain my lungs and proclaimed I would live and not die. Dena sat by me while Jane was out of the room, praying fiercely for my survival. I found out later that the pulmonologist wanted to follow Jane out of the room, not wanting to witness the inevitable, but he needed to remain in the room to certify the time of death.

About thirty minutes later, Jane returned full of faith, believing that God had heard her prayer, and I would not die. Shortly after that, the doctor told her that, amazingly, they were able to get my lungs to start draining. I still wasn't out of the woods, though, due to the amount of fluid still on my lungs. It could take several hours for them to drain, as draining them too quickly could cause other problems.

Jane and Dena went out to the hall and praised God for his miraculous intervention, which had caused my lungs to start draining. Several hours later, my doctor and the pulmonologist told Jane that I was still in serious trouble, but they were cautiously optimistic because my heart rate had suddenly and unexpectedly improved. Jane went home full of faith that I was going to make it because God had answered her prayer.

They allowed me to remain in a deep sleep, as I was worn out from the trauma my body had endured due to the lack of oxygen to my brain. Even before I was admitted to the hospital, I was hallucinating, and I could have developed cerebral hypoxia, which can cause severe brain damage and even death.

A couple of days later, they decided to see if they could get me to wake up. They were concerned because I was exhibiting signs of hallucination. I imagined I was at a Cincinnati Bengals football game, sitting in the owner's box and enjoying a delicious cinnamon roll. I felt a woman rubbing my face and whispering in my ear. That disturbed me because she caused me to spill my coffee, so I tried to push her away. A nurse wiped my face with a damp cloth and tried to wake me.

When I awakened enough to be cognizant, I was only able to recognize Jane, who was smiling and mumbling something. Later, she told me that she was praying in the spirit and speaking in tongues. I was only aware for a moment before I drifted back to sleep.

An unknown period of time later, I felt a damp cloth on my face again and heard people talking to me, but this time I recognized Jane's voice. I was somewhat coherent, but I insisted I wanted the rest of the cinnamon roll I thought I had been eating. I continued to drift in and out of consciousness, but they decided I had improved enough to move me into a regular hospital room, where I would get the type of care that I needed.

The doctors told Jane and Dena that they believed that I had been totally exhausted mentally and physically due to sleep apnea for some time before I came to the hospital. These issues had caused congestive heart failure, which, in turn, caused my lungs to fill with fluid, creating pulmonary edema and cerebral hypoxia, both of which are life threatening. Because they were able to get my lungs to start draining as soon as they did, my heart had recovered somewhat and was able to function at a higher rate. The prognosis for my recovery had improved, but my brain had been starved of oxygen for so long that they were still concerned about my brain function.

Dena asked who had made the decision to go against her warning regarding the Ambien derivative, which exacerbated my problems. The doctors would not or could not give her an answer. Jane, normally a quiet, gentle woman, became angry and told them she expected an answer, as it had put my life in further danger. She also pointed out that they had not been able to get my lungs to drain completely, which concerned her.

Dena contacted a pulmonologist whom she respected and asked if he would look at my case to make sure that he agreed with the prognosis that had been presented to her and Jane.

Later that day, he called back and said he believed the prognosis was correct, but he agreed to check on me daily. Dena also spoke to another RN who was aware of the situation. She said Dena and Jane should go home to rest, as there was nothing else they could do. She also agreed to update them if they were needed for anything. Dena was living in Arizona at the time, so she arranged to stay with Jane while I was in the hospital, which was a great relief to my wife. Dena was better equipped to get information, and she could help Jane make informed decisions about my care.

Fortunately, our janitorial company continued to operate smoothly during this time. The independent contractors who were with us were all Christian men who attended the church we had attended previously, and they treated the business as if it was theirs. My wife was able to check my voicemails and emails to see if we had received any complaints. Thankfully, there were none. That allowed Jane to turn her attention to the bookkeeping, ensuring a steady cash flow.

During the next week or so, I was in and out of consciousness. I had some weird hallucinations. The weirdest one had me believing I was at a piano bar enjoying the music when I realized I was going to be out after curfew. I walked out of the bar into the street (which was the hospital hallway) when I saw a police officer (a nurse) who wanted to know if I was okay. I told him I was good but that I needed help to find my house.

As time went by, I was progressing well physically, gaining strength by walking the halls, but I was not well mentally. I was still hallucinating and couldn't recognize my visitors, which included people from church, people we did business with, and my son, Brent, who had arrived from Texas. I wasn't sure who he was at first.

One day Jane called me very excited and told me I needed to get to a window because we were having freaky snowfall in Upland, California, where it never snows. She joked that she thought God was giving us a sign that I would be getting out of the hospital soon. As strange as it may sound, the next day, a couple of doctors and the pulmonologist came in to see me. They asked me questions and watched me walk up and down the hall. Surprisingly, they said I could go home as soon as Jane arrived. Say what you want, but that is a true story.

When I got home in the first week of March, an oxygen machine had been delivered to the house. I was told that I had to use the machine during the day, if needed, to keep my oxygen level at ninety-one or above. I was also required to use it at night, even while sleeping, or I could wind up back in the hospital or worse. During the day, it was not a problem, but at night I had to be watched closely because I would pull the tubes out. Jane and Dena took turns staying up to make sure the cannula remained in my nose.

By the end of the second week of March, things were slowly returning to normal. I was able to sit up most of the day, carry on a coherent conversation, and breathe mostly on my own. So, we told Brent it would probably be good for him to get back to his home and his job. After having a conversation with Dena about my health, he agreed. Jane called Stacey, who was working as a math teacher in San Diego County, to let her know what was transpiring.

She arrived late in the morning the day Brent was to leave, so we ordered lunch and had a great time remembering their younger days. About midafternoon, it was time for Brent to head out, so I asked that we pray and thank God for the wonderful day that He had given us together. As Jane started to pray, the Holy Spirit fell on us, binding us together. What a joyful, marvelous time we had. Brent, who is very pragmatic, hugged his sisters, who were crying tears of joy. But the crowning moment was when Brent went to his mother with tears of joy and said, "Mama, I love you more deeply than you will ever know." The Spirit of God had wiped away the heartache, stress, and worry of the recent trauma and replaced it with His love. As my grandpa used to say, "Ain't God good?"

After that day, things began to improve dramatically, to the amazement of the six doctors who had been treating me, beginning with my ability to sleep in my own bed without the oxygen machine. My brain began to function so that I could recognize people, my health improved so that I could go out to the market with Jane, and most importantly, my kidneys regained their function, so my body weight was almost back to normal. I was able to do things again that I had taken for granted just a month earlier.

By the third week of March, I had recovered physically and mentally enough that when Jane asked me if I felt I could sit through a church service, I was ecstatic. I had been living in sweats and T-shirts, so when I found that my dress clothes fit, I felt like a new man. My only concern was the reception we would get at church. I wasn't ready for a lot of interaction with the people who always greeted each other with hugs. I asked Jane if we could be a little late and then leave a bit early to avoid the greetings and goodbyes. She called me silly, but she agreed.

When we got to church, I had forgotten the guys who

watched over the parking lot would be there, and sure enough, they had hugs for Jane and me, praising God for His healing power. I realized they were happy to see us and that they were exhibiting God's love.

As soon as we walked into the church sanctuary, Pastor Doug stopped the service and gave thanks for God's healing power that had brought me back from near death and had sustained Jane through the entire trauma. After he finished praying, the church members who had been supporting us during the situation greeted us, exclaiming, "Praise the Lord!"

One dear lady whom I had grown quite fond of looked at Jane and said, "I've been praying for you because I know what you 've been going through." Unfortunately, she had lost her husband under similar circumstances.

During my sickness, Darnell had been emailing Jane about the progress he was making with the entertainment side of the business, all of which was costing money and raising our debt level, but the negotiations with the studios looked promising. Tim was recording an album and playing a club gig to help cover costs. The girl who sounded like Whitney Houston had been difficult to deal with. Her father, acting as her manager, requested a higher percentage for her, but Darnell opposed it. Things were going well with the actors who were in talks to act, direct, and invest in my story, though. They were ready to sign a letter of intent, all of which sounded great.

After catching up on the news, I called Darnell, requesting clarification on how the money was being spent. He said he would call back soon, as he was speaking with the singer's father about signing her. When he called back, he was excited because the girl's father had agreed to Darnell's offer, but wanted to talk to his daughter first, who had taken a trip to Miami with her mother, and she wouldn't be back until after the first of May. Then Darnell said he was going to meet with the actors later in the week. They had agreed to the deal and would sign a letter of intent. He said he'd update me about the studios, but he wanted to meet after the letters of intent were signed.

Toward the end of the second week of April, Darnell asked to meet with Jane and me for lunch, saying he had some good news to share with us. When he arrived at the restaurant, he presented letters of intent to us from the actor and director and had the investment clause for $100,000 contingent on studio signings included. We were ecstatic. When I asked about the studios, he had no new information, but he said he would set up meetings with both studios the following week and report back on the results. At the end of the next week, Darnell called to say both meetings went well, but he couldn't get a commitment from either one.

The next day, Darnell called and said he needed to take some time off for a vacation in New Orleans because he was stressed out from everything he had been working on. He also needed to check in on his mother in Missouri, who wasn't doing well, and he would be back the following Friday. I agreed, but I asked him to email all of his reports to me before he left. After reviewing them, I did not feel comfortable. Our debt continued to climb.

The following Friday, Darnell called to say he would be available to visit with me that evening if needed, but he wanted to meet the following Monday instead to lay out his plans for the next couple of months.

On Saturday morning, Jane and I were going to drive to San Clemente to have lunch with Stacey at one of our favorite restaurants on the pier. As is our custom, we asked God for traveling mercies and protection before we left. After we prayed, we turned the radio up and hit the road, looking forward to the drive.

Just after we got out of our neighborhood and onto the main boulevard, Jane grew eerily quiet, which was not normal. After a few moments, she told me that God had spoken to her. He said we had a stronghold of arrogance, pride, and greed that was destroying our businesses.

I pulled into a parking lot and asked her to pray it away because a stronghold is not a physical place but sins that God opposes and which lead to destruction. She began to pray, but then she stopped. "God just told me that Darnell is our stronghold, and he must be dealt with." We were stunned because we had been told in the beginning that God was sending someone to help us with our business. From the first conversation I had with Darnell about his past business success, which I confirmed, to the meeting Jane and I had with him, even up to and including the letters of intent he showed us, everything appeared to prove that he was the guy God had sent.

During the two-hour drive to San Clemente, Jane and I had an open, honest, in-depth discussion regarding what had come to pass. We began to understand that God gives us all free will, and He will not interfere with our choices. At that point, we realized that God had allowed us to make the choice to hire Darnell for our purpose. He had warned us through His word to our pastor to "stop," but we decided to go forward with

Darnell anyway, and at some point he had let pride, arrogance, greed overtake his spirit.

When we got home from lunch with Stacey, I told Jane that I was going to ask Darnell to meet me at a nearby Starbucks. I wanted to have a conversation with him, but I also wanted to avoid accusations. I told Jane that we needed to pray that God would keep me in peace. I wanted the truth about the time we had spent together so far and what Darnell thought about the future, but I have a tendency to be confrontational.

When I pulled into the Starbucks parking lot, Darnell was already inside. After a quick prayer, I walked in and waved a greeting, which he returned with a smile. We shook hands, but when I asked if he wanted a coffee, he declined. He said he was short on time and wanted to take care of my concerns. I told him I would like to get an update on how he felt we had done since he had come aboard, starting with the online stores. His response was curious. He said those stores were my ideas, and I couldn't hold him responsible for their failure, to which I agreed. I asked him to talk to me about the entertainment portion of the business. After staring at me for a moment, he got a strange smirk on his face. "What do you really want?" he asked. "You want to blame me for everything when I've busted my ass for very little pay?" He continued to speak to me with a raised voice, causing a commotion that made other customers uncomfortable. Then, to my surprise, he began to shriek, almost unintelligibly. Cursing, he picked up his laptop and ran to the restroom.

I sat very still, contemplating what had just happened, when a couple of employees came over and asked if I was okay, wanting to know if they should call the police. I told them that I wasn't sure what had just transpired, but I was sure that when I left, Darnell would become rational, and everything would be okay.

"That guy is demon possessed," one of the employees, a young guy, said, visibly shaken. I nodded in agreement and assured them that Darnell would calm down as soon as I left. I asked them to wait for a while before they called the police.

14

THE GREAT I AM SPEAKS

WHEN I GOT HOME, I told Jane about the incident. She decided that we needed to pull all the emails and expense reports we had received from Darnell, so we could go through everything with which he had been involved and figure out where we were at. I agreed wholeheartedly, figuring it wouldn't take long. In his current frame of mind, I had no clue what he might pull on us, so we went right to work. Later that night, we were beginning to get an idea of where we were financially with him, but we couldn't get a true picture until Monday, when we planned to talk to our CPA.

When we went to bed that night, we had our normal prayer time where we seek God's wisdom. We needed help to get to the truth, no matter what we found. Normally, after prayer, we are able to drift right off to sleep, but we were still troubled, so it was a long, sleepless night for both of us.

The next morning was Sunday, so we got out of bed, determined to follow our normal routine: reading the Bible, praying together and watching our favorite television church service while we had breakfast. We were set on not letting the spirit of fear overcome us because it is impossible to please God without faith.

By the time we went to church, our faith was strong because we focused on remembering the things He had done throughout our lives. If He has done it before, He would do it again. The Bible tells us, "Do not forsake the assembling with others," (Heb 10:25) which means we need other believers around us to help build our faith. That day, it was truly a blessing to be with our brothers and sisters of faith. The worship service was marvelous, and it seemed as if God was speaking to us directly through our pastor. He began by reading from Psalm 91, which invokes God's protection if we trust Him.

After the service, we went to the pastor and told him about Darnell's seemingly demonic behavior in Starbucks the previous afternoon. He prayed for protection over us, pleading the blood of Jesus to cover us. Satan and his demons cannot cross the bloodline. By the time we left church, our faith was even stronger. We were praising God at the top of our voice with songs because He inhabits the praises of His people. Fortunately, He gladly accepts when we just make a joyful noise unto the Lord because our singing was a little off key at times.

That night we decided to go to bed early because we didn't sleep well the night before. We were looking forward to our regular nightly prayer meeting with God. When we finished praying, we were saying goodnight to each other when, to my surprise, Jane started praying in the spirit and speaking in tongues. It was followed by the interpretation. "My children, I am here. I love you deeply. I will never leave you, nor forsake you. Trust me only. Do not doubt my word. Fear not. I love you. I am the Great I Am."

When she stopped speaking and was quiet for a few moments, I said, "That was comforting," thinking she had spoken those words herself.

"Buddy, that was God," she replied. I was skeptical, but I wasn't about to argue.

At about 4:00 the next morning, I was awakened by her speaking in tongues again, along with the same interpretation. No more skepticism on my part.

The next morning over coffee, we discussed what had occurred during the night. I repented for my skepticism, but I had never heard of tongues and interpretation in bed. After our devotion time and breakfast, I called our CPA to tell him what had happened with Darnell. His response was chilling. He said our bank accounts were okay, but he was concerned about some credit card use that he had seen recently. He said he would check things out on his end, but we might want to look into one of our corporation's accounts that he didn't handle.

By the end of the day, we were devastated. Somehow Darnell had been able to get a credit card under the corporation but in his name. He had used it for trips to Las Vegas, New Orleans, and gifts for his girlfriend. Our corporation was accountable for the repayment. When we added up what he had spent and the debt we had incurred doing business with him, we owed nearly half a million dollars. The only income we received came from our janitorial company and Social Security. We found ourselves in a challenging financial situation with limited options available. At our age, there appeared to be no way out, but we still believed that somehow God would see us through.

That night when we went to bed, we had our normal prayer time with very little enthusiasm. But just as we said goodnight, once again, Jane began speaking in tongues, along with the same interpretation.

The next morning after our devotional, I told Jane that we were facing something we had never faced before and that desperate times called for desperate measures. We needed to do whatever was necessary to survive, including declaring bankruptcy. She asked if we could pray before we did anything. I told her that she would have to be the one to pray. I spent the rest of the day on the phone, taking care of our janitorial business. I was rummaging through our desk drawers when I came across a credit card that had $10,000 of credit on it. I was at the point where I didn't care how it came. We would be able to survive for a little while, using the credit to pay our other debts and living on the money from our janitorial company.

That night before we went to bed, I asked Jane if she thought God would speak to us after finding out what we were doing. She laughed. "God's ways are higher than our ways." Just then I remembered Psalm 37:25, which says, "I have never seen the righteous forsaken or their children begging for bread." Sure enough, the tongues and interpretation came, and I'm not ashamed to say I cried myself to sleep.

The next Saturday morning was May 6, 2023. Jane came into our home office and said that when I brought up filing bankruptcy before, she was against it. Now she felt like we needed to do it quickly, calling an attorney that very day.

"Hallelujah!" I exclaimed. "That's a great idea." Then I

asked her almost mockingly where she thought we were going to find an attorney on a Saturday morning. She insisted I try, but she also said we should pray first, which she did. To my utter amazement, once again, she started speaking in tongues, followed by an interpretation. "Choose wisely, my children." That was wise counsel, but I doubted there would be attorneys to choose from because they would need to answer the phone.

I started calling bankruptcy attorneys and, to my amazement, one of them actually answered, but he wasn't interested in us. So, I called another one, who also answered. He spent about thirty minutes telling me why we couldn't file chapter seven, which was what we needed to do. He said he could help us file chapter eleven, which would be of no help. I made three more calls, but there were no answers. I was ready to quit, but Jane asked me to make one more call, so I did. To my surprise, a man's voice came on the line. When I told him I wanted to speak to a bankruptcy attorney, he asked what I needed. I asked if he was a bankruptcy attorney, as he had not identified himself as such.

"I'm talking to you about what you need," he said. At that point, I lost it. I almost yelled, "I am a half million dollars in debt, and I have no money. What are you going to do?"

I will never forget his next words. "Am I pissing you off?" he asked. I was flabbergasted.

"Hell, yes!" I exclaimed.

He laughed. "Good. Now tell me your troubles."

After I shared my woes, I was stunned when he told me I was going to be his customer for a couple of years. He gave me a price that I could handle and even told me he would take monthly payments. He said his office would send me a contract on Monday, then he thanked me for our visit and hung up.

Afterward, I just sat and stared at Jane, wondering what had just happened. Much to my surprise, she started speaking in tongues again. When the interpretation came, it was "You have chosen wisely my children." I couldn't help laughing because I hadn't chosen anything.

On Monday, we received the contract, as anticipated. It was apparent we had chosen wisely, but it had to be God who arranged the phone call because the attorney I spoke to was one of the premier bankruptcy attorneys in our area. He'd been a partner in the firm for over twenty-seven years and taught bankruptcy law at one of the elite universities in southern California.

The attorney's firm was so professional, competent, and caring that by Wednesday we were feeling as though everything was going to be okay. To add to our comfort, they directed us to contact a paralegal firm in northern California that handled their paperwork. The paralegal company would make direct contact with all the creditors, eliminating us from the process. When I called the firm, I was transferred to a lady named Patricia. Jane had many questions about the bankruptcy process and was quite anxious. Patricia addressed Jane's fears and answered most of her questions before she even asked them. She also told Jane that she could call anytime with any additional questions that arose. At that point we really understood God's words: "You have chosen wisely."

By the time our nightly prayer time came, we were completely at peace with our circumstances. We were even more comforted when the tongues and interpretation were the same as the first time we heard them.

Even though we found a solution to our problems and were legally safe from creditors harassing us, we were living in a horrendous nightmare every waking moment. It wasn't just a difficult situation financially but also mentally. Our previously excellent credit score of over 800 had disappeared, and we chose not to discuss our situation with anyone. We felt that by filing bankruptcy, we were stealing from our creditors. We became isolated, but we vowed that we would not blame anyone for the mess, as it was our decisions that put us in this position.

We continued to attend church with a cheerful countenance, believing that God would uphold us. We knew that the God we trusted was not a vengeful God but a loving God who would be with us always. That belief was solidified one night when we heard Him ask, "*My children, if I can die for you, can I not provide for you?*"

Eventually, we talked to Pastor Doug in whom we had complete confidence. We told him of our concerns, and we wanted to keep everything private which he agreed was right, but he was adamant that we continue living as we had always done. He made it clear that if God didn't condemn us, we shouldn't condemn ourselves. After he prayed for us, he assured us that if we continued walking in faith and obedience, God would make a way for us. Our relationship with Him was covered by the blood of Jesus.

We did as our pastor suggested and continued living just as before, keeping everything as normal as possible. Our janitorial company was not affected by the bankruptcy, as it had no creditors, and our clients would not be notified, so our income would remain steady. The independent operators who worked with us had no knowledge of our situation and continued to perform wonderfully with very little help from me. Jane continued to keep the books, so we had no problems with receivables either.

One night after our Tuesday night Bible study, Pastor Doug asked us to wait because he wanted to speak to us in private. After everyone left, he told us that God had spoken to him, saying the situation we were in was not our fault. We had been abused and deceived, and God held nothing against us.

The next Sunday, Pastor Dan stood up before the church and said, "The prophecy that you are going to hear was given to me the week before, but I was just given permission by God to speak it publicly. Buddy and Jane Mercer, you will receive justice for all the injustices you have wrongly endured."

The rest of 2023 moved along smoothly as we continued our regular activities. We attended church and enjoyed the Tuesday night Bible study. We took day trips to Big Bear, Palm Springs, and various other places. It is not necessary to spend a lot; occasional outings and maintaining regular daily practices are sufficient. It was about this time that God told us that He was controlling the bankruptcy, and He was making our path clear.

In November, we celebrated our fiftieth wedding anniversary. We had planned to just stay home and be thankful for all the wonderful years we had enjoyed together, but God had other plans. In October, we received an unexpected check for enough money to allow us to go to the Pismo Beach area for a week. We stayed in a hotel with a beautiful view of the ocean and evening sunsets. How did the money come? When I contacted the owner of the business to find out what was going on, he said, "It was the darndest thing. I was in my car driving when I was reminded that your company had performed extra services for us, but I had never paid the invoice." After I thanked him and hung up, I praised God at the top of my lungs. The Great I Am had provided so that we could have a marvelous fiftieth anniversary.

Prior to going away for our fiftieth anniversary, I had gone to our family doctor because I was experiencing back pain. He had me undergo a blood test. After reviewing the results, he said that surgery on my lower back would be necessary. However, I'm strongly opposed to undergoing any surgical procedures. So, I told him that I wouldn't be considering that option, and I would talk to him when I got back into town.

After a beautiful time in Pismo, on the way back it was raining, and when we got to Santa Barbara, there was a bad accident. The freeway was nearly closed, so it took seven hours, instead of two, to drive from Santa Barbara to Rancho Cucamonga. Upon our arrival, I felt extremely fatigued. The next morning, I went to the gym, but the pain persisted. I was having problems just getting into and out of a chair.

Unable to deal with the pain any longer, in January I made an appointment with a rheumatologist. I was instructed to have blood tests, with the results available the following day. The doctor invited me into his office. He wore a bow tie that matched his overall persona. He informed me that I was experiencing inflammation and gave me several prednisone pills. By Saturday morning, things had settled down, and on Saturday afternoon, I was able to be out and about. The next week I picked up my prescription for prednisone and did away with my family doctor who wanted me to have an operation.

A few days later, I received a call from my cardiologist's office, requesting that I undergo an echocardiogram. When my doctor got the results, he told me that he wanted me to come into his office.

"Mr. Mercer," he said during my appointment, "your heart isn't responding like we were hoping. It's not an emergency, but six months ago, it was at forty-five beats per minute, and now it's at thirty beats per minute, which is low. I believe you need to go to an electronic cardiologist, so he can put a device in and keep your heart up at forty-five beats per minute."

I didn't want an electric device in me, so when I walked out of his office with Jane, I said a little prayer: "God, if you want me to have that device, so be it. If you don't want me to have that device or I don't need it, please slam the door."

I made an appointment to see the electronic cardiologist, as suggested. He was a young guy with a terrific attitude. "What makes you think you need the electronic device?" he asked. I told him that my cardiologist, the one they called "the plumber," had sent me to him. The electronic cardiologist asked me about the medications I was taking, and Jane had to step in to give him the basic information.

"I am not familiar with the medication I receive," I added. "I rely on doctors for information about it. I understand that I take the medicine and go from there. So far, I've done well. I'm able to do pretty much anything I want to do, including going to the gym three days a week. Everything was proceeding as expected until an issue arose with my heart rate, which has been dropping into the thirties."

He turned to Jane. "Who's managing his medication?" She told him that nobody was and that we were just taking it as a cardiologist prescribed it. He turned back to me. "I will not put that device in you," he said, "because you don't need it. How old are you?"

"I'm eight-one," I replied.

"The hell you are," he proclaimed. "You don't have the mentality of an eight-one-year-old man, you don't talk like an eighty-one-year-old man, and you don't move like an eight-one-year-old man. You're more like a sixty-year-old guy. I'll have you start a different medication, then get another electrocardiogram."

When Dena heard about the absurdity going on with our doctors, she suggested that I get rid of our family doctor. She had a different doctor in mind. She also recommended a different cardiologist in Pomona. I went to the new family doctor and the new cardiologist, as directed.

During my initial visit to a cardiologist, an EKG was performed. Afterward, the cardiologist discussed changes to my medication regimen. He took me off Lasix and some other things. Then he told me to come back in ninety days.

"Is that it?" I asked.

He smiled. "Get some exercise."

I followed his instructions, and ninety days later, I returned for another appointment, during which he stated there was improvement. I am continuing to follow his orders, and now my heart is back up to forty-five beats per minute.

We had a relatively quiet December, enjoying Christmas with our kids and grandchildren and looking forward to 2024. In early January, I received an email from the largest property management firm that we worked with. We had nine properties with them, and they were demanding some new items be put in place immediately, including some ludicrous insurance requests that did not pertain to janitorial services. I contacted the company's regional vice president to ask why they thought we should provide these items. He said that, if needed, they would find a more professional company to service their accounts. This left me stunned. I knew that if we tried to meet their demands, it would be impossible for our guys to make any money. I called each one of them, explained the situation, and asked them to pray and then get back to me with their thoughts. One of the guys was ready to drop all his properties with this management company because the board of directors was so demanding, and he wasn't making enough from them even without the new stipulations. The other two got back to me within the hour with the same answer. I called the regional vice president and told him that, in accordance with our contracts, we were giving him thirty days' notice to terminate services via email for all nine properties. Since I had already sent the email, I just hung up.

About an hour later, he called back to say his property managers weren't ready for us to quit. Sounding angry, he explained that the email they had sent was just to give me a heads up, and they thought we would find a way to meet their request. I was confident that God had something better in store for us and that we would be able to pick up some other accounts that were equally profitable and less demanding. I told him that we had prayed about his demands, and we would no longer service his properties after thirty days, then I hung up again.

The next day, the nine property managers arranged for a conference call, during which they said they wanted us to drop our thirty-day notice and continue our service according to our original contract. Knowing what my guys had said, I told the property managers they could call my independent contractors and see if they could work out a deal. I wanted nothing to do with them, even though it was costing me money. I found out later that two of my guys told them, "No, thanks," and one of them retained two properties and enforced the contracts. Within sixty days, we picked up enough business to cover what we had lost with a lot less stress on all of us. God has provided for us miraculously, with unmerited grace and favor since the founding of HOA Janitorial in March 2009, and this event was no exception.

We carried on with our lives, receiving monthly calls from our bankruptcy attorney, whom I respected for his honesty and concern for our well-being. We spoke to Patricia so often that we developed a personal relationship. We engaged in a discussion regarding our shared values, my background, and the positive changes I experienced following a significant personal transformation. She asked me to send a copy of my story to her because she was a published playwright herself and would love to read my story of redemption. I sent it to her and was blown away when I received a letter from her with a testimony of what Jesus had done in her life. She had a troubled past beginning at thirteen years of age but was now happily married with two children.

15

CONFOUNDING THE DOCTORS

ONE SATURDAY MORNING in early 2024, Jane and I were sitting on the patio enjoying a cup of coffee together. We were having a pleasant conversation when I noticed Jane giving me a strange look, so I asked her why.

"I don't see psoriasis on your elbow or your knees," she said. That was a complete shock to me because from the time we'd gotten married, I had dealt with psoriasis. As a matter of fact, I went to the doctor's office after we got married and told the doctor I had an incurable disease, and it was probably going to kill me.

"What is it?" he asked.

"Psoriasis," I replied.

"That's not going to kill you," he said.

"Can it be cured?"

"No."

"Then I'm probably going to take it to my grave with me," I

said. He saw no sense in my humor. I was serious. Without a cure, I would have to live with it permanently, and it certainly appeared that way. I began using a costly topical cream prescribed by the doctor, but a few days later, the psoriasis returned and began spreading to the sides of my calves and legs. I had it in my hair, and as embarrassing as it sounds, I also had it in my navel. It even appeared in my ears at times.

Then I found a dermatologist in Downey who specialized in skin conditions. After an extensive evaluation, he agreed to give me steroid shots. Sure enough, after taking the shot, the psoriasis began to disappear. I was ecstatic because I didn't have to use the topical cream, and I could wear my swimming trunks and not have people staring at the scabs and flakes all over my body.

I continued going to the doctor. Then one day he said, "I'm not going to be able to give you any more steroid shots. The steroids can do damage to other parts of your body, and medical science says we shouldn't continue this treatment."

My psoriasis returned and worsened, but I learned to live with it. I kept putting cream on my elbows, but then it would be on my knees and ankles. So, when Jane told me I didn't have psoriasis, it was a real shocker because it's incurable.

Shortly after that, I had an appointment with my rheumatology doctor and asked him about psoriasis, during which he also said it's incurable.

"Then, Doc, if you'd take a look, tell me where my psoriasis is."

He looked in my hair and my ears, on my elbows, on my knees, and on my ankles. "There's no sign of psoriasis now," he said, "but it can go dormant and return later."

I went home and waited, looking for signs of psoriasis every day, but finally I just forgot about it. Then one day Jane said, "I believe you're healed."

I returned to the doctor, who said there was no reason why the psoriasis should not be present, but he concluded that it appeared to be cured. When I told my church that God had healed my psoriasis, one of the members replied that it's incurable. Well, over two years later, I still have no signs of psoriasis, no itches and no ugly red marks. That's why I'm putting this in my story because when the Great I Am heals something, it stays healed.

It seemed as though everything was moving along nicely, with only a few issues with janitorial customers for me to deal with. By this time we had let our kids know about our financial situation, so they wouldn't be surprised if things didn't go as planned. However, our world was shaken on the Friday before Mother's Day 2024 when Jane developed a cold, clammy, sweat with horrific pains in her abdomen.

We went to emergency, and they took her straight past admitting and called for a doctor who started running tests. Then they came to me with a dire diagnosis. Jane had been trying to lose weight through a weight-loss clinic and apparently, the over eighty ounces of water that she was required to drink every day had depleted her potassium and sodium levels. As they processed her for admission to the hospital, when I asked the emergency room doctor what was going on, he said the only thing he could tell me was that she wasn't dying at the time, then he walked away. I became angry and started after him, but a nurse grabbed my arm and asked me to calm down.

She explained that the doctor wasn't sure what was wrong with Jane, but she wasn't in critical condition.

The next day, Jane's primary doctor conducted further tests that confirmed the initial diagnosis and identified a severe infection as the underlying issue. They started an IV to eliminate the problems, but it would be some time before he could tell if his diagnosis was complete. She was very tired and just wanted to sleep, so we prayed for Jesus's healing power to flow through her and give her a restful night's sleep.

The next morning, Jane called and asked me to bring her phone, some makeup, and some clean clothes. That indicated she was already feeling better, but when I got to the hospital, she had been pulled out of her room for more tests. A nurse told me that Jane was improving but that she wouldn't be released for a few days, which made sense given her exhaustion after such a traumatic experience.

When Jane returned, I told her what the nurse said, but she refused to accept it, believing she was well enough to go home. We talked for a while, then she became very tired and wanted to go to sleep. I went home, knowing she was going to be there for a couple more days at least, as she was wiped out.

A few days later when they were ready to release her, I went to the hospital early, hoping to see the doctor before Jane was released. When I got to her room, one of the ladies from our church was there, talking and laughing with Jane, so I waited in the hall, not wanting to interfere. When the lady came out, we greeted each other, but she told me that I should wait before I went in. After a while, Jane came to the door with her belongings. She appeared ready to leave, but then she set her stuff down and went back into the room, making me wonder what was happening. The lady from church who I had talked to before told me I shouldn't be concerned. Minutes later, Jane came to the door with a huge smile, picked up her stuff, and walked down the hall, leaving me totally befuddled.

We walked in silence until we got out of the hospital, then she turned to me with that same smile and told me that as she started to leave the first time, the older lady in the other bed said, "I feel the presence of the Holy Spirit in the room. Would you please pray for me to be healed?" Jane prayed with her and then picked up her things to leave. When she got to the door, she became filled with the Spirit. God told her to go back into the room because He wanted to heal the woman. After she prayed with her again, the older lady started weeping, saying, "I felt a warmth going through my body." Jane believed the woman was healed, but she didn't feel it was her place to inquire further. It reminded me of the young man in the bank who laid hands on me and began praying in the Spirit. I too had felt a warm glow going through my body.

On June 15, we celebrated Jane's seventy-sixth birthday, against her wishes. We kept it very low key and personal, but that night God spoke to us in prayer, telling us that He was going to speed up the bankruptcy process and that we should be ready.

A couple of days later, we received a call from our attorney. "When we first spoke, I told you we wouldn't be filing your case for two years," he said. "However, I just got a feeling that we should prepare to file as soon as possible, maybe by the end of August. I need to make sure you don't have any liens against your home, that you don't have any lawsuits filed against you, and none of the creditors have put a hold on your bank accounts." I informed him that we had none of those problems. Furthermore, we were still operating the janitorial company and receiving income from it, but we expected to conclude operations by the end of July.

Since our children didn't want the company when it came time for us to retire, we wanted to make a way to have our independent contractors receive the money from the properties they serviced. That would give them a lot more money for no additional labor cost. In the middle of the night, I was awakened with a beautiful plan that would allow them to receive the properties they serviced on August 1, as we had discussed. After November, though, they would remit a stipend from the money they had collected to us for December and January. This would cost them nothing out of pocket.

The next morning when I explained my proposal to Jane, she was amazed and happy. When she asked how I had come up with the proposal, I had to confess it was given to me in the middle of the night by the Holy Spirit in a dream. I also proudly proclaimed that the practice was biblical. In Acts 2:17 it says, "your young men will see visions, your old men will dream dreams."

When I presented the proposal to the men, they were taken aback with the sudden turn of events. I assured them that we were well, but it was time for this change to happen. They were ecstatic, realizing they would start receiving the extra money quickly because they would start invoicing their customers for August, with the payments due to them by the fifteenth. As Steven Covey wrote in *The Seven Habits of Highly Effective People*, it was a "win-win situation."

We were busy in August as we prepared to file our bankruptcy case. Questions regarding our household items and their value as well as current and previous financial records had to be addressed. These inquiries were part of the bankruptcy court proceedings and could be posed by the court trustee. Our attorney told us that we had to be prepared to live on Social Security until our case was discharged. That would be about ninety to one hundred days from the time we filed. Our bank account could not have more than $2,600 in it during that time. This created a problem because we were still receiving money from the July invoices for HOA Janitorial. Our first thought was to increase our charitable donations, but we could not, as it could draw the ire of the creditors who would be monitoring our financials.

We were highly concerned about doing everything by the rules. We wanted to avoid any problems when we went to court in front of the trustee. Then one night at prayer time, the interpretation was comforting as we heard, "Have no fear. I am going before you and all will be well when you go before the court trustee. Just be wise in your daily living."

The next day while reviewing our budget, we realized that relying solely on Social Security would leave us short by the end of each month. I thought about how wise animals stored up food to make it through the winter. God told us to be wise in our daily living, so we began to store up food, paper products, and any other consumables we needed. A friend told us she had, through a divine inclination, found a fantastic food pantry and was buying most of her groceries there, so we checked it out and found we could cut our grocery bill in half. Once again, God made a way.

By late August, we had nearly completed all the necessary

preparations when our attorney informed us that the bankruptcy court date had been rescheduled to October 10 due to an unforeseen development that, according to him, was remarkable. If the court proceedings went smoothly and no creditors objected, we would be finished once the court trustee dismissed us. My thoughts went instantly to the night that God had told us He would be speeding things up.

On August 26, our attorney told us to be ready to sign all the papers required to present to the bankruptcy court on Wednesday via a Zoom meeting, which would take about forty-five minutes. He would watch us sign the papers via Zoom, which would prevent us from having to go to his office.

That Wednesday, we were nervous because we had never done anything like it before, but Patricia called us at 10:00 to tell us not to worry. "Gods got this," she reminded us.

At 11:00, the Zoom meeting started, and everything went well until the attorney appeared on the screen. To our dismay, he said he couldn't see us, so he couldn't watch us sign the papers. He waited while Jane tried frantically to get our camera to work, to no avail. He told us not to worry; we could do it on our smart phone, but that didn't work either. He apologized, then said he had other clients to take care of and turned things over to his assistant. She told us not to worry, that we could do it on September 5, right after Labor Day. Despite his assurances, after the call, we felt totally dejected, but we prayed that God would continue to take care of us.

We started to close the laptop, but then I remembered that the camera had been working not two weeks earlier. What could have gone wrong? I shared this with Jane, so she attempted to do another Zoom call. To our surprise, the camera worked perfectly. I called the attorney's assistant back and told him the good news, but the attorney's schedule was filled for the day and through the rest of the week, so we would need to wait until the following Tuesday, as planned. While expressing my appreciation for his assistance, I informed him that should a cancellation arise, he could contact us, and we would be prepared to respond immediately. He laughed. "You don't understand. We're overbooked. Other people are like you and want to file their cases before Labor Day. I'm sorry, but we won't be getting any cancellations."

The next morning, I heard Jane shouting and praising the Lord as she came down the hallway from our bedroom, almost running. She entered the living room to tell me that we had to be ready for a Zoom meeting with the attorney at 11:00. One of their other clients had canceled. We laughed with joy because we believed that God had given us His unmerited favor.

We got everything ready, making double sure the camera was working, then waited to hear from the attorney at 11:00. To our surprise, the attorney called us at 10:15 and asked if we were ready for him. When we said we were ready right then, he laughed. "I don't know what's going on, and it's too crazy to explain, but we can do the Zoom call right now. A paralegal will call you afterwards to go over everything to make sure your numbers are what we need. When it's all confirmed, we can file."

That afternoon, the paralegal called to review our documents before filing. She had a great personality, and when she asked where I was from, we started talking about our past lives. She had overcome many addictions. "It was meant for us to speak," she said. "I am also here only by the grace and mercy of God."

After we finished reviewing our papers, I asked if she could file them right away. She said it was unlikely, but she would do her best. Filing depended on the court's schedule, so it would likely happen on September 5 or 6.

The week after Labor Day, we didn't hear anything, so we went on with our lives, realizing the situation was out of our hands. On September 6, we received a letter from one of the creditor's attorneys, threatening to file a lawsuit in superior court. Jane sent a copy of the letter to Patricia. She called and told us that the attorney was the type of guy that she really didn't like because he was trying to bully us. She would send him a letter to let him know we would be filing a lawsuit against his firm and his client for harassment. Her next words stunned us both. "You guys have nothing to worry about because your case was filed on the third, so enjoy your weekend." Somehow our case got filed early, against all odds, so once again, all we could do was praise God, the Great I Am, for His divine intervention.

The rest of September went by smoothly as we adapted to our new budget constraints and continued to look forward to our evening prayer time with the Great I Am as he expressed His love for us. At times His message was varied, including what was going to be happening in His Land of the Eagle (America), a promise that evil and wickedness would be diminished, that He was in control, and how much He loved *all* His children.

On October 9, we received a phone call from an attorney who introduced herself as the one who would be at our Zoom meeting with the bankruptcy court trustee. She wanted to do a mock run of what we could expect. This was a huge relief to Jane. The attorney acted as if she was the court trustee by asking questions regarding our financial situation. When she was satisfied that we were comfortable, she explained that she would be at the meeting in a side room, but she would only speak if she felt we needed her help. She was confident that we were competent enough to handle the meeting ourselves, and she assured us that if any of our creditors were at the meeting, she would deal with them.

The next morning, we were up early, spending time in prayer, asking for God's wisdom and peace and the ability to answer all the questions that we had gone over with the attorney. At 8:00 a.m. sharp, we logged onto Zoom. We watched a couple of cases before us involving people who weren't as prepared as we were, but the court trustee was patient with them, which gave us comfort.

When it was our turn, we were sworn in, then the trustee asked for our names and if we had prepared our papers and signed them. She paused as she went through a couple of our papers, scrutinizing each page. Then asked about something we did not remember, but before we could speak, our attorney identified herself and said it was a standard antiharassment act that we had signed in the beginning. The trustee thanked her for the clarification and then asked us a couple of more questions. We were astonished by her next words. "Well, I have everything I need, and since there are no creditors here to contest your case, it is dismissed. Thank you." That was it? The Zoom meeting was over? There's a song from long ago by Peggy

Lee entitled, "Is That All There Is?" which fit us perfectly at that moment.

After a year and a half of living so differently, it felt as if time had stopped. Jane and I just stared at each other in stunned silence. Then our emotions burst out as Jane did a happy dance, shouting praises to God. All I could do was laugh. After a few minutes, we realized the nightmare that we had been subjected to, through no fault of our own, was gone, wiped away by the Great I Am, as He promised. He won't remember any of it again.

From that day forward, we have walked through life free of any guilt or shame, totally forgiven by the only One who matters. Since we have been forgiven, we have come to a place in Jesus Christ, our Lord and Savior, that we have completely forgiven the poor soul who gave in to pride, greed, and arrogance and caused the issue in the first place.

Following our Zoom call, Jane reminded me that I had a routine appointment with the pulmonologist who was in the room when I nearly died. I looked forward to visiting him because of his straightforwardness and the relationship we had developed, but when I arrived at his office, the receptionist directed me elsewhere. "The doctor is going to be in a bit later," she said. "Be prepared." This confused me because it was a routine appointment to check on my sleep apnea, my lungs, and related issues.

Normally when he came into the room, I was greeted with a cheery smile and "Good morning, Buddy. You're looking good. How are you doing?" However, on that day, he arrived without wearing his white smock or having stethoscopes around his neck. Instead, he was wearing a casual, button-down shirt with his sleeves rolled up, and he did not say a word to me as he entered and then closed the door. He had some papers in his hand. After glancing through them, he placed them on the desk, then turned to me. "I'll be asking you some questions, and I want straightforward answers," he said. "You and I have a cordial relationship, but this time, it is doctor-patient, and that's what it's got to be. I need straight answers."

"Whoa, Doc," I replied. "I'm not used to this, but if that's what you need, let's get started."

"I'm going to ask you a question, and I want you to think about it before you give me an answer."

"Fire away," I replied. "Let's get her done."

"Do you think you have any reason to feel that you are getting younger?" he asked.

I stifled a laugh. "Doc, it's hard to keep a straight face and a straight thought when you ask me a question like that because I have no idea what that even means. Before my open-heart surgery, I routinely did four two-minute planks at the gym, even when I had three blockages. I also did push-ups and sit-ups, used workout machines, and spent twenty minutes on the treadmill. I've returned to my regular routine, but I'm uncertain if these activities are affecting my age. I feel great."

"Please just tell me your age for my records," he demanded.

"I'm eighty years old," I said.

"Your vitals are all here," he replied. "Your blood pressure is 115 over 75, which is very good, and your other vital signs are nearly ideal. As for your sleep apnea, you're on the CPAP machine with the mask. For mild sleep apnea patients, it's normal to have five to fifteen events per hour each night. You're averaging less than two events per hour. It's usually fewer than one event per hour—about 0.4 on average. According to that, you don't have sleep apnea."

"Then I guess we can get rid of the CPAP machine and the mask," I replied.

"That's not the course of action we'll be taking," he said. "I'm just trying to understand the situation. Your sleep has improved from five to six interrupted hours to six to seven continuous hours. There are times when you're up at night because of restroom visits, but even those are no more than two a night. People your age are normally up three to four or more times each night. That tells me your urine situation is good, so you don't have prostate problems. I want to make sure that what I'm seeing is what you think and what you feel."

"I feel great!" I exclaimed. "I wear the mask while sleeping, which allows me to rest well, I wake up feeling refreshed, and I proceed with my daily activities, including going to the gym."

"I'm going to leave it at that," he said. "I've recorded our conversation and will check back in with you in six months. It's good to see you. Give my best to Jane and Dena. I recall them well from when we were in the hospital, thinking that you weren't going to make it. It's quite a joy to have had this conversation with you today. I'll see you in six months."

The rest of the year went wonderfully well. We came into a completely new life of celebrating God's love every day, knowing He is with us. We continued looking forward to our nightly prayer time where we would hear, "I am here, my children. I love you. I will never leave you or forsake you." We also began receiving the stipends from the guys at HOA Janitorial, as they had agreed to do. This gave us the opportunity to take day trips on occasion to the various places that we used to go for lunch at some of our favorite restaurants.

On November 1, we heard from the Great I Am, that we should celebrate the birth of His Son for the rest of the season. At God's insistence, we decorated our home for Christmas with a new spirit of love and joy. Throughout the holiday season, we celebrated the birth of Jesus in ways we had never done before, culminating with having our family together in our home for Christmas. We celebrated in love, peace, joy, and the Spirit.

16

GOD BECOMES A REALTOR

JANE and I began 2025 grateful for our health, daily gym visits, and for growing closer to God and each other through His mercy and grace. I have often said I would not wish what we had to endure on my worst enemy, but I'm grateful for the opportunity to have walked through it. We began looking at our future. In the middle of January, we talked about where we wanted to be and what we might want to do for the rest of the year. Both of us felt a divine inclination to sell our mobile home. We had happily lived in our 1973 Oldham mobile home for nine years, investing significantly into it to make it suit our needs. It was designed and decorated by Jane. Even though we had lived at that location for some time, we became concerned that some issues may have been overlooked. Upon further observation, we noticed some activities in the mobile home park that made us feel uneasy. It was restricted to people fifty-five and older, but it appeared that younger people were being allowed to move in, and we didn't like that. There were other issues too, including the hot water heater, the furnace, and the appliances, all of which were ten years old or more. It wouldn't be long before we would have to replace those things. We decided not to invest any more money into such an old mobile home.

I knew we needed a real estate agent, so I spoke to a young lady who worked for the mobile home park and also as a real estate agent. She viewed the property, then estimated a price that matched our expectations. We were hopeful because the asking price would allow us to make quite a bit of money that we could use for living expenses as we grew older.

On February 7, we signed the listing contract, then she put the sign in the yard and in the window. She planned to hold some open houses and was confident it would sell quickly. I was dubious because it was early February. Reports indicated that sales during that period were not expected to progress rapidly. However, when they had the fires in Los Angeles, all those poor people who got burned out were looking for places to live. It just so happened that the people in Altadena were looking down south, which is where we lived, and mobile homes were an inexpensive way to get back on their feet.

The available real estate information indicated that the home could sell quickly, and our actions were consistent with recommended practices. But as time went on, we weren't getting any offers. I'm not saying anything that the real estate agent was doing was wrong, but it wasn't working. She provided us with additional options to consider. After waiting for some time without receiving any follow-up communication, we decided to search for another agent. After ninety days with no offers or even any walkthroughs, we had to try something different.

During this time, I got another call from my pulmonologist's office, which concerned me since I already had a routine appointment scheduled for six months after our last visit. They said the doctor wanted to see me right away, which made me uneasy. I told Jane that she was required to come with me this time because I needed a witness. During my last appointment, the pulmonologist had said I looked younger, but without a witness, no one really believed me.

The appointment was scheduled for the following day. When we arrived, the staff greeted us courteously, then directed us to the waiting room. When the doctor came in, this time he was wearing his white smock, his stethoscopes dangling around his neck.

"Well, at least this time you look like a doctor," I said. "What's going on?" He smiled but ignored my comment while he greeted Jane and asked how Dena was doing. Everything was very congenial. "Okay, I'm over here," I called out. "Let's talk about me. You said I need to come in to see you. So, what's up?"

"Normally, I would not do this," he replied, "but you've been on my mind since I saw you. The last time I asked if you felt like you were getting younger." He acknowledged my surprise, saying he was glad I brought my wife. "Your inner strength is increasing," he continued, "which is unusual for someone aged eighty-one. Normally, they recede a bit." He stated that my blood pressure was within the normal range but slightly low, which, given my circumstances, was preferable to having high blood pressure. "You don't have sleep apnea, but I advise you not to discontinue using the machine. I checked your records and reviewed the data from your CPAP machine, and you are seldom over 2.0, which is three points below where it would be to have sleep apnea. When I check your lungs, they're perfectly clear.

"I also have the records from your primary doctor," he added. "Everything is right on. You're not having the normal problems with your prostate that most men your age have, and you're not having any kidney problems. Everything is just right. Do you know what you're doing differently?"

"Doc, I know you and I have a different outlook on life," I said, "but right now I have to tell you the truth. I know for a fact that I'm walking through a miracle of God because I'm doing nothing different. I'm just taking whatever medication that I need to take and going to the gym. I'm still doing what I'm doing, and anything that you see internally in me, I have no control over it, as you know. So, that's my story, and I'm sticking to it."

He laughed. "I appreciate your honesty. You can leave my office now, and I'll meet with you again in six months."

Shortly after my visit with the pulmonologist, I had a routine checkup with the new cardiologist that I had been seeing recently. I was looking forward to that because we had a great relationship even though we didn't communicate very well. He spoke broken English, but we could still yuck it up.

"Hello, Buddy. How are you?" he asked as he entered the room.

"Hey, Doc," I replied. "How are you? I need to look after you and make sure you're fine. I can't risk anything happening to you since you're my cardiologist. I need you to be healthy until I get out of here. So, are you eating well, sleeping well, and working out?"

He laughed. "I am. And now, how are you?"

"I'm good, but I have a problem. My pulmonologist told me back in October that he thought I was getting younger. I didn't say anything about it because it spooked me. But I just saw him again about a week ago, and he said I was still getting younger, and my vitals were even stronger."

"Well, let me check you," he replied. He put his stethoscope on me in a couple of places. "Yep, I agree with your pulmonologist," he said. "Your heartbeat is stronger than it has been. So, why don't I see you in about ninety days?" Then he grinned. "Okay, young man, make it one hundred and twenty days."

In mid-May, we discovered that another mobile home, also built in 1973, was for sale down the street. It had been totally gutted and redone on the inside, and they were asking a lot more money than we were asking for ours. It didn't make any sense to go look at it. I wanted to find a new agent to review our asking price, but I didn't care to look at that one.

A couple of days later, I went to the market to get Jane some ice cream. On the way, I noticed that every weekend, cars would line up outside the other mobile home for an open house. It made me doubt our deal. On the way back from Ralph's, it was like God told me to stop and take a look. In my spirit, I couldn't go any farther without going inside.

When I entered, I greeted the real estate lady, whose name was Irene. "I'm just looking, so enjoy your day," I said. "I'm only observing it and don't wish to discuss it." Despite my polite rebuff, she was friendly, and soon we got to talking. I told Irene that I was looking for another agent, but we were the poor folks down the street. "You're selling this one for a lot of money, and ours won't sell for that."

"Well," Irene replied, "I'd love to be able to help you, but you have an agent already, and there's nothing I can do until you decide that you want me to do it. You'll have to give her a note explaining that you won't be using her anymore."

"We'll get that done in a hurry," I replied.

"Have you signed a contract?" she asked.

"Contracts are made to be broken if things aren't working," I said. "You know, when I was in the third grade, my teacher told me, 'Mr. Mercer, you have a propensity for being legally right and morally wrong.'" I heard laughter coming from behind her. It was her husband.

"That's our quote for the day," he said. He explained they were looking for a quote of the day that they could put on their advertising. That ended up being the actual quote for the day.

"I'm very serious," I said. "Because I've had our home for sale for a while. We haven't been getting any prospects, and it's beginning to get a little nerve-racking because we need to sell it. I don't want to keep paying high rent for this space. It feels like we're wasting money."

"I really can't help you until you get back to me with a notification that you have terminated your current agent," she said.

"I'll have it done by tomorrow," I assured her, "so be ready to take her place."

That evening at around 8:00 p.m., Irene called to inform me that, after checking, my home wasn't on the Multiple Listing

Service (MLS). No wonder we weren't getting any calls! The next day, I went to visit our current agent to inform her that we were ending her services. She wasn't there, but her boss was. I said we would be terminating the lady because we were getting no prospects, and it wasn't listed as promised.

"Well, you know she isn't here," she said again.

"You're here, and you're her boss," I replied. "I'll provide you with the note, and you'll need to inform her, as this will take place immediately. I don't want any problems. In the letter, I've listed the reasons why we're terminating her, including breach of contract because she hasn't done what she said she would do."

"I don't want any problems," our realtor's boss said, "so I'll go ahead and take the signs down."

The next morning, Jane said we'd received an unpleasant email from our former agent. "Well," I said, "let's go get it taken care of."

When I walked in to see her, she was very angry. "You know you can't terminate me like that," she said. "We have a contract."

"I apologize," I replied, "but that is what will occur."

"Where did you get this breach of contract?" she demanded.

"You didn't do what you promised. I don't want any problems. I just want to get somebody who's going to do the job."

"You do know," she added, "you have a contract with a ninety-day notice. If you break it, you owe us one thousand dollars."

"If you would like to come after me for one thousand dollars, let me know," I said, my voice calm. "I'm going to small claims court against you personally for five thousand dollars for breach of contract. From February through May, you haven't performed as agreed by the contract. We've been wasting time, and I found out that our home's not on the MLS, so I'll get the $5000. If you want to do that, go ahead."

At that point, her supervisor interrupted. "We don't want any issues," she said. "We're not going to cause you any problems."

"I have no desire to have any problems," I replied. "I just want to sell my mobile home and move on."

Shortly thereafter, Irene listed our property, held an open house the first weekend, and immediately attracted prospective buyers. We hid across the way in the parking lot, watching people visit our home. When we spoke to Irene later, we noticed she seemed a bit sad. "I think we have a problem because you have solar panels on the roof. There's a twenty-five-thousand-dollar contract that the new buyer will have to absorb."

"It's only a hundred and twenty dollars per month," I replied. "We'll lower our asking price, so they won't have to pay that." She agreed and then set to work, doing everything she could do.

Every weekend we had an open house. There must have been thirty-five or forty people that went through our home. All but one of them thought it was beautiful, but only one person gave us an offer. Unfortunately, she couldn't qualify for a mortgage, so here we were still stuck.

Then the Great I Am talked to us one night. "I have a special buyer for you," He said. "Do not be concerned." With His assurance, we were completely at peace.

A few weeks later, Irene told me she had three appointments for Saturday: one at 10:00 a.m. where she represented both buyer and seller, another at 1:00 p.m., and a third at 3:00 p.m. where she again represented both parties. *Now, we'll get some action,* I thought.

At 10:00 a.m., we watched from across the way as the prospective buyers parked in front of our house. However, Irene wasn't there, so I went ahead and opened our house, so they could view it. Then I called Irene.

"Did I mess up?" I asked, only to realize she hadn't made a mistake like this before. *What's going on?* I wondered.

That afternoon at 1:00, the next potential buyer came. After the client left, I caught up with their realtor. "Oh, they loved it," she said. "We need to have a conversation with your agent, then I think we'll have an offer that you'll be happy with."

At 3:00, along came Irene with a pickup truck right behind her. I turned to Jane. "I bet you we have a buyer there."

When Irene got out of her car, her husband was with her. He had never accompanied her when she visited us. Two men were in the pickup truck. I told Jane that I sensed something unusual was happening. At that moment, I realized in my spirit that our home would be purchased by a real estate agent. We had dropped the price enough that they could completely redo it and then sell it for top dollar like the one where I had met Irene. It would make them money, which was fine with us.

We had a meeting scheduled with Irene the next morning at 11:00. When she showed up, her husband was with her. *Whoa,* I thought. *What's going on here?*

As she began to explain the offer, I stopped her. "Irene, you talk really fast when you're nervous,"

"Would you like to know who the buyer is?" her husband asked.

"Could it be you?" I inquired. They laughed. It was a cash deal, but I didn't care. He stated that with the price reduction, they could restore the mobile home, sell it, recoup their investment, and earn a profit. It was a win-win situation.

One night shortly thereafter while we were praying, the Great I Am told us that He liked the people to whom we had sold. That ended that, but now we needed to find a place to live. "Do not worry," God assured us. We would have a place to live.

While we were waiting to close escrow, we packed and prepared to move. As I was moving a box to an upper shelf, I felt a severe pain in my left arm, between the shoulder and elbow. The pain dissipated rapidly, so I continued with the tasks at hand.

The next morning, I felt minimal pain but noticed the area had turned an ugly red and black. As the day progressed, the discoloration became more pronounced, but because there was no pain, I opted to spend twenty minutes on the treadmill at the gym. I was on my way out of the gym when the manager approached and asked what had happened to my arm. When I explained the situation, he noted that I had a ruptured muscle and informed me that surgery would be necessary. I laughed. "Ain't no operations at my age."

The next morning the pain had intensified, and the discoloration was terrible. The skin under my arm was sagging as if blood was gathering there, but I still had very little pain.

The following day, I went to see my primary doctor. "How in the world did you do that?" he asked as he examined my arm. "Buddy, I can't help you. That's going to need surgery."

That afternoon, with minor discomfort, I returned home and helped Jane pack boxes. On Sunday, we went to church as usual. Everyone asked the obvious questions and said they would pray for me.

After the service, I went to talk to our pastor regarding an appointment we had later in the week. We started our conversation, then without a word, he held my arm and said a quick prayer for healing.

Two nights later, I was awakened with an itching, burning feeling inside my arm. It intensified, then about two hours later, it subsided, so I went back to sleep. Jane and I were having coffee the next morning when I told her of my experience. She laughed and said, "The Great I Am was probably healing it, so you can continue to help me pack boxes."

Later that afternoon, the pain was almost completely gone, and the colors were not as ugly. I told Jane that she was right; my arm was being healed, and there would be no surgery. Over the next few days, I continued packing boxes and going to the gym, eventually regaining the strength I had lost. The next Sunday, it was evident that my arm was healing, so I testified to the church about what the Great I Am had done.

Once escrow closed on our mobile home, we had less than a week to vacate, so we had to start looking for a place to live. It had been a long time since we had rented an apartment, a condo, or anything else. Wherever we looked, they required three times the monthly rent up front. Due to our Social Security benefits not being sufficient, combined with bankruptcy and less-than-ideal credit, we were unable to meet that requirement.

While driving on a main street one day, I saw a large, well-maintained apartment complex. "Look at that!" I exclaimed. "With all those trees, it looks like a park." Jane said she didn't want to live there because she knew people in the area and preferred not to be around them. "Well, that's funny," I replied. "It's a big place," but she was adamant.

We went farther down that street, but when we got to the original place that she wanted to see, something tripped inside of her. "Nope," she said. "This isn't the place."

We went back down the same street, and just as we went past the attractive apartment complex that Jane had nixed, I felt in my spirit that we needed to stop there, so I made an illegal U-turn and went back.

As soon as we entered the building, I knew we would be living there. The office was cheery and bright with an air of freedom. The young leasing representative was professional and congenial. After discussing our financial situation with her, she said she was sure that we would get accepted. She asked me to come back after our house sold and escrow closed.

We did as she suggested and then filled out the application right there in the office. It was a comedy of errors on my part, as I am not computer literate. But the leasing agent was patient and helpful, and with Jane's help, we completed it. Afterward, she introduced us to the manager, who was working in her office. They said they would let us know within seventy-two hours if we had been accepted.

On Saturday afternoon, as promised, the young lady called and said, "You've been accepted, so get ready to move in on June twenty-fifth."

We were elated. All arrangements were made for the scheduled move-in date, and it went without a hitch. As expected, we were and are extremely happy with the apartment. The ladies who manage the property have been fantastic, helping us with any needs we may have. The apartment has been decorated according to Jane's preferences, and she appreciates the park-like environment of the property, particularly the presence of numerous butterflies.

ACKNOWLEDGMENTS

Gratitude to the Great I Am

With the deepest reverence and humility, I wish to acknowledge the almighty God, the Great I Am. Throughout every stage of writing this book, I have continuously felt His unmistakable presence guiding me. God has revealed Himself as the "Golden Strand," skillfully weaving together each part of my journey and ensuring that I never walked alone. I am continually reminded that without His divine guidance and boundless love, the completion of this book would not have been possible. For His steadfast support and continual presence in every moment, I am profoundly grateful.

Appreciation for Pastoral Support

I extend heartfelt appreciation to Pastor Doug Hefly of Radiant Church International in Upland, California, and his wife, Pastor Cindy. During some of our most challenging and darkest moments, we placed our trust in Pastor Doug, relying on his confidential counsel, which became a wellspring of comfort and wisdom for our family. Pastor Cindy's leadership in the weekly Glow Women's Ministry has been of immeasurable value. My wife's participation in these gatherings has allowed her to experience love and fulfillment, even during times of stress, all thanks to the nurturing and supportive environment that Pastor Cindy so thoughtfully cultivated.

Honoring Apostle Dan Sherstad and Pastor Sue

Our gratitude also extends to Apostle Dan Sherstad and his wife, Pastor Sue, who are connected to our church as Evangelists. They have become not only trusted spiritual guides but also cherished friends, providing us with a safe space to share our deepest concerns. Their wisdom and friendship have been a true blessing in our lives. We remain committed to supporting their ongoing evangelistic work, now and in the future.

ABOUT THE AUTHOR

Born Glen Roy Jacobs Jr. in Marlow, Oklahoma, on August 7, 1943, my journey has been marked by significant transformation. At the age of twelve, I was adopted and became known as Buddy Roy Mercer. My life stands as a testament to enduring faith, redemption, and the transformative power of family, community, and spiritual commitment. This story is one of both hardship and triumph, showing how resilience and belief can lead to profound personal and professional fulfillment.

Visit https://buddymercer.com

www.ingramcontent.com/pod-product-compliance
Lightning Source LLC
LaVergne TN
LVHW041314080426
835513LV00008B/453